Portraits of Power

MARK GEVISSER

Portraits of Power

PROFILES IN A CHANGING SOUTH AFRICA

To Inga,

with all my love

[signature]

PHOTOGRAPHIC EDITOR HENNER FRANKENFELD

DAVID PHILIP
MAIL&GUARDIAN

First published 1996 in Southern Africa by David Philip Publishers (Pty) Ltd,
208 Werdmuller Centre, Claremont 7700
in association with the *Mail & Guardian*, Johannesburg

ISBN 0 86486 314 4

© 1996 text Mark Gevisser
© 1996 photographs Henner Frankenfeld
© 1996 photographs Ruth Motau
© 1996 *Mail & Guardian* (photographs by Anna Zieminski, Angela Buckland,
    Naashon Zalk, Karina Turok, and Monty Cooper; see page xii)

Printed in South Africa by Creda Press (Pty) Ltd
Eliot Avenue, Epping 7460

Contents

Foreword by Professor Kader Asmal — ix
Acknowledgements — xii
Introduction by Mark Gevisser — xiii

1 The don who wants an ebony tower — 2
  Malegapuru William Makgoba: Former Deputy Vice-Chancellor,
    Wits University
2 Wits's whitey in the woodpile — 7
  Charles van Onselen: Wits University historian and senator
3 If not a mother, then a witch — 11
  Mamphela Ramphele: Vice-Chancellor Designate, University
    of Cape Town
4 A Steve Biko for the '90s — 16
  Barney Pityana: Chairman, Human Rights Commission
5 Olive Overboard! — 21
  Olive Shisana: Director-General, National Department of Health
6 What all the song and dance is about — 25
  Mbongeni Ngema: Director of Sarafina 2
7 Sarafina of the health system — 30
  Nkosazana Zuma: Minister of Health
8 Giving the media a black eye — 34
  Thami Mazwai: Head of the Black Editors' Forum
9 Working-class hero: something to be? — 38
  Sam Shilowa: Secretary-General, Cosatu
10 Head of the class struggle — 42
  Blade Nzimande: Deputy Chairman, SA Communist Party
11 Nkosazana with a knobkerrie — 46
  Sibongile Zungu: Chief of the Madlebe tribe
12 Ethno rehab at the Civic — 50
  Welcome Msomi: Creator of Umabatha and image-consultant to the
    ANC
13 Priest who takes no prisoners — 54
  Sipo Mzimela: Minister of Correctional Services and IFP National
    Deputy Chairman

Contents

14 *Ulysses in the canefields*   59
Farouk Cassim: Dissident IFP Member of Parliament

15 *Whirlwind in a sari*   63
Fatima Meer: University of Natal sociologist and SABC Board member

16 *Queen of her own soapie*   67
Cawe Mahlati: Acting Chief Executive of Bop Broadcasting

17 *No longer His Master's Voice?*   72
Zwelakhe Sisulu: Chief Executive of SABC

18 *A Lois Lane in tweeds*   76
Jill Chisholm: Chief Executive: Television, SABC

19 *Klerksdorp Icarus*   80
Riani de Wet: Former MEC for Public Media, North West Province

20 *Too damn straight to leave the laager*   84
Roelf Meyer: National Party Secretary-General and chief negotiator

21 *SANDF's new brothers in arms*   89
Brigadier Roland de Vries and Colonel Solly Mollo

22 *Onward, Christian soldier …*   93
General Tienie Groenewald: KwaMakhutha murder accused and
    Freedom Front senator

23 *The Prussian of Pritchard Street*   97
Klaus von Lieres und Wilkau: Former Witwatersrand
    Attorney-General

24 *The ultimate test of faith*   101
Archbishop Desmond Tutu: Chairman, Truth and Reconciliation
    Commission

25 *The Desmond Tutu of SA Jewry*   106
Cyril Harris: Chief Rabbi of South Africa

26 *The taxpayers' bouncer*   110
Gill Marcus: Deputy Minister of Finance

27 *Minister of common cents*   114
Trevor Manuel: Minister of Finance

28 *Cinderella-in-waiting*   118
Geraldine Fraser-Moleketi: Minister of Welfare

29 *The Nats' blackface Elvis*   122
Peter Marais, MEC for Local Government, Western Cape

30 *The Tina Turner of the provinces*   126
Tokyo Sexwale: Premier of Gauteng

31 *The street-fighting premier*   131
Mathews Phosa: Premier of Mpumalanga

32 *Mr Dial-a-Quote and the gravy boat*   135
Eugene Nyati: Former Consultant to the Mpumalanga government

33 *Mama's boy of the Kalahari*   140
Manne Dipico: Premier of the Northern Cape

Contents

34 *Oom Ray of the Wild East*   144
   Raymond Mhlaba: Premier of the Eastern Cape

35 *More Biggles than Bokassa*   148
   Bantu Holomisa: Deputy Minister of Environmental Affairs and
      Tourism

36 *An unlikely Tarzan for our red-tape jungles*   152
   Zola Skweyiya: Minister of Public Services and Administration

37 *Wild woman, big soul*   156
   Brigitte Mabandla: Deputy Minister of Arts, Culture, Science and
      Technology

38 *Strijdom Square's merry prankster*   160
   Hugh Masekela: Assistant Chief Executive, Performing Arts
      Council of the Transvaal

39 *The Sam Goldwyn of South Africa*   164
   Anant Singh: Independent film producer and creator of 'Cry, the
      Beloved Country'

40 *Weekend Special bites back!*   168
   Brenda Fassie: South Africa's bad-girl singer

41 *Go, Feeeesh!*   172
   Mark Fish: Bafana Bafana superstar

PROFESSOR KADER ASMAL
Minister of Water Affairs and Forestry

Foreword

I have often thought, during my weekly pilgrimage through the pages of the *Mail & Guardian*, that I should have liked to be the subject of a Mark Gevisser profile. That is natural, considering their excellence. Yet the fact that I have not, equips me with the detachment to write this foreword to a collection whose appearance is, I believe, an event.

Most of our newspapers in South Africa are governed by the lowest common denominator of what is decreed 'newsworthy', all too often a superficial mixture of money, sex, crime and political gossip.

In both style and layout our newspapers still suffer from the stifling legacy of a post-war influx of Fleet Street professionals, with a recent and curious admixture of North American and European norms. We therefore endure the daily dichotomy of a largely superficial press in a serious country, immortalised in the words of a Johannesburg Sunday newspaper editor, who promoted his paper as 'qualipop'.

A characteristically local style has largely eluded the South African press, with the possible exception of the developing *Sowetan* – and, of course, long-forgotten black newspaper efforts that flourished before white power pushed them into the bland establishment mould or out of existence.

There were other exceptions in the now largely deceased 'alternative press'. There was one particular alternative newspaper which managed to create a unique style, and which not only survived, but prospered. The *Mail & Guardian*, which falls into a category of its own for excellence, as has been internationally recognised, has systematically attempted to get behind the news with an investigative approach, detailed features, substantial, skilfuly composed articles and high-quality writing.

While this generally intelligent approach may have limited its readership, it has, nevertheless, allowed it to play a crucial role over the past decade, and particularly during this turbulent period of transition and transformation. Its success gives the lie to the traditional view that circulation is king. The *Mail & Guardian* has also, in a newspaper world sadly lacking in style and quality of writing, provided us with both, often couched in the subjective and creative mould of the best in new journalism.

Mark Gevisser, presenting serious analytical writing in the guise of profiles, is essential to the *Mail & Guardian*'s excellence. He marshals his words like the delicate and precise tools of a plastic surgeon to peel away the masks of people usually presented as the mere sources of statements, comments, or actions, or the blurred figures of newspaper photographs and TV footage.

Gevisser gives us a nuanced, subjective and emphatic insight into the authentic people behind the news and what drives them, in a subtle and creative way that rises above journalese into compelling and delightful reading. He provides the reader with a privileged window through which to view leading players on the South African stage, a view which enables us the better to understand the political, cultural, and psychological complexities that interact to make up the real 'new South Africa'.

It is unusual for public figures to open themselves to this kind of acute scrutiny. These profiles, now transformed from the transience of newsprint to the relative permanence of a book, are testimony to the openness which characterises the new South Africa.

They are also testimony to the contradictions, ambiguities and tensions that shape our project of nation-building. Gevisser quotes Charles van Onselen, in a philosophy (if not words) that could well be Gevisser's:

'I want to convey that not everyone here is an oppressor or a victim, that there's a whole middle terrain here where our interactions are a lot more complicated, and our loves run a lot deeper than people think; as do our hates … you peel away the racial thing and you say, Jeez, the crossover here, the cultural osmosis, is quite extraordinary.'

Perhaps the Van Onselen/Makgoba debate highlights most clearly the subtlety in Gevisser's work. In a battle which (if the letters pages of the daily press are a guide) polarised public opinion along alarmingly racial lines, Gevisser managed to portray each man as a complex, deeply concerned individual with his own purpose and history in life; each, as he writes in his introduction, with a consciousness that is 'swirling and contradictory and multi-layered'. It provides those interested in the future of this country, those concerned with issues of race and identity, with a kaleidoscopic lens through which to view a seminal debate.

Yet in his support for Van Onselen's curt rejection of nationalism as 'bad stuff', Gevisser reveals his own contradictory and multi-layered consciousness. It is understandable in relation to the xenophobic fervour of Nationalist rule, but is too sweeping in relation to African, and hopefully South African, nationalism which in its best aspects is generously inclusive. The needs of the current South African context are, perhaps, not fully recognised. One of our greatest challenges is to weld one nation, out of (and in) diversity and difference. The new patriotism called for by President Mandela incorporates a progressive and inclusive nationalism, a national consciousness that is a necessary step in building unity. The Yugoslavian option of sectarian fragmentation based on appalling violence still hangs over us. Interestingly, work such as Gevisser's, by bringing us all a greater understanding of each other, of the actual behind the image, serves to build that nationhood.

In his approach to the alleged 'new black elite' Gevisser's touch is less sure. The group that he chooses is neither a cohesive and select group drawn from a particular background, nor a group of people who all wield real power – something that should not be confused with office and status. The creation of a new elite is dependent, ultimately, on the transfer of the control of power – economic, social and political.

In this sense, the book's title, *Portraits of Power: Profiles in a Changing South Africa* is a misnomer. Perhaps the next challenge for Gevisser is to cast his beam onto the shadow of that which has not changed, onto that (white) minority of (white) minorities who still wield vast economic power and wealth: not those who, after years of

Foreword

humiliating Verwoerdian Bantu education are sending their children to private schools for the first time, but those whose ancestral lineage, all the way back through the fading sepia pages of family photographs, went to private schools which gave direct access to privilege and power.

The great debate about the massive sweep of change in South Africa, about the layers of power in our society, and the way that apartheid and racism have impacted on the 'faces at the bottom of the well', has eluded many of our intellectuals, black and white. All too often I turn another page to find, once again, that 'the best lack all conviction, the worst are full of passionate intensity'. This, in a country to which the world turns an ever-expectant gaze, hopeful that the promise of our negotiated transition to democracy will be fulfilled.

Gevisser, on the other hand, has the intellectual calibre and the political courage to leave behind the tired slogans and to engage, not so much with the 'new South Africa', as with the 'now South Africa'. But this sense of engagement is not without its pitfalls.

I have been interested to observe, when reading these profiles, how Gevisser negotiates the tightrope on which, because of the very nature of the work he attempts, he must teeter – a tightrope which is strikingly topical in the context of the recent completion of our Constitution. South Africans are now amongst the privileged few throughout the world protected by a justiciable Bill of Rights. Freedom of expression, fought for so bitterly in the dark days, is now a guaranteed right, limited only by respect for and the upholding of other rights, such as dignity and privacy. Gevisser walks this ethical tightrope with integrity, revealing personal detail about his subjects not in order to boost purient readership, but to give substance to his portraits of controversial public figures.

It is this integrity, combined with flair, that makes Gevisser's profiles comparable to the best written in the international press, reminiscent of the work of Hugo Young or Patrick O'Donovan in England and Fintan O'Toole in Ireland. Gevisser refreshes and provokes as he takes the genre on, two, even three steps beyond the mundane. He paints with oils in a world of watercolours.

Gevisser, like many of his subjects, provokes strong reactions from his readers. Some see him, as one wrote to the paper, as an 'idiotic praise-singer to the new bourbons', some as insensitive, even arrogant – but whether they love him or dislike him, thoughtful people still read his profiles, assiduously. Most would admit that he is one of the most incisive and compelling writers in South Africa today.

I am, finally, relieved that I am not one of those on the Gevisser operating table. Let me admit that I am too aware of my own frailties to want to see them exposed by a mind which has the renaissance features of a true polymath.

Kader Asmal, May 1996

Acknowledgements

These profiles have been nurtured by three people in particular. Anton Harber was prepared to risk the idea in the beginning, and has been unstinting in his support and guidance ever since, both as *Mail & Guardian* editor and as my weekly reader. David and Marie Philip have guided the publication of this volume with vision, with insight, and with their renowned bonhomie. They understood instinctively what I was trying to do, and helped me achieve it. To all three I owe the greatest debts of gratitude.

I would like to thank all at the *M&G*, particularly Henner Frankenfeld, with whom I share the vision for this project, and who provided most of the photographs, Christian Figenshou and Christian Stephen, who copy-edited and designed most of the profiles, Shaun de Waal, who designed the cover of this book, Reedwaan Valli, who went way beyond the call of duty doing photoscanning and copy preparation, and all my colleagues in the newsroom. Thank you too to Caroline Creasy, for her contribution to the marketing, and Barbara Ludman, who edited many of the profiles; to Thuli Mavi, Adele Steenkamp and Maxine Rautenbach for their administrative assistance; and to Russell Martin, Bridget Impey and all at David Philip Publishers.

South African journalists are unusually generous with their sources, their information and their time: for their camaraderie I thank my colleagues, in newsrooms across the country, who assisted me in one way or another. Michelle Leon and her staff at the Times Media library, where I did most of my research, were unfailingly helpful. Thank you too to the *Daily Dispatch*, the Independent News-papers library in Johannesburg, and the staff of the TNP videoteque at SABC.

Friends and family too have assisted with insight, critique and support. Thank you especially to all the Gevissers, to Charlotte Bauer for helping with the final selection, and most of all to Chetty for his love, his patience, his support and his infallible insight.

Final thank-yous to all those who spoke to me, often at considerable length, about my profile subjects. And of course to my profile subjects themselves, who gave of their time and ideas – and often their souls – so generously and openly. This book charts their moment in history. It is dedicated to them.

Mark Gevisser, May 1996

As photographic editor, I wish to thank the following for additional photographs provided: Anna Zieminski (pp. 11, 30, 122); Angela Buckland (25, 46, 63); Naashon Zalk (76); Ruth Motau (93, 131); Karina Turok (110); and Monty Cooper (144).

Henner Frankenfeld, May 1996

MARK GEVISSER

Introduction

In April 1996, almost two years to the day after South Africa went to the polls in its first democratic election, I gave a lift to the writer Mandla Langa. In a silence somewhere along Louis Botha Avenue, he turned to me and said, 'You know, I was watching the news last night, and the announcer spoke of President Mandela. I was shocked. President Mandela? It just didn't sound right. I find myself having to pinch myself almost every day.'

Society has an astonishing capacity for re-invention. What was unimaginable a few years ago is now our lives. There is a new language of power, a new pigment of authority, a new morality of governance. While most of us – black or white, rich or poor – have not experienced any radical shift of material circumstance, we have nonetheless lived through a revolution. We should all, like Mandla Langa, be pinching ourselves daily; instead we go about our business as if we had merely blinked our new society into being.

The project of my weekly *Mail & Guardian* column, then, has been to freeze-frame South African democracy into a series of profiles, so that we may somehow make sense of it. I want to try and render visible all those skeins that hold us together by profiling those who *have* experienced a change of circumstance, material or political, due to South Africa's transition.

I chose to do this by focusing largely (but not exclusively) on the first generation of new South African leaders, because I wanted to track the coming into being of a new elite. I wanted to understand what, exactly, the nature of power is in a new South Africa, how former street-activists deal with the power that has been so suddenly thrust upon them, and how former soldiers of apartheid handle the equally sudden loss of it. It has been fascinating to chart how different our new leaders are from those who preceded them – and sometimes how similar they are.

And it has been exhilarating to touch base, every week for a year, with people trying to make a dream work. If indeed there is new power in South Africa, one of its key fuels is idealism. Despite our plunging rand and our escalating crime rate, there cannot be another society on the planet as devoid of cynicism, as engaged in its destiny, as our own. Which is not to say we are not subject to our own unique set of pathologies. Race remains a matter of central concern in South African public life, and one of my projects too has been trying to track the way in which old obsessions and conflicts have mutated into our new society.

This is by no means a 'Who's Who' reference book; it is neither comprehensive nor unbiased. These are not neccessarily the 41 most powerful people in South Africa; nor are they my personal 'Top 41'. I chose them for any one of a number of reasons: because they raise the defining dilemmas of our time; because they are larger than life and embody the difficult contradictions of our society; because I found them enigmatic and wanted to 'get to the bottom' of them; because I found them inspiring and wanted to have an excuse to spend a day with them; because they were available, because they were newsworthy, because they are volatile.

Most of the profiles I have included in this collection will make immediate sense to the reader as 'portraits of power': the premiers, the cabinet ministers, the cultural mandarins, the media bosses, the generals. I've thrown in some wild cards too, because they offset or throw into relief the new elite. Conversely, many obvious power-players – from both the political and the economic sphere – do not appear. This is sometimes because they didn't spark my imagination; sometimes because they declined to be interviewed; sometimes because I felt that, because I knew them too well, my judgement might be compromised; sometimes because, even though they are on my list and will appear in my column, I simply didn't have time to get around to them before the deadline for this book. There are also some people whom I profiled in my column but who do not appear in this volume: this is not because I deem them in any way unworthy. I made my final cut based on an assessment of the quality of my writing rather than the quality of my subject.

It must be remembered that all of these pieces first appeared in the grubby temporality of newsprint; often written and published in the heat of the moment. I have tried to contextualise them in this volume by beginning each profile with an update, explaining the circumstances of the interview and, where appropriate, the subsequent reponse to it. In our fast-changing society, though, even these updates risk being outdated: following FW De Klerk's May anouncement that the National Party is quitting the Government of National Unity, many of the people profiled in these pages could well have been promoted into the cabinet – or dropped into obscurity – by the time you read this book.

My approach at the time of writing was to take names off the banner headlines – people like Mbongeni Ngema, Eugene Nyati, William Makgoba, Trevor Manuel – and render them three-dimensional; to deal with the controversies surrounding them, certainly, but to put them into context too. I wanted to afford my readers the chance to get to know them.

Which brings me to the question of subjectivity. I do not write myself out of these interviews; my approach, rather, is to recreate the experience of meeting my subject so that my readers can live the encounter through me. I have my biases, I have my foibles, I have my own idiosyncratic ways of seeing and interpreting, I have my own strongly held beliefs. These, I hope, are all manifest.

I do feel, though, that it is presumptuous to form an opinion about my subjects after spending a mere couple of hours with them, and so an essential part of my writing process is research: not simply looking at old newspaper clippings but, more importantly, talking at length to people who know my subject far better than I do. For any given profile, I will often speak to up to a dozen sources.

Most journalists' mailboxes are awash with hate-mail, and columnists more than any – perhaps because we are name-branded correspondents. Beneath our photobylines, we foist our opinions, rather than simply state the facts, upon our readers. So people develop relationships with us; some get very cross with us indeed. In my introductions to the profiles in this book, I've reproduced a few of the more strident

Introduction

or revealing of the responses to my column.

Sometimes our fans write to us too. One letter I cherish was written to me personally, following my profile of Human Rights Commission chair Barney Pityana, published at the height of the controversy over his calling legal academic Dennis Davis a racist: 'This is the first piece I've seen on the issue,' the correspondent wrote, 'which uses the human faculty of empathy to describe/consider what Barney is saying. Rather than the much cruder one of judgement/criticism/cognitive logic. We always seem to be asked to pronounce an expression of people's hurt/pain/opinions, rather than trying to understand them.'

Whether it's Barney Pityana or KwaMakutha murder accused General Tienie Groenewald, that's exactly what I try to achieve in my profiles. Using a roughly psycho-analytic approach I try to understand my subjects rather than judge them; I then share my insights with my readers. Thus I attempt to make sense of apparent contradictions; to deconstruct their public personae by looking at their politics, their psychology, their class, their ethnicity within the context of the work they do. Of course, in the process, unwittingly or consciously, I do a fair bit of judging too – it would be disingenuous to pretend otherwise – but I do not set out to be a kingmaker or -breaker.

I sense that a lot of the anger or unease that my columns generate is because in South Africa we are used to accepting public personae at face value. It is not only disres-pectful but downright dangerous to demystify power, because in so doing you also often disarm it. But as many people get angry with me for being 'too soft' on my subjects. This, I believe, is the classic portraitist's dilemma. When you spend a day with someone, when you enter communication beyond the conventional Q and A interview style, you develop a certain level of empathy – not patronising, just human – with your subject. Often I would respond positively to someone, but that impression would clash, sometimes violently, with the opinions of people who knew my subject much better than I did, or with the objective facts surrounding the person. This is what I find most challenging about writing political profiles: trying to reconcile these apparent contradictions, and to reflect the fact that consciousness is swirling and contradictory and multilayered rather than linear and easily explicable.

I have presented the profiles, not chronologically, but rather in loose thematic order. The book begins with a series of profiles of people who all engage, in one way or another, in what has established itself as the prevalent intellectual and political discourse of our times: the clash of Africanism or 'black empowerment' on the one side and non-racialism or 'white liberalism' on the other. The book then meanders through a range of themes – transformation of the public sector; Zulu politics; broadcasting; Afrikaner identity; militarism; justice; finance; regional politics; the arts. I have also often grouped people together according to ethnicity: Western Cape coloureds; Eastern Cape Xhosas; Zulus; Afrikaners; Jews; Indians. This is not because I am interested in recreating the ghettoes of apartheid, but rather because one of my preoccupations is looking at how people with power deal with their roots, with where they come from, their ethnicities, their histories, their places within the South African rainbow.

But every single profile can be cross-read with a dozen others, no matter where it is placed in the book, and I urge readers to dip and dive through this book accord-

Introduction

ing to their own interests rather than simply following it from beginning to end. Cawe Mahlati, for example, is placed amidst the broadcasters; she also holds fascinating views on Africanism and black empowerment, and on Xhosa politics. Welcome Msomi is juxtaposed with other people looking at 'Zuluness'; Mbongeni Ngema with those looking at black upliftment and with those in the health sector. Both showmen, they could just as well have been put with each other and with Hugh Masekela.

One of my agendas has been to track the phenomenal increase, in South Africa, of women in power since the transition began: I have not grouped these women together, but Nkosazana Zuma, Brigitte Mabandla, Geraldine Fraser-Moleketi, Olive Shisana, Mamphela Ramphele, Jill Chisholm, Gill Marcus, Sibongile Zungu and all the other women profiled talk to each other, in fascinating ways, about gender and power.

The book ends with two of my favourite profiles, Brenda Fassie and Mark Fish. They are not easily at home with the rest of these profiles, as the power they wield is over our imaginations (not to mention our ghettoblasters and sports stadiums) rather than over our material lives: pop icons of decay and regeneration respectively, though, I am thrilled to conclude this collection with them. Brenda telling it like it is, stubbing all the grime of our existence into the ashtray of the New South Africa as if we were little more than one of her lipstick-stained cigarettes. A stadiumful of the most racially mixed crowd South Africa has ever seen all shouting 'Feesh!' in unison; all living the experience of patriotism together through the on-field antics of the mop-headed defender who carries our dreams. They are flipsides of our freshly minted coin of democracy.

There is, finally, one more very important agenda to these profiles, and that has to do with the craft of writing in this age of television, of soundbites and fast-food commentary, where nothing is left to percolate the imagination. I have taken much delight in crafting these profiles; I hope you will take as much delight in reading them.

Mark Gevisser, May 1996

MALEGAPURU WILLIAM MAKGOBA

Former Deputy Vice-Chancellor, Wits University

The don who wants an ebony tower

No intellectual debate defines our times more than that which racked the University of the Witwatersrand in 1995. I interviewed Makgoba in July 1995, just after he had launched a public media campaign against Wits's 'liberal hypocrisy', but a few months before the so-called 'Gang of 13' senior Wits academics was to question his CV and call for his resignation. Makgoba responded by showing that highly qualified scientists could also be streetfighters: he publicly disclosed confidential information about his critics, for which he was suspended. Makgoba became the hero of many black students and staff. But that image was compromised when, in January 1996, he accepted a mediated solution that removed him from office and gave him a chair in medicine: why, his supporters asked, had their hero backed down?

Malegapuru William Makgoba

Two things happened on the day Professor Malegapuru William Makgoba went to the Wits University Senate for the first time: he dressed as an Arab sheikh, and his boss, vice-chancellor Robert Charlton, forgot to introduce him. The outfit was given to him by a cousin of the Sheikh of Kuwait, whom Makgoba had supervised in Britain, where he was a research head at the Royal Postgraduate Medical School in London. Now Wits University's new deputy vice-chancellor for academic affairs, he swears that, 'I had not worn the outfit intentionally. In fact I had quite forgotten that I was to be introduced to the Senate that day.'

Makgoba, a stellar Oxford-trained medical scientist in his early forties, may be vain, but he has both humour and self-reflectivity. He is prepared to admit that his subconscious might have been at work. One way or the other, those were the flowing robes of both difference and flamboyance, sartorial reminders of how exotic a black man in power still is at Wits, of his alienation from it (signified too by his lack of introduction), and his dogged desire to shake it up.

Makgoba must be the dons' worst nightmare come true. He was chosen, according to insiders, because he was 'the right kind' of black man: scholarly, academic, seemingly unpolitical (he lived in England, but was not in exile), and impeccably credentialed. The university had, in fact, been wooing him since 1987 and, once he was appointed, several faculty members were to be found crowing that they had found a 'black Charlton' – another highly decorated doctor who believed above all in keeping the ivory tower burnished.

What they got instead is a man who has declared war on the hypocrisy of white liberals who, he tells me, are 'arrogant, sluggish, and cannot accept the fact that they no longer run things'. This is the man who believes that the university must discard the 'pursuit of knowledge and truth for its own sake' along with its 'English-speaking and liberal images'. This is the man who, from a position of scholarly superiority, seems to take immense pleasure upbraiding his faculty for how parochial it is – one of his most oft-repeated swipes is about how few of them have foreign qualifications.

Vice-chancellor Charlton admits that there are problems – 'we haven't melded into a senior adminstrative team as fully as I'd like' – but says that Makgoba has played 'an important role in helping transform the institution'. But he betrays the way Makgoba has been used as a token in the two examples he volunteers: that Makgoba's presence 'lent credibility' to the administration during the negotiations with black workers and students, and that he 'has credibility with the government, which some of us don't seem to have'.

This, bluntly, is the affirmative action appointment who bit back. And it hurts. These days, the letters pages of the *Wits Reporter* read like an extract from a Malcolm Bradbury or David Lodge novel: 'The racist vapourings' of Professor Makgoba, writes Henry Kenney of Business Economics, are 'arrogant, offensive, and symptomatic of where Wits is going.' Eminent historian Charles van Onselen – Makgoba's most formidable foe in Senate – weighs in with an acerbic refutation of some of the deputy vice-chancellor's more provocative allegations.

Makgoba replies, replete with sarcasm: Van Onselen is 'the dear professor' who has his facts wrong. His detractors are issuing 'a direct challenge to my authority', because they believe that 'any constructive criticism of the institution is a criticism to

3

them or all white people', and cannot accept that 'a competent African can be in authority'. In a rhetorical flourish, he charges: 'I hope all of them will remember the fate of the great Procrustes!'

I'm afraid I don't remember the fate of the great P: I've done some research, and it appears that he was a robber who made travellers lie on his bed and either shortened them or lengthened them to fit it. The Athenian duke, Theseus, accorded him the same treatment and killed him. I do remember that Theseus killed the Minotaur and conquered the Amazons; that he was a national hero of epic proportion. I am sure that Makgoba – who is also the chair of the parastatal Medical Research Council and of the National Science and Technology Forum – chose his allusion carefully.

Certainly, he has become the champion of black people on campus, but, says a black academic who is certainly no Uncle Tom, 'if he were to take a walk around this place and check it out, he would be shocked at how unpopular he is among the majority of faculties here. He has not taken the time to get to know this institution. He doesn't have a clue about how the university works.'

Now that there is a reaction to Makgoba's sweeping statements, the academic continues, 'rather than slowing down, he interprets them as typical of a group of racists who don't want to change. It reinforces his attitude that this place is beset with racism, and it provokes him to push harder.'

In the arcane workings of the insitution, things only change at Wits by committee. But, notes a progressive white academic, 'Makgoba has now gone and alienated the very people he needs to help change things.' Furthermore, 'I find myself lumped into a category of retrogrades simply because I'm white. If I criticise his ideas, I'm automatically a racist.'

The public rage over Makgoba's pronouncements on the future of Wits have provoked an outburst of indignation which, like the furore over 'black' voices and accents on the new SAfm, only goes to prove that there is more than a little substance to allegations of *rooinek* chauvinism: English-speaking South Africans really do often believe that they hold the copyright on civilisation.

And Makgoba's diagnosis of white South African liberalism is acute: 'It is a mixture of guilt and arrogance. Black people at this university feel alienated here, as if they are just passing through, as if they might be the noble project of Wits, but they don't belong, and their input is not required.'

Certainly, this bastion of free thought has been notoriously slow to transform: the number of black academics is unacceptably low, and those few black academics who have passed through its portals have been shabbily treated. But, while his diagnosis might be correct, the treatment Makgoba has publicly prescribed – the 'Africanisation' of the university – is inexplicably fuzzy for so precise a scientist.

He wrote in the *Mail & Guardian*, for example, that, 'When Europeans decide about their institutions, be they French, German or British, the first principle is to capture the essence of France, Germany and Britain. The primary principle of a South African university should be to capture and encapsulate the essence of Africa.'

So limited a description of universities is all the more remarkable for the different standards it applies to Europe and Africa: there, universities may be 'French', 'German' or 'British'; here, they must simply be 'African', as if there were one 'essence of Africa' that pulses through the veins of this vast, complicated, heterogeneous continent of ours.

It is, of course, precisely this reparative nationalism that is at the heart of the political philosophy of Africanism, which Makgoba embraces. He was present at the birth of the South African Black Consciousness Movement, in Steve Biko's very class at the Natal University Medical School's Non-European Section, and some of his statements come almost verbatim out of Biko's writings. 'The time for whites to determine or articulate what they presume are the wishes and destiny of blacks is over,' Makgoba writes.

His harsher detractors accuse him of articulating the primitive politics of another era: 'He has been away for the past 20 years and so has missed out on the sophistication of the ANC's non-racialism,' says one don. But, Makgoba shoots back, 'nothing has changed. Whites still presume to talk for black people.'

Makgoba comes from a prominent Sekhukhune family: his great grandfather was Chief Makgoba, defeated by the Afrikaners at Magoebaskloof, and his father, a schoolmaster, was a secretary to the local chief: 'Being a country boy from a relatively well-off family,' he says, 'I grew up relatively free.' He became aware, from an early age, of the inherent democracy in his home-society: though he denies that he romanticises 'the African way', it is difficult to get him to articulate a critique of the customary society he grew up in.

He gives one cogent example of how the institution should 'Africanise': 'We have not brought traditional healers into the system … If we Western doctors were to interact more with traditional healers, we might learn a lot, and we might be able to teach them too. The point is that, without the participation of these people, we'll never be able to institute the primary health care system we need.'

Note the way Makgoba says 'we' when speaking about Western doctors. What Makgoba's critics don't get is that he is, in so many ways, one of them. He is an unashamed 'elitist' who is in the business of 'creating elites' – he just wants them to be black. When pressed on what transforming the institution means, apart from the above example and some elementary multiculturalism, what he speaks about is changing its complexion. He wishes it to be a black-led institution where black people can finally be comfortable. But he, as much as any of his critics, believes incontrovertibly in 'standards' and 'excellence'.

Listen to his plans, and you'll hear the workings of a mind that feels that white South Africa has betrayed the essential ideals of liberalism; ideals which he locates in his father, an iconic figure in his life: 'He always took the middle road. He was not an extremist. He imparted knowledge in a very democratic way. We were brought up to question.'

Perhaps that is why he never became a South African Students Organisation stalwart: 'I perceived the beginnings of mob psychology at work. They were missing Steve's message, which was, Learn to think for yourselves and work out who you are. Rather, they were saying, He has thought for us! – let's just do as he says! That might work for mobilising masses, but it doesn't work for mobilising intellectuals.'

It's not just that Tony Blair – that liberal, middle-class saviour of the British Labour Party – is the political leader to whom he feels closest. It is, notes a Wits insider quite close to him, 'his belief in the Great Man theory of history; that individuals can change institutions. His major weakness is that he, being such a traditional intellectual and also being an academic luminary, hasn't had experience in progressive and collective politics.'

So here's the dirt on William Makgoba: he is a great liberal himself.

CHARLES VAN ONSELEN
Wits University historian and senator

Wits's whitey in the woodpile

There is tragic irony in the fact that the 1996 publication of historian Charles van Onselen's brilliant book, **The Seed is Mine**, *remains to some extent overshadowed by his involvement in the William Makgoba affair of 1995, which branded him in many eyes a 'racist hardliner'. I interviewed Van Onselen in November, in the midst of the Wits debacle. His uncompromising stand was reflected, two months later, when he, along with two others, refused to sign the agreement in which Makgoba resigned. Perhaps, though, the very fact that Makgoba did resign is evidence that I was wrong when I wrote, in this profile, that Van Onselen's campaign against Makgoba had 'failed miserably'.*

Charles van Onselen

Perhaps the problem Charles van Onselen has, I think as we sit together on a Sunday afternoon, is that he looks – and sometimes sounds – like the enemy: bulging eyes beneath a balding pate, *ware-ding* khaki shorts, blustering physicality, bombast and belligerence. He talks with the overdramatised stress of a 19th-century Shakespearean actor; his discourse is filled with the building crescendoes of rhetorical interrrogatives, with hammed stage-whispers and sneering mimicry; verbal capes he flourishes over his earthy features. As he talks, I imagine him playing a platteland Lear.

But it is all too easy to miss the ironies and perpetual self-deprecations and qualifications embedded in his bombast; to tune, instead, into the crackle of righteous indignation that has made him one of the most contentious figures in current South African academia. Here, for example, is a classic torrent, in response to the allegation that he has irrevocably torn Wits University apart with the tome of allegations of fraud and incompetence he has compiled against Wits deputy vice-chancellor William Makgoba:

'According to your newspaper and everyone else, the university is bleeding to death anyhow! Here, at last, is the opportunity for an operation which might save it. The patient might die! I'm saying, Christ, I acknowledge that! But what do I do? Do I sit back and say, I know I've got an incompetent fraud in senior office who's in with a good chance of running it, but I'll tell you what, I'll be your good white South African teaboy and keep quiet about it? I'll roll over? I'll behave politely?'

His vision of Wits is millenarian; the scenarios he paints are all-or-nothing ones. Makgoba reciprocates in kind with rhetoric of 'the firing squad' for coup-plotters who fail. Van Onselen is an academic street-fighter, a campus tough who towers over the Wits Senate, where he pulls fellow academics onto his side with his rough-hewn eloquence, or alienates them with his frequent extremism. His sneering refusal to become, in his words, 'a client' of the liberation movement in the 1980s has earned him the undying antipathy of many of his fellow left-wing academics. Academic reputations were made and lost in the African Studies seminar over which he presided: he was ruthless and brutal in his criticism, particularly of people who cut their academic coats to suit the political cloth.

As June Sinclair's primary adviser when she was acting vice-chancellor in 1993, Van Onselen advocated the hard line against rioting students. Characteristically, he fought extremism with extremism, vigorously opposing mediation, and laying himself and Sinclair open to charges of 'liberal fascism' by calling the security forces onto campus.

And yet this is the man who writes with a subtlety and sophistication unparalleled in South African historiography. His account of black banditry on the reef at the turn of the century, *The Small Matter of a Horse*, is a masterpiece; one of the greatest works of literature – let alone scholarship – to emerge from South Africa. This is the man who has spent the last fourteen years on the monumental biography of an illiterate black sharecropper. The result, a 700-page volume entitled *The Seed Is Mine*, is one of the most moving re-inscriptions of black dignity onto a landscape scorched by colonialism and apartheid I have ever encountered.

He tells me he chose his sharecropper – an old man called Kas Maine whom his researchers found in a Pilanesberg resettlement camp – deliberately to upturn the stereotype of 'black people as totally deracinated victims'. He talks, with passion, about the shared skills, shared languages and values, between black sharecroppers and white farmers: 'I want to convey that not everyone here is an oppressor or victim, that there's a whole middle terrain here where our interactions are a lot more complicated, and our loves run a lot deeper than people think; as do our hates … you peel away the racial thing and you say, Jeez the crossover here, the cultural osmosis, is quite extraordinary!'

Peel away the bombast of Van Onselen and you see that, Jeez, this guy who has been branded an unreconstructed Marxist by some liberals and a 'liberal fascist' by students is, in fact, a romantic at heart who is seeking universality with black people and who is deeply hurt when they won't reciprocate.

Van Onselen has built an academic reputation on his attention to detail and on the advocacy of absolute and unassailable principle. He cannot stomach expediency, but, notes a colleague who knows him well, 'while expediency is the mark of poor academic work, it is absolutely essential to politics. The very things that make Charles a good scholar make him an ineffective politician. He will not negotiate, he will not concede, he just sallies forward with the blazing guns!'

The dossier of evidence Van Onselen has compiled against Makgoba is compelling, but critics and supporters alike say that the way he has gone about attacking and isolating the highest-ranking black academic at Wits has had the opposite effect to that intended. Most damaging was his attempt to disguise an inquiry into Makgoba's record at the University of Natal as an 'esoteric piece of social history'. Even though this instance of what one of his supporters calls 'typical Charles irony' in no way compares with the alleged level of fraudulence in the Makgoba dossier, it weakens the campaign to remove Makgoba by shifting the allegations away from Makgoba onto the process of how he was entrapped.

Several Wits players note that Van Onselen's *sine qua non* is academic independence, and that he worries that the state, having designs on Wits's independence, is using Makgoba as its can-opener: the irony, though, is that the current crisis might force state intervention. Likewise, if the intention was to bump Makgoba out of the race for the vice-chancellorship, it has failed miserably: the 'Save Willy' campaign has apparently filtered up to the highest levels of government, and Makgoba's political future is guaranteed. He has become our O J Simpson, the lightning-rod for all the complex and painful racial politics of our times: black upliftment pitched against reactionary racism on the one hand; the maintenance of standards pitched against fraudulent black nationalism on the other.

Van Onselen sets himself up against – and apart from – what he calls 'rollover liberals', whites so dominated by guilt that 'they are prepared just to roll over in the face of this new breed of African nationalist, because it's just too painful for them to engage with the fact that a black man might be a fraud!' He will not, he says, 'have a set of double standards for black South Africans', and he will not shy away from his path, which is to ensure that 'black South Africans inherit their birthright – a first-class institution at Wits'.

Although he denies that he is a 'rightwing liberal' (as claimed by Makgoba), he quotes Jill Wentzel's *Liberal Slideaway* – the new bible of right-wing liberalism – approvingly. When you define a position in absolute terms, anyone who disagrees with you is sliding away, rolling over.

Makgoba and Van Onselen were doomed to conflict from the start: 'Most of my colleagues', he says, 'are softer, gentlemanly liberals' who didn't fight back when the new deputy vice-chancellor attacked them as 'sheeps and goats', as 'inbred' and 'mentally deficient', as 'juntas' plotting 'coups'. 'But I sure as hell am not gonna take that from someone else, and so early on Makgoba singled me out as a problem, and quite rightly so.'

On top of that the historian is, in his own words, 'totally allergic to nationalism. I'm in a constant rash from it. I spent my whole family life reacting to Afrikaner nationalism, and I react in the same way to African nationalism. It's bad stuff.' Van Onselen's own family was a victim of nationalism – after his father was expelled from the police force in the early 1950s for being a *bloedsap*, the family lived an unsettled, migratory existence.

He was an outsider from the wrong side of the tracks who pulled himself up by his bootstraps and made it – with a PhD from Oxford – into the very heart of the academic elite. His attitude towards contemporary black students – whom he often caricatures, in conversation and in print, as the 'young, noisy, frustrated, illiterate, poorly cultured victims of a racist and oppressive society' – seems to be informed by his own experiences: if he could buckle down, why can't they?

His analysis of nationalism as a scourge is spot on. The bad politics come in when he refuses to acknowledge that it might mean something to others: you cannot dismiss a political force just because you think it is wrong-headed. One veteran player in Wits politics accuses Van Onselen of a 'lack of sensitivity to racism; a denial that racism exists at Wits. Not only is his wilful insistence on non-racialism often interpreted by blacks to be a covert form of racism, but people with explicit racial agendas attach themselves to him. And so Charles has a lot of supporters on campus whose motives are truly racist. Whether he intends it or not, he has become something of a reactionary hero on campus.'

Many of his detractors believe Van Onselen is driven by bitterness: for years, his generation of Wits academics have been fighting conservatism from above and preparing themselves to take over the running of the institution according to their non-racial principles and model of transformation. Now, at the very moment they should be given their chance, the vagaries of history mean that black people must be at the helm. Others feel that if Makgoba is a dud, then Van Onselen and the other academics who selected him must be held accountable: they went out of their way to find what they believed was an 'apolitical' scientist unconnected to the African National Congress. When they thought they found one, they jumped at him. The result was that they didn't vet their candidate carefully enough, and they were landed with someone who still believes in a retro-Africanism that went out with Nkrumah.

Charles van Onselen ends his new book with the suggestion that, had his subject lived to see South Africa's transition to democracy, Kas Maine would have treated the current dispensation with the same measured peasant caution as he had all the others he had survived. He then concludes with a quote from Giuseppe di Lampedusa's brilliant novel, *The Leopard*: 'I belong to an unlucky generation, swung between the old world and the new, and I find myself ill at ease in both.' It is not clear whether Van Onselen is talking about Kas Maine or himself.

MAMPHELA RAMPHELE
Vice-Chancellor Designate, University of Cape Town

If not a mother, then a witch

The crises at Wits University are often contrasted with the smooth process of transition at the University of Cape Town, where, at the same time as the Wits debacle, Dr Mamphela Ramphele was appointed the first black (and first female) Vice-Chancellor of an historically white university. I interviewed her, by sheer coincidence, the day after the appointment was announced and her autobiography launched: she was understandably hyped-up. Entitled A Life, *her book is controversial for the upfront way in which it deals with her relationship with Steve Biko.*

Mamphela Ramphele

It's the day of the anouncement of Mamphela Ramphele's appointment to the vice-chancellorship of the University of Cape Town, and she's in a fire-engine-red powersuit with fingernails to match. This woman is hot, seriously out there. Up on campus, she waves at black students who pass her, 'Hi-i-i-i!', acknowledging their felicitations. 'They have always wanted to love me,' she says of the university's black students, 'but somehow they couldn't do it, because I was being projected as a witch.'

When she was first made deputy vice-chancellor, responsible for the Equal Opportunities Programme, in 1991, 'they thought, here's our mum coming to solve problems and look after us. But I'm not the mothering type. When students came crying to me with their problems I didn't accept them unconditionally, the way a mum is supposed to. I pushed them. I challenged them. I wouldn't let them use UCT's racism as an excuse for not performing.' You're a woman. You're powerful, you're successful. If you're not a mother, you must be a witch.

In the far-northern Transvaal, from which Ramphele hails, 'many of the women branded as witches are single parents who manage to live successfully without men'. People with problems 'look for signs of taboos that have been crossed. Aha! You see that Mamphela is doing x or y or z and she's not supposed to be doing that. By breaking the taboo she has become the reason for your personal misfortune'.

So what taboos has she broken? She says it's the fact that she doesn't ask for permission; that she speaks without the imprimatur of any political party. But there's also that nifty little castrating knife she keeps in her handbag: the sharp-edged sexual harassment policy she developed as her first project at the university. ('Ha! Mamphela is really trying to emasculate us African men, and create a division between us and our women!'). And then there's her refusal to identify with black people just because she is black herself: in 1991, just months after her appointment, the campus staff went on strike. She made no bones about how wrongheaded she thought they were – and about how naive and stupid the students were for following them.

Affirmative action and black upliftment are 'strategies imported mindlessly from America, where they haven't even worked, because it was all about just giving black people a leg-up rather than profoundly transforming society'. She'll have 'no part' of reverse discrimination. 'Equity' is what she wants; 'equity and excellence'. And don't let anybody tell her that the latter is a social construct: she knows exactly what it is. Medical doctor, PhD, corporate board-member, national agenda-setter: in the face of all obstacles she – the child of rural schoolteachers – has attained it.

Oh, yes, and then there's the Biko thing. Anybody who has spent more than an hour with Mamphela Ramphele will know that she clearly doesn't need the crutch of her association with Steve Biko, her comrade, her lover and the father of her older son. She is fearless and hyper-confident, intellectually razor-sharp, refreshingly independent-minded in a world full of hacks. But what she has done with Biko is radical: she has turned herself into that stock figure of novels and tabloids alike – the Gennifer Flowers of the Black Consciousness Movement; the mistress who spills the beans.

In her autobiography, *A Life*, she has taken that innuendo-laden and dismissive one-liner attached to her, 'former Biko associate', and reappropriated it. You want to know about me and Steve Biko? she seems to taunt. I'll tell you about me and Steve

Mamphela Ramphele

Biko! It has become, overnight, the great romance of our struggle, coming into the full bloom of the public eye at the very moment of Nelson and Winnie's decline.

If you haven't already heard about their relationship in the TV and radio interviews she has given, you can read all about it in extracts published in *Femina* or the *Mail & Guardian*. In fact, next month you can go on a Mamphela Tour of South Africa with *Femina*, visiting all the haunts of the relationship: the clinic they started outside King William's Town; the office where they had their trysts; the Tzaneen community to which she was banished, pregnant with his child.

Why is she doing this? She calls it an act of self-healing, of self-definition in the face of others who would define her. She tells me about an article, in *Executive*, that announced: 'Mother of Biko's son becomes deputy vice-chancellor.' She writes in her autobiography that her public persona 'is an uncomfortable one for patriarchal society to deal with, and has to be given respectability by summoning Steve from the grave to accompany me and clothe my nakedness. In summoning him to my side, society chooses to forget the multi-dimensionality of the relationship I had with him as colleague and fellow activist and only dwells on the aspect which presents me as an instrument of his nurture and a bearer of his son.'

And so the book offers that multi-dimensionality; shows her as more than the vessel for his progeny; his child and his ideology. It's a difficult two-step, though. On the one hand she is saying, 'Treat me as my own person, not as Biko's appendage.' On the other she is gaining vast publicity for her book – unparalleled by any in recent South African publishing history but for Mandela's – through the sexiness of her relationship with Biko: star-crossed political lovers caught in a difficult triangle; a son being born at the moment of his father's brutal murder; his filing of divorce proceedings (and therefore the possibility of a marriage with her) just before his devastating death. And then, later, self-knowledge and the redemption that comes with it.

When describing, in her book, her early years and her current life as an academic, Ramphele performs the perceptive but not always interesting act of auto-anthropology; applying the tools of her trade to her own life. The middle section of the book, though, from the time she went to the University of Natal Medical School and met Biko, through to her banishment to Tzaneen and her gradual recovery from the shock of his death, is something altogether different. It is novelistic in narrative drive and deeply moving: there were at least three occasions where I found myself weeping. This, clearly, is the story she really wanted to tell.

Perhaps that is what makes people so angry with her. Three weeks before the book's publication, she wrote an opinion piece in this newspaper, slamming the Azanian People's Organisation (Azapo) for abusing Biko's legacy.

The following week, Azapo's ex-president, Itumeleng Mosala (now head of higher education at the department of education) wrote a response that was vituperative in the extreme: Ramphele, he said, was guilty of a 'continual anti-black ... diatribe'; 'a systematic and constant rubbishing of the black community as a way of climbing up the ladder of white privilege'.

He alleges that it is Ramphele, and not Azapo, who is misusing the Biko legacy towards these self-serving ends, and recalls only 'two outstanding things' about her from the early 1970s: that she defiantly smoked through meetings, and that she slept with Biko.

One of South Africa's most brilliant intellects is thus reduced to a chainsmoking concubine by virtue of the fact that the author disagrees with her politics. The point about Mosala's invective, though, is that it reflects, not inaccurately, the way many black people at the University of Cape Town (where Mosala taught before moving into government) feel about her.

When the letter was published, it was brandished about campus. One professor recalls that 'there was something so swaggering and triumphant in the attitude of some of my students, it made me quite sick. Why did they feel so vindicated?'

One of Ramphele's circle of BCM leaders and one of her oldest friends, Barney Pityana, notes that 'there is a feeling that Mamphela has been less than committed to the radical cause. She hasn't always been very understanding of the protest movement, and sometimes seems to be out of touch with the political reality. If she had a sharper political sense, she might have been able to engage students over issues, and brought them round to her point of view. Instead, she tends to dismiss their attitudes as naive and wrong.'

Recently, Ramphele had to submit to a public grilling by students at Jameson Hall as part of the selection process for a new vice-chancellor. The black students present did not spare her – many of them, in fact, mocked and goaded her. Ironically, there was a simultaneous campaign against her by many of the university's white faculty: word spread that she wanted to rid the campus of 'good little Englishmen' and that she had called for mandatory proficiency in Xhosa.

But according to a senior faculty member, 'attitudes changed because of the way she handled herself at that Jammy Hall meeting. She dealt with the students in a way that was both empathetic and firm. She wasn't defensive; she completely disarmed them. We were impressed!'

Towards the end of the race, the other remaining candidate, David Woods, was offered the rectorship of Rhodes (the self-effacing Njabulo Ndebele had already withdrawn, stating discomfort with the brutal publicness of the process). Only Ramphele was left. Even so, she came perilously close to not being appointed. At a crucial Senate meeting, she gained only five votes more than the 66 percent she needed to be approved. The main concern there seemed to be her managerial style. One professor, a supporter, describes her as 'bossy and headstrong. She is brusque, and doesn't suffer fools. Because she is often a step ahead, she is seen as intolerant.'

In her book, Ramphele describes a major breakdown she had in 1990: she had linked her own destiny too closely to that of South Africa's, and felt so responsible for the fate of the land, then extremely unsure, that she was unable to cope. Retreating to a friend's home at Simon's Town, she watched the 'inner energy and logic' of the waves, 'which no human being can alter', and asked herself: 'Who am I to think that I can change the course of history through sheer determination? Why should I think that my shoulders can hold up the sky above South Africa?'

Even though she writes that she has now managed to uncouple herself from South Africa's destiny, the mere fact that she ever thought in that way is testimony to her tendencies toward omnipotence-fantasy. But she is no unsexed Thatcher. Certainly, like Thatcher, she has pulled herself up by her own bootstraps, and does not tolerate whingers.

But there's something more unstable – and thus both more interesting and more human – about her power than that of a Margaret Thatcher or a Stuart Saunders (her predecessor at UCT). Beneath the 'carapace of confidence', as one of her friends terms it, there is an edgy and uncomfortable personality, whose authority often feels performed into being rather than innate.

She writes, as few men would dare, that she has made 'repeated disastrous choices in my personal relationships' – the main one being a wrong decision to marry her childhood sweetheart rather than Biko.

She does herself a disservice, however, by letting Biko off too lightly: even after describing how he shuttled between her and his wife Ntsiki, and also had several other affairs, all she writes is that 'there was a side of me which felt that he was not really trying, and that he might well be enjoying having the best of both worlds.'

Say it, sister. It is a rare moment in which Mamphela Ramphele unwittingly allows her readers to see her as a victim.

*A Steve
Biko for
the '90s*

*If the Makgoba/Van Onselen debate was the first incarnation of the battle between
what is inadequately caricatured as black nationalism versus white liberalism, then
the row between Human Rights Commission chair Barney Pityana and legal academic Dennis Davis was the next. Davis had written that the HRC was not performing adequately; Pityana fired back that Davis was a 'racist' who could not
accept that he and his 'ilk' didn't run things; Davis countered that he had been criticising white right-wingers on the commission and not blacks. It all culminated in
a furious TV debate, in March 1996. I interviewed Barney Pityana days later.*

Barney Pityana

When Geoff Budlender visited one of the many trials of Barney Pityana in the early 1970s, he ran into his fellow student-leader's mother, whom he did not recognise but who clearly seemed to know him. She revealed herself as Budlender's aunt's domestic worker, and told Geoff that he and Barney often used to play together as kids.

At the time, Budlender was a leader of the National Union of South African Students (Nusas), and Pityana was a leader of the South African Students Organisation (Saso) – the organisation, founded by himself and Steve Biko, that had led black students out of 'nonracial' union with Nusas. Relations between the two organisations were immensely troubled and, remembers Budlender, 'what amazed me about Barney is that in our debates he never used it against me that I was the madam's child who didn't remember the nanny. What made Barney so extraordinary is that he showed us that you could be pro-black without being anti-white. He never personalised the issues ...'

Twenty-five years later, Barney Pityana has attained notoriety (or fame, depending on which way you look at it), by going onto national television, in the very week he was inducted as chairman of the Human Rights Commission (HRC), and branding legal academic Dennis Davis a 'racist'.

Davis is one of South Africa's most celebrated left-wing lawyers, a *pro bono* legal counsel to the labour movement, a stalwart of the United Democratic Front. Pityana is an ordained priest, a theology PhD, a political visionary and the former head of the World Council of Churches' Programme to Combat Racism. Both are mensches; the former an archetypal Jewish intellectual, the latter an archetypal Anglican cleric. If Davis is volatile, impassioned and not a little shrill, then Pityana is temperate, modulated and not a little sanctimonious.

Their public row was a searing and painful spectacle of the dominant political debate of our times. Both men came to embody racial composites representing Black Rage and White Racism, Grasping Black Arrogance and Sneering White Cynicism. There on our TV screens, hovering over the befuddled head of Max du Preez, were all the genies we thought had been tightly bottled by our official ideologies of Reconciliation and Nonracialism. There was the dreadful reality writ large: democracy has not freed us from the race-bound shackles of our past; we all still live in Potgietersrus.

The accusations are even more acute than they were during the Wits University debate, but the lines are less clearly drawn. Political columnists Mondli Makhanya and Wilmot James, both black, have slammed Pityana for ill-advisedly playing the race card against a man who, they believe, has displayed no evidence of racism. One black colleague of mine believes Pityana's attack is 'the right battle, but badly fought'.

On Sunday, however, I listened to Radio Metro deejay Grant Shokoane tell hundreds of thousands of listeners about how Pityana had made his week by telling Davis exactly where to get off. If Davis wanted to leave the country, said Grant, well, 'good riddance'. Either Shokoane and I watched different debates or we truly live in different countries: in the Focus debate I saw, Pityana was manifestly unable to substantiate his claims that Davis had been motivated by racism into criticising the HRC's composition.

Last week, however, Pityana's phone was ringing off the hook. ANC officials who know Davis might be 'horrified', as one very senior (black) source told me, at Pityana's 'error of judgment'; many others see him as the standard-bearer of a new campaign against racism.

The Barney Pityana I met was clever, engaging, affable, not in the slightest bit defensive, and imbued with a quiet strength that gives way, very frequently, to a hearty guffaw. Around 50, he is of youthful demeanour, yet well on his way to clerical avuncularity: if he were my shepherd I'd feel safe in his flock.

He will go back and read the offending article, he says, and if he was wrong he will publicly apologise. In the meanwhile, he is 'delighted' that this has all happened in the very week of his inauguration because 'as the Human Rights Commission, we have an obligation to raise awareness of how things work in our society or we'll never be able to deal with them ...'

Pityana's mission is to to get South Africans to acknowledge that we are all victims or perpetrators of more subtle manifestations of racism than the crude Potgietersrus variety. Pityana, remember, was Steve Biko's other political half. Together they pioneered the notion, in South Africa, of racism as a culturally embedded phenomenon rather than simply a political force. Although he entered the Black Consciousness Movement via the ANC at Lovedale and in his native New Brighton township, and although he strenuously resisted the notion of black separatism to begin with, his political work in the student movement was to challenge not the brute force of the apartheid regime, but the more subliminal racism of 'our liberal friends in Nusas'.

Budlender writes, in a collection on the legacy of Steve Biko co-edited by Pityana, that 'the feeling of rejection was painful and profound' for white liberals. 'Part of the pain was caused by the fact that so much of the Black Consciousness rhetoric and argument seemed to be aimed directly at white liberals rather than at government supporters.'

Plus ça change: Pityana used the inauguration of the commission to eulogise the Freedom Front's Chris De Jager, who has since left the HRC for the Truth and Reconciliation Commission. Davis had slammed the Volkstater's appointment, but, says Pityana, De Jager was 'a model member of the HRC ... we actually marvelled at his capacity – and this is part of my anger with Davis – to really come to understand, to work within what the changes of our country are about'.

He allows that conservative Afrikaners, for reasons both cultural (they respect authority) and strategic (they understand where the new power lies), are more likely to be acquiescent to the new power elite than bolshy lefties like Dennis Davis. But sometimes, says Pityana, 'my liberal friends still seem to operate from a paradigm of the past. They've contributed so much to the struggle that they've now become intolerant of viewpoints different from their own. They're intolerant of Afrikaners coming in to participate, and they're intolerant of the class they often pejoratively call the black elite.'

After their televised row, Pityana and Davis had something of a rapprochement in the SABC parking lot: 'I told him', says Davis, 'that I found it deeply ironic that he should lash out at me in this way. When I came to university in 1970, the Black Consciousness Movement had just got going, and it had a profound effect on me – it made me rethink liberalism and moved me towards Marxism. What is ironic is that I'm *not* a liberal because of you, Barney Pityana!'

The point, says Davis – who stands by his criticism of the HRC – is that 'there's a huge dichotomy between nation-building and democratic culture. Pityana is angry with me for criticising nation-building. Of course you've got to have nation-building, the Bafana Bafana thing, but if you run away with that and get intoxicated by it, you lose the context of a democratic culture. You cheer thoughtlessly for the home team rather than holding it accountable.'

If indeed Pityana is to be a thoughtless cheerleader for government policy, then he is the wrong person to head a statutory body that has been set up to protect ordinary South Africans against human rights violations – a project that will, sooner rather than later, bring it into conflict with the state. But the vision Pityana articulates for his commission is precisely one that will hold the government to account. The commission has more powers than any other of its kind worldwide – not only powers of search and seizure, but the right to intervene directly in the legislative process and to call government officials to account for policy decisions.

Under his guidance, it has expanded its brief 'beyond just taking complaints of violations. We're going to find out what socio-economic human rights are being violated, and be proactive about solutions.' By the end of this year, he envisages a head office staff of 39, and offices in every province. If there has been a slow start, he says, this is because of bureaucratic red tape.

There is a bigheartedness, a broadness of vision, to Pityana that is difficult to square with the extremity of his rage over Davis's criticism. He is, in fact, an ecumenical humanist at heart. In his doctoral thesis on transition and theology, accepted by the University of Cape Town last year, he exclaims in a delightfully unscholarly way, 'I love freedom. Being free to think and act according to one's conscience. A religion that imprisons the mind will fail to capture my imagination.'

He is, in fact, a lawyer by training, but he soon came to see law's limitations. He recounts a seminal moment in his life – when Desmond Tutu, chaplain at Fort Hare, crossed a barricade of policemen, to be with protesting students in 1968: 'I saw that as a lawyer, I'd always be pushing against the bounds of possibility, fighting with a law intent on limiting my sphere of activity … But for meaningful human existence, you have to be transcendent, you have to think beyond what is possible.' The transcendent image of a levitating Bishop Tutu, faith-sailing over the barricades, seems to have powered his decision to become a cleric: in 1978 he left the country after five years of banning and detention to study theology at London University.

Now, say those who know him, much of his ire at Dennis Davis is rooted in an irritation at the self-righteousness of white leftie lawyers who think they liberated the country, and who are currently writing the Constitution in a process to which blacks remain marginal. Fellow commissioners recall that, at roughly the same moment he fired his salvo at the *Mail & Guardian* and Davis, he lost his temper for the first and only time within the commission: in response to some white members' complaints that they were being deliberately left out of the appointments process. He even snapped at Helen Suzman: 'You thought we couldn't make a good appointment without you.'

His approach, says one commissioner, 'was to deal, there and then, with what he perceived to be ingrained racism'. A friend talks about the racial slights he and his family – used to the gentility of Milton Keynes (where he was a curate) and Geneva – have endured since returning to South Africa: 'The Davis criticism was the last straw,' the friend says. 'And while I personally believe Barney maybe acted ill-advisedly, I know one thing for sure: he gets angry so rarely that, when it happens, you need to sit up and take notice. There's something going on.'

There is most definitely something going on. It's the second wave of Black Consciousness, and it makes sense that one of the prime originators of the first wave has emerged as its most strident advocate. He is a man intent on linking the tenets of an earlier age of struggle – psychological liberation, the combating of racist culture – to the current reality of the political power that black people have and the economic empowerment and control over their destinies many of them seek. He may well be a Steve Biko for the '90s.

OLIVE SHISANA
Director-General, National Department of Health

Olive Overboard!

So controversial is the national director-general of Health that, a year after I pub-lished this profile – in June 1995 – people still approach me, outraged that I was either too kind or too hostile to Olive Shisana. She was appointed to the post a few weeks after the profile was run: a year later, she was no longer the 'darling' of the funding sector, as I report in the profile. This was one of my earlier profiles, signifi-cant for me because it flagged what was to become the dominant theme in my col-umn and the power-politics of our times. Long before William Makgoba and Barney Pityana took it on publicly, Olive Shisana was raising the race issue in our new democracy.

Olive Shisana

When Olive Shisana was appointed special adviser to the minister of health in 1994, she found herself dreaming the same recurrent nightmare that had dogged her through her first five years of exile: 'I am locked up in the borders of South Africa, trying to get out and I can't. The police are after me and I can't escape them. This dream kept coming and coming, and so every white South African who was in government was to me part and parcel of those police out to get me.'

And so, when she entered the Civitas building (a Pretoria monument to banality and enclosure carefully designed to make civil servants feel they are being detained without trial) for the first time, 'I looked at these people, and in my mind what was coming through was, Oh my God! They're gonna get me! Therefore I must be defensive. I must defend myself, otherwise I'm going to be trapped within and I'm never going to come out.'

Olive Shisana comes from a family and a part of the world – the far-North – where dreams and visions are taken seriously; where the lines between this world and those of the spirits are not clearly defined. She listens to her dreams. To her immense credit, she is one of the few, in the new black elite, who will articulate the traumas and agonies that accompany sleeping with the former enemy.

And she has been working on it: 'It has taken a long time to deal with this, but I've begun to see these people as human beings and colleagues rather than as parts of an evil machine.' Not that this admission has made it any easier for those who have borne the brunt of her paranoia (she quotes Kissinger: 'Just because I'm paranoid doesn't mean there aren't people after me').

As the woman charged with restructuring the health sector in this country and the leading contender for the position of director general, she is without doubt one of this country's most controversial new technocrats – the quick-witted counterpoint to her phlegmatic minister, but as politically clumsy as Dr Zuma is wily.

When she first started, notes one of her supporters, 'she blundered around in a very self-opinionated way, and she trod on a lot of toes – not only in the department, but in the health policy world. She just didn't trust anyone.' That is an understatement. She apparently reduced outgoing director-general Coen Slabber – an easy-going gynaecologist from Bloemfontein – to a gibbering wreck, and has incurred the wrath, at one point or another, of almost everyone working in health.

She came in, says one of the leaders of a provincial strategic management team, 'shooting from the hip. She wanted to change things, to shake things up, and she had a very poor understanding of the sector. The fact that she was offhand, dismissive and arrogant meant that the people who could have helped her didn't.'

Shisana tells the story of how, when she first arrived in the United States in the mid-1970s to study clinical psychology, 'I was too scared to open my mouth. I thought, I'm the only black, a rural girl from Africa, what do I have to say?' But a friend – a Jewish woman – took her on, and once pushed her hand up in class, saying, 'Sir, Olive has got something to say!'

'She literally forced me into speaking. I'll never forget that experience. I had no self-confidence until then, but once I started talking, I went overboard! Only after a while did I start toning down …'

Although she disputes it, that seems to me to be the very model of Shisana's first year at Health. Call her Olive Overboard. She has ridden bareback into a whole plain of windmills, the most razor-edged of which was the ill-considered Deeble Plan for national health insurance, which would have guaranteed universal access to health by collapsing the private and public sectors into each other – and bankrupted the system.

Despite opposition from almost all quarters, she insisted that it be implemented, pre-empting the work of a further committee to be chaired by health economist Dr Jonathan Broomberg.

In the storm that ensued she relented. Now, after having chaired the committee with Broomberg, she has co-authored a plan that is by all accounts exactly what the doctor ordered. Her comment? 'I don't even think Deeble would believe in his plan now, given the process we've gone through and how much more we know and how many people we have consulted.'

It is a clear admission of her earlier impetuousness, and a sign of how quick – and willing – she has been to learn. Just like that first year in America, she has begun to tone down. 'There has been a definite wind-change,' notes her associate. 'She now listens to people. She seems comfortable. She delegates. She has begun to smile.'

Her detractors and supporters agree that she is both intellectually brilliant (she has a doctorate in public health from Johns Hopkins, perhaps the most prestigious institution of its kind in the world) and belligerent. She claims that she has had to be 'tough and firm' to get results: 'I came in here,' she says, 'and I found a department that was unwilling to look at substantive change. I was not put here to reform the system. I was put here to transform it, and I am succeeding.'

A more neutral observer, Dr Craig Househam, who runs the Free State health system, says: 'She has a strong personality, but she gets things done. She has driven the process of change and the result is that health is one of the departments further along the road than any other.' Indeed, the funding community has estimated that health is at least nine months ahead of any other department in terms of restructuring, and has thus made Shisana its darling.

She has shaken things up, in terms of staffing, budgetary allocation and inter-provincial co-ordination. But there are, once more, many who disagree. Yes, they say, there has been movement. But to what end? They accuse Shisana of academicism; of worrying unduly about policy and restructuring when there is, in fact, a crisis of delivery that needs to be sorted out first.

These people – and they are the ones in the front line, the superintendents of crumbling hospitals and resource-starved provinces – want a manager first. The vision stuff, they say, can wait.

The vision stuff is basic, and powerful: 'There is still one thing about the Deeble plan I stick to, and that was its insistence on universal access to health. I will fight for that as long as I live. And, whether or not I am appointed director-general, I will stay in government until I see a national health system in place.' If this is not heartfelt, then Shisana is an excellent politician.

She claims that her detractors are a small group of people who have been left out of the process. 'Let's be frank,' she says, 'there are people who are uncomfortable about Africans taking on a leadership position. We are challenged as if we are intellectually incapable and we are challenged about our political background.' This last point in response to a rumour that Shisana, in contradiction to her CV, was not allied to the ANC in exile, a rumour that is easily disproved.

She is patently wrong when she says that her critics number only a handful and when she implies that they are all not African – critics of Olive Shisana come in all colours, and they are all over the place. But let's be frank, there is a major race issue happening in the upper echelons of the new technocracy; one about which everyone will hold forth at great length off the record, but no-one will tackle publicly.

It goes like this: Africans are bitter that the supposedly progressive coloured/Indian/white intelligentsia is nabbing most of the senior posts (and indeed, there are very few African directors-general), while appropriately qualified, progressive non-Africans fear that they are being left out because they are not black enough. The one side cries 'racism!' and the other 'Africanism!'; both sides over-exaggerate the issue, but both have a point. And Shisana has become a lightning-rod in an ever-intensifying storm.

She responds with indignation. 'Wait a minute! Where do I come from? I come from the very people I'm trying to help! It's not academic or theoretical for me! I'm talking about my brother, my sister, my mother, my neighbor; I'm talking about the people I grew up with, in Mamelodi, in Makotopong. Why do I have to prove anything beyond that?'

In a day spent with Olive Shisana one sees both the flickers of embattlement and the ease which comes with a sense of arrival. She talks, with much emotion, about the guilt of bringing her two children, born in the United States, back to the captivity of South Africa (they returned in 1991), and of the house she built with her husband – who lectures at the University of the Western Cape – at Tableview, 'with a picture-perfect view of the sea and the mountain'.

She had never before been to Cape Town – she and her husband chose it from the pages of a book while in Washington DC as the place they would 'return' to. It says something about the single-mindedness with which she is pursuing a sense of emplacement; a sense that was first shattered, perhaps, when she was forcibly removed with her family from their ancestral land at Makotopong, outside Pietersburg.

She was 17 at the time, and her memories of life before removal are pastoral and idyllic – all dew-covered berries, the twittering of birds, and the welcoming hearth for wayward travellers. Even the poverty of having to sleep around a fire under blankets made from mielie-meal bags is remembered as being 'close to the ancestors'.

There is, in Olive Shisana, both a quest for unattainable perfection, and a manifest self-consciousness of her own imperfections. That combination results in the kind of drive that propels a black woman, against all odds and in the face of much opposition, to the very top of the civil service.

MBONGENI NGEMA

Director of *Sarafina 2*

What all the song and dance is about

I met Mbongeni Ngema in Durban in February 1996, in the midst of the Sarafina 2 *scandal, when it was disclosed that he had been given R14,2-million, through dubious procedure, to make a play about AIDS. He is another subject I am often accused of being 'too soft' on. My answer is that the job of the psychoanalytic profile is to understand its subject rather than to judge it. I wanted, here, to put Ngema into the context of black South African theatre, and to get to the psychic roots of his creative impulses. This last project took me into shaky ground indeed: is it ethical for the journalist to examine the sexuality of his subject? I decided that, in this case, it was: if a man is given R14-million of taxpayers' money to teach sexual responsibility, then we are entitled to know how he deals with these issues in his own life.*

Mbongeni Ngema

Depending on which way you look at it, Mbongeni Ngema is the very best or the very last person you'd want to give a R14-million Aids education contract to. Even his biographer, Laura Jones, was moved to chide him, in an otherwise salutary *Nothing Except Ourselves*, for his sexual 'recklessness': 'No matter the consequences to himself or his lover, (...) he has always found it impossible to pass up any appealing woman, especially one who seemed attracted to him.'

Ngema, rooting his polygamy in the customs of the rural Zululand whence he hails, at one point had three wives. His first, Xoliswa, divorced him. Now he has two: his star, Leleti Khumalo, with whom he lives in that Kloof home all over the Sunday papers, and Cebisila, 16 when he married her in 1990, who lives in another Durban house.

So yes, says Ngema about the relationship between his theatre and his sex life: '*Sarafina 2* has made me change my life. I'm living through a revolution with my own customs. It's difficult for an African man, particularly for a successful one, to say he has only one partner.' Understanding Aids through the play has made him 'keep women at arms' length. I've had to go through a struggle within myself – if I'm attracted to someone, I have to ask myself so many questions.'

Like whether to use condoms? 'A beautiful option. If I have to go out of the way, that's the only option I have.'

Sarafina 2, which has been dormant for the past few weeks, re-opens on 15 March at the Eyethu Cinema in Soweto, where it will run until the end of the month. On Monday, four days before this unexpected opening (brought forward because of the scandal), Ngema gathers his cast in a Durban hall: 'I'm warning you,' he says, '... the journalists will not be on your side. They'll be thinking you're a massive scandal, a waste of taxpayers' money. So every step you take they'll be judging you. The stakes are high ...'

The stakes are high, and so I cannot blame Mbongeni Ngema too much for giving me the runaround. I chased him, usually unsuccessfully, around Durban for two days. He lived up to his notorious reputation for disorganisation. When we did connect, he was charming, cool in floppy linen suits, shorn of those trademark peppercorns around the mouth, fresh-faced rather than dissolute. Despite the fact that he was working those 'so sue me' spaniel-eyes for all they were worth (far more than R14-million – Ngema is a multimedia superstar), I found him refreshingly artless. A country boy from Hlabisa quite at home in an imported silver Camaro with personalised plates, calling the shots at a fab post-modern office, all curves and views and shiny black surfaces, up on Morningside Ridge. The Umgeni Road is most certainly not Sunset Boulevard, but this is as close to the Hollywood Hills as you're going to find in the canefields.

Depending on whom you believe, the offices were decked out by you and me, dear taxpayer, or by our equivalents on the polders and in the *petites villes*. Ngema confirms that *Sarafina 2* was the brainchild of Minister of Health Nkosazana Zuma. The truth is that conventional AIDS-awareness methods – pamphlets, posters, even worthy educational theatre – have not worked, and so Zuma is to be commended for trying something new, and for roping little Sarafina, pop-liberation icon of the 1980s, into the act: who ever thought the matronly minister could be so funky?

Whether it is worth R14-million – equivalent to a fifth of the annual Aids budget and the total cost of the entire annual provincial Aids allocations – is another matter altogether. People in the Aids field can be forgiven for finding it offensive and even grotesque that even Ngema's stage-hands earn R2 000 a week, the salary many of them earn in a month, and that Ngema has bought, with the department's money, items like a R1-million luxury bus.

Citing what amounts to a gag from the minister's office, Ngema will not respond to allegations of 'unaccounted for' money, save to say that he has 'no knowledge' of the R1,1-million in dispute.

Like his political principals, he has decided to brazen it out. About the bus, he says, 'Yes! It's about time our artists were transported in dignity. Why must we be transported in luxury buses in the United States, but come to our own country to be put in the back of Kombis? No way! I'm proud of our bus.'

Are his own services worth R300 000, particularly given the fact that he is paid another full-time salary, worth R90 000, by the state through his position as musical director of the Natal Playhouse? 'No, they are not. I should be earning at least a million.' But does any director in this country earn those figures? 'I don't think you can compare me to anyone in this country.'

He is unrepentant about the cost of the production, putting a race-spin on it: 'I'm not prepared to do a second-class production. Why should whites get state-funded first-class productions in the State Theatre, while blacks in the townships get flatbed trucks? No. Blacks deserve Broadway standards.'

Apart from the fact that he is now a senior official at one of these 'white' state institutions where he has successfully produced three of his own plays using state money, the problem here is that he – a creative artist – is dealing with the Health Department's budget as if it were his own private performing arts council rather than funding for health education.

Sarafina 2 marks a crucial turning point in indigenous South African theatre, one that has been a long time coming. Now, given the severe budgetary constraints on arts funding, the only way performing artists will get money for their work is if they tie in to one aspect or another of the RDP: this year *Sarafina 2* uses AIDS and throws in a message about condom use; next year *Sarafina 3* might tap Kader Asmal's budget and throw in a message about sanitation: 'Ventilated Privies Are Coming, To-mor-row!'

Ngema, who has no problem with the concept of 'RDP theatre', sees it another way: black South African theatre has 'always been issue-based. What I'm doing with *Sarafina 2* is an exact continuation of what I was doing with the original *Sarafina!* The only difference is that when we were doing freedom theatre, the government wouldn't pay for it. Now we are free, we are shifting to other stories, and the government is finally paying.'

Some might say that by calling this *Sarafina* a continuation of a previous one, the director is revealing his own expediency. He was frequently slammed, in the 1980s, for capitalising on the struggle. Is he now capitalising on another?

It's worth putting Mbongeni Ngema into context. His *Woza Albert!*, developed with Percy Mtwa and Barney Simon, heralded the birth of South Africa's world-renowned protest theatre in 1981. Then with *Asinamali!*, Ngema demonstrated his exceptional technical abilities, and his ability to turn the wrenching political dynamics of the time into an entertaining and challenging theatrical form. Both are among the most brilliant and defining works of art to have emerged from this land.

Asinamali! became a *cause célèbre* in New York. The Lincoln Centre gave Ngema hundreds of thousands of dollars to produce his next work, *Sarafina!*. He recruited 30-odd kids, housed them in a refurbished warehouse in Newtown, and set to work, from scratch, to create the play over nearly a year. Certainly, his patriarchal position made the situation ripe for exploitation, and there were controversies, not least allegations that he used the casting couch, and the cane and belt to 'discipline' his wards. Ngema admits to the corporal punishment, saying that it was because the families of the 'kids' had entrusted them to him, and that it was his duty to discipline them.

One way or the other, *Sarafina!* became the benchmark musical of the time, and launched a generation of young stars. The play defines the way most Americans think about South Africa, and it defines the way most young black South Africans think about theatre. Go to any community theatre group, and you'll see a dozen teenage girls trying to be Sarafina – all 'Broadway-here-I-come' mug-faced delivery and brazen sexuality. At every community theatre festival in this land, there is at least one group that puts on a tape of the play and lip-synchs its way through it. The pastiche of political anger and comic burlesque, fused into a form of struggle-minstrelsy, has become the almost inescapable formula for how to make black South African theatre: liberating in the possibilities of success it presents, oppressive in the limitations of style it imposes.

Oppressive, indeed, even to its own creator. Since *Sarafina!*, Ngema has produced little of note. His latest musicals have been pale shades of *Sarafina!*, with narratives becoming more and more inconsequential and self-referential. His work is formulaic, and often seems half-baked, precisely because he is trying to be everything from director and composer to choreographer, producer, manager and writer. But Ngema professes to be thrilled with the formula: 'Yes, my musicals do work to a formula, but it's a formula I like. And more important, a formula the people like.'

Now the brassy schoolgirl returns to our stages as a condom-toting social worker; the revolutionary aspiration of the 1980s has matured into the social responsibility of the 1990s. Perhaps South African theatre's most famous son is to be commended for his inventiveness: using Aids, he has found a way of bringing theatre back into the townships, to the rickety halls and grubby cinemas and open fields he once played to with 'Bra Gib' Kente. It remains to be seen whether, in the process, he has resparked his own creative muse and re-energised the genre of township theatre.

I can trace my coming to political consciousness, as a white schoolboy lurking around the Market Theatre, to a performance of *Woza Albert!* I'll never forget Ngema. I wept at the shame of my ignorance while black folk guffawed all around me. Later in my life, I remember watching Americans on Broadway at *Sarafina!*, smugly leaving the theatre believing that, by simply paying $25 and sitting through a couple of hours of song and dance, they had personally done their bit in liberating South Africa, by literally applauding black children from slavery into freedom.

To invest R14-million blindly in such an unpredictable medium is a costly risk. The odds are not improved by the fact that Ngema knew little about Aids to begin with, and was given little backup from the Department of Health until the very last minute. Even now, his understanding is rudimentary. No wonder some spectators felt his first productions perpetuated the problem that women face in the Aids epidemic by showing women to be subjugated 'gifts' spreading the virus.

Laura Jones writes, in her biography, that Ngema's 'tender answer to the questions I've put to him about the numerous affairs in his life – many of which seem to have been highly irresponsible – is always the same: "But she loved me".'

Hey, if Mbongeni Ngema speaks the truth and *Sarafina 2* has precipitated an internal sexual revolution, maybe Dr Zuma's risk will pay off. This man is no prissy health professional: he has been there in the sexual trenches, done it all. Perhaps he does, after all, know what he's on about.

NKOSAZANA ZUMA
Minister of Health

*Sarafina
of the
health
system*

I interviewed Dr Zuma in March 1996, at a time when the Sarafina 2 *scandal, was tarnishing her previously clean record and making her an object of both derision and fury. The allegations of funding irregularity were referred to the Public Protector. One of the things that troubles me most about being a journalist is that you get people when they are down. Dr Zuma was, understandably, defensive; she was also gracious enough to give me many hours of her time, even though she clearly did not want to be interviewed.*

Nkosazana Zuma

There's a lesson Nkosazana Zuma learnt from the African National Congress training manuals when she was an operative that she continues to apply, now that she is in Cabinet: 'If you sell your people out by giving in to the enemy, the enemy will respect you even less for it.'

The commonsensical health minister chooses to recount this particular struggle homily when asked what she has read, in her life, that has influenced her most: it says much about both her down-home intellect and her current state of embattlement. She accepts, of course, that the enemies she has to deal with in her current job are of an entirely different order from those she confronted when she was working underground, out of Swaziland, for the ANC. Sometimes, though, she feels that the 'enemies of transformation' she has to fight now are 'more difficult to deal with' than those she encountered during the liberation struggle.

She reminds me of a middle-aged Staffordshire bull terrier or two I have known. She is stolid and doughty, thickset and lowslung, unfashionable but powerful; wilful and driven; self-contained, diffident, and sometimes downright crabby; possessed of an astonishing economy of motion (she sat through a three-hour interview with barely an eye-flicker) that masks an equally astonishing capacity for action: she kicks, as they say, ass.

Her image is that of a country doctor you would both trust and fear: prematurely matronlike (she is only in her mid-forties) with a bonnet of unstyled grey curls framing her features, she is given to sensible two-pieces and low-heeled pumps.

Phlegmatic and undemonstrative by nature, she does not reveal any agony at the fact that her carefully maintained image of dependability has been scorched by the *Sarafina 2* fiasco. On the streets she has become a figure of parody: the taxi-drivers laugh about Sarafina 4 and Sarafina 5; the cartoonists fashion her unlikely frame as a Broadway chorus girl chucking dollars about the stage of her profligacy; even her fellow parliamentarians joke about *Sarafina 2* on public platforms.

There is no doubt, though, that she has been deeply hurt by the affair. If this was her first major political test, she failed. Not because the whole thing was her brainchild and she still insists that 'I stand by the principle of an Aids musical like this', or because she finds no problem with the inadequate and unsavvy way that the project uses drama to effect behaviour change. Not because of the poverty of the play's message; not even because the justification for spending so much on the project was that Mbongeni Ngema apparently has the power to pull black people back into township theatres, and the day I went – last Saturday afternoon– there were no more than 80 souls in the thousand-seater Eyethu Cinema.

No: she failed because, rather than acknowledging that there might have been irregularities and instituting an immediate inquiry, she rushed, hackishly, to the defence of a department that seems to have acted indefensibly; and then demanded of the ANC that it rush, as hackishly, to her own defence. Of the several canards she pulled out of her hat, the most ill-advised was the race card (her critics were whities who just wanted to pull black people down): it has been effectively trumped, not only by *The Star*'s political editor Kaizer Nyatsumba's condemnatory column, but also by the anger and derision of many ordinary black men and women.

Sitting in her home on the Groote Schuur Estate last week, she did allow herself self-reflection on the issue: 'I looked seriously at my intentions; I genuinely believe

I've done nothing wrong.'

What about her department? She answers by speaking generally rather than specifically: 'If, in any matter, I don't see any deliberate wrongdoing or bad intention or sabotage from the people in my department, I should not leave them in the cold. It doesn't mean I am saying they did everything right, but if someone was trying to make an honest day's work and they made a mistake, I'm not saying the mistake should not be pointed out ...' Lift the haze of obfuscatory double negatives, and one thing becomes clear: Nkosazana Zuma has realised that she needs to distance herself, even if slightly, from the actions of her department.

Her comportment over the last few weeks notwithstanding, she strikes one as a person of immense integrity. She has always been, says one senior health professional who knows her well and is deeply dismayed by the *Sarafina 2* mess, 'on the side of the angels; deeply committed to health reform and bringing the right of health care to ordinary people'.

A senior comrade from exile describes her as 'refreshing; very simple and uncomplicated and frank; open, honest and direct'. Another colleague describes her 'capacity for hard work' and her 'genuineness' as 'legendary' within the ANC. The source adds, though, that 'when the situation calls for it, she can be tough and difficult, and can get very stubborn indeed'.

From very humble Natal midlands beginnings – the oldest of eight children of a Catholic rural primary school-teacher – she got to the University of Natal's non-European medical school in 1972, just as Steve Biko was leaving. She became a vice-president of the South African Students Organisation, but left it – and her studies – to join up with the ANC abroad, because 'being proud of what you are and asserting yourself is a great start, but it doesn't liberate the country – you need a bit more than that'.

She finished her degree in Britain and, as a good medic to the movement, she came to the attention of ailing older men like Oliver Tambo and Harry Gwala, as well as the younger and healthier Thabo Mbeki. She met and married Jacob Zuma; committed her life to the struggle. She was one of the first batch to return to the country, and played a major role in re-establishing the ANC in the tense southern Natal region. Friends say that she fully expected the ANC to win the province, and was readying herself for a career as its MEC for health.

Then Nelson Mandela called her to Pretoria. It was unexpected and difficult: her children, the youngest of whom is six, remain in Durban. Nkosazana Zuma is extremely uncomfortable talking about her personal life: all she will say about the fact that she is not the only wife of Jacob Zuma, is that 'I am his only legal one'. There is something dislocated and lonely about her current existence.

Despite her paranoia about the media –'I've never received good press; everything I touch is attacked' – she has developed a sturdy reputation as a minister, perhaps for the very reason she got into trouble over *Sarafina 2*: she stubbornly stands her ground, and insists on action. This publication alone has twice awarded her eight out of ten in its annual Cabinet review.

What has been the greatest achievement of her tenure? 'Undoubtedly, the free health care for children under six that President Mandela announced after his election ... the fact that it was done in the first 100 days was a real highlight, because if it hadn't been done then, so many questions would have been asked that it would never have happened.'

The logic reveals, perfectly, the 'shoot now and fight the fires later' approach she shares with her controversial director-general, Olive Shisana. And that is the basis of most of the criticism the two women receive from their colleagues in public health.

Despite the fact that there has been more reforming movement in this sector than almost anywhere else, there have also been a string of ill-fated and ill-conceived plans, the latest of which is Shisana's pet project, the National Health Information System; a hi-tech fantasy that would have all South Africans carrying smart cards with their entire medical histories on them, and the most sophisticated centralised database in the world. 'It's a brilliant end-point for ten or fifteen years' time,' says one highly placed critic. 'For now, though, how about electrifying the clinics and training the nurses in basic diagnostic skills?' So outlandish is the project that the European Union has withdrawn its funding for the first phase.

Then there is the troubled National Health Insurance plan, which finds itself once more on the rack after having been sent back from Cabinet a few weeks ago. Zuma does some damage control by saying, 'I'm not committed to health insurance. The most important thing is to bring free health care to the people: if we can do it through taxation, then that's preferable.'

The latest dazzle-'em announcement is that there will be free primary health care in clinics for all South Africans starting 1 April. 'It's absurd,' says one provincial director. 'The homework hasn't been done. There's no attention to detail. It's all quite meaningless.' Zuma probably knows this: once more, though, her strategy is to commit her sector to reform, and deal with the problems it creates later. It's the combat mode of progress: advance now, count casualties later.

Several health professionals note that there is a pattern to all the schemes she has introduced, ranging from those mentioned above, through the import of Cuban doctors, down to *Sarafina 2*. They say there should be more substantive process; that complex reforms are often implemented in a scattershot manner, with little consultation and nowhere near enough planning and research or pilot programming.

There are, nonetheless, some exceptionally good reforms coming out of the health department: the new district system, for example, and innovative new plans for hospital management. Whatever her problems, one thing is invaluable about Nkosazana Zuma: she is both a steely activist and a committed professional in the field of her portfolio. If you have any doubts about the latter, ask her about what it's like to watch a child under your care die unneccesarily due to lack of facilities.

At the end of our time together, I ask Dr Zuma – who was chair, before she became minister, of the committee that drafted South Africa's exemplary Aids policy – why she has been so high-profile about anti-tobacco legislation and yet so silent on Aids.

She disputes the premise of my question strenuously: she speaks much more about Aids than she does about smoking; it's just that 'everyone thinks about me every time they have a cigarette, because of the warnings on the packets and the ads'.

I josh that she should institute a similar campaign promoting condoms – then people would think about her every time they have sex too. She lets loose a deep ripple of laughter; her face opening into the broadest of grins. In one of the most difficult weeks of her life, I am afforded a brief glimpse of her teeth – and her humanity.

THAMI MAZWAI
Head of the Black Editors' Forum

Giving the media a black eye

At the time of the Sarafina 2 *scandal, both Nkosazana Zuma and Mbongeni Ngema accused the white-owned media of being opposed to black-led transformation and initiative, because its inevitable result was the relinquishment of its own power. This critique was pioneered by Thabo Mbeki and Thami Mazwai at a conference on state media at Arniston in August 1995; I interviewed Mazwai shortly thereafter. Following my profile, Mazwai took up the cudgels against me in his* Business Day *column, asserting that I was part of a 'spontaneous white conspiracy against the black intelligentsia'.*

Thami Mazwai

L ast Saturday night at the Carlton Hotel, while a band trundled tonelessly through a rendition of 'Stand By Me' in the function room next door, Thami Mazwai's Black Editors' Forum (BEF) gathered to contemplate its relationship to press freedom, to the white mainstream media, to the African National Congress government, and to guest speaker Thabo Mbeki.

About 60 people were there – black editors, journalists and professionals. If there is such a thing as a black middle class, then its publicist is Mazwai, editor of *Enterprise* magazine. He introduced Mbeki to the gathering by quipping that, in some circles (the 'white media' that have been lambasting him for his call for state regulation of media to ensure affirmative action), he is seen as Mbeki's subaltern in a sustained assault on press freedom and independence.

The room erupted into laughter at the absurdity of the notion. Mbeki then gave one of the more masterful speeches of his career. With his trademark style of the elegant assailant – creeping up on you with the knife-edge of an argument beneath the night cover of Proustian syntax – he urged the BEF to join his government in the task of black upliftment that must remain a central part of transformation.

When his speech was over, *Sowetan* political editor Mathatha Tsedu rose to challenge him. It's all very well for you to speak about black empowerment, he said, but why aren't you helping bail out the African Bank? Why aren't you making sure that small black businessmen get government contracts?

Mbeki countered by singling out one of the few palefaces present: 'I see Anton Harber is here,' he said, looking over at the *Mail & Guardian* editor. 'Now criticism and complaining is what I expect from him. This forum, on the other hand, has to see itself as a change agent, and not just criticise.'

Roll up your sleeves, Mathatha, and stop whingeing like a whitey. Get with the programme. It dovetailed perfectly with perhaps the most cynical conceit of Mbeki's speech, when he rallied his audience by quoting, at length, from a newspaper editorial attacking African National Congress policies as 'the very antithesis of reconciliation' and accusing the party of fighting a struggle that is already over.

Here's the cynicism: anyone who reads Johnny Johnson's daily rants on the *Citizen*'s leader page will recognise immediately the crusty style of this reactionary campaigner. He is way to the right of a mainstream print media that behaves, on the whole, like a kindly – if occasionally reproachful – aunt to the ANC. But Mbeki pointedly did not identify the author: he wanted its misguided opinions to stand metonymically for the entire corpus that is the white media.

Interestingly, though, his audience did not rise to the whitebait. One woman asked what Mbeki had done, since taking power, to help the ordinary black person. He responded very sharply indeed: those who were starving and who now get one slice of bread a day are very pleased with the government's performance. It is only those 'who have not yet graduated from a Toyota Corolla to a BMW who are saying to the government, "After sixteen months, what have you achieved?" '

Mbeki knew he was among a group of people who are dissatisfied with the slowness of transition. While white South Africans – in the private sector and in government – bemoan affirmative action, many black professionals still believe, often quite correctly, that there is a glass ceiling to their upward mobility. And so the deputy president was simultaneously wooing his audience (Come on board, chaps, and the end result will be your own advancement) and gently rapping it over the knuckles.

It may indeed be risible to say that Thami Mazwai is acting on Mbeki's behalf in an assault on press freedom. Firstly, Mbeki, for all his expressed irritation at media criticism and his ill-conceived plans for TV airtime, has never once suggested curtailing press freedom. Secondly, Mazwai was correct when he wrote, in the latest of his fortnightly *Business Day* columns, that 'if it is press freedom we are talking about, then we black journalists ... know more about the subject than anyone else. We went through detentions, torture, exile, personal and newspaper bannings.'

But it is equally correct to say that, at the moment, Mbeki and Mazwai are allies, in that they have both taken up arms against the whiteness of the mainstream media; the former because he perceives it to be hostile to the government's transformation agenda, the latter because he believes it is thwarting black economic advancement. Perhaps it comes down to the same thing.

But if Mbeki uses the scalpel so gently it takes a while to notice the incision, Mazwai prefers the battering-ram: 'The white media goes out of its way to hammer black enterprise and achievement. If you look at the history of apartheid, there has been a systematic campaign to portray blacks as failures,' he tells me. 'The white media is interested only in scandals, corruptions and failures of the government.'

There is only one way to remedy this situation, Mazwai says: the state must regulate the media. It should do this by sticks – placing its immense advertising accounts only in publications that have the requisite number of blacks – and by carrots – funding media organisations owned by blacks. It should also limit foreign ownership in the media. This would enhance rather than limit press freedom by encouraging a diversity of voices: 'I and my colleagues in the Black Editors' Forum oppose a government-owned media,' he wrote in *Business Day*. 'However, ownership and control by the minority is just as undesirable.'

Cape Times editor Moegsien Williams, who worked with Mazwai on the *Sowetan*, says that his commitment to press freedom is irreproachable, and credits much of the paper's success to 'the way Thami drove his journalists, expected the best from them, sent them back again and again'. Mazwai was the day-editor of the *Sowetan* for over a decade. Before that he helped lead the team of black journalists on the *World* which, some say, provided the only real coverage of the 1976/77 uprisings.

He has had two spells in prison: the first in the early 1960s, for Pan Africanist Congress activism; the second in the early 1980s, for withholding evidence against one of his sources. He helped found one of the anti-apartheid media unions in the 1980s. He has been at the very typeface of media activism in South Africa.

His political trajectory – from PAC hothead to strident capitalist – is not as surprising as it may at first seem: 'black upliftment' (shorthand for the establishment of a black middle class) has always sat, uneasily, alongside radical socialism in the PAC and the Black Consciousness Movement. Mazwai finally parted with the PAC in 1990, but notes now that most of the 28 000 members of the black elite who buy his magazine are 'Africanist in orientation, whether they are PAC, ANC, IFP or even National Party. There is an immense pride in being black and an achiever.'

Thami Mazwai's blustering persona – flailing arms, spluttering inarticulacy weirdly at odds with the facility of his written prose, and rumpled and distracted image – often leads those who dislike him to dismiss him as a buffoon.

But to highlight the obvious contradictions – a strident free-marketeer calling for state regulation – misses the point: Thami Mazwai lives and dies by the credo of black economic advancement. That, rather than the free market, is his ideology, and if a regulated environment suits it, then so be it. He has set himself an agenda that he is pursuing singlemindedly; he has tapped into the currents of the ever-expanding black elite and developed a product second only to the porno-market in growth.

Enterprise, he says, 'focuses on achievement by blacks in the business economy. I've gone out there to look for those stories of measurable success and come back to write about them. Obviously, some of those stories turned sour. Some couldn't per-form, although we gave them lots of coverage. That's not my problem. My task is to let blacks see themselves in a positive light.'

He is using exactly the same approach to black advancement in government as he does to black advancement in private enterprise. In an *Enterprise* special series, for example, every provincial minister is getting a whole page of uncritical publicity-fluff: Mazwai, a good journalist, is doing the government's job better than the inept South African Communication Service ever could. 'Previous apartheid governments were given this opportunity, and they were then measured against what they said after a year or two. Why must this not apply to blacks?' Mazwai wrote in his July 1995 *Enterprise* editorial. Little wonder government official Frank Meintjies singled him out, in a recent broadside against media coverage of the RDP, for special praise. Little wonder some might think he is acting as Mbeki's agent.

His critics allege that he is setting himself up to be one of the black editors whom the newspaper groups might be bullied into hiring by his own campaign; or setting his own publication up as one of the beneficiaries of selective government advertis-ing. He certainly wasn't complaining about foreign media ownership they say, when he seemed about to launch a business daily, with Swedish funding.

But listen to Moegsien Williams, the first black editor ever of a traditionally white daily: '62 percent of my readers are black. And yet I am only the sixth black person to be hired here, out of a total staff of 60. So Thami's stand helps me immensely, in that he is sensitising my bosses to the need to fix up these problems. When I go speak to them, I can say "Look, this is what Mazwai is saying." The pressure is good.'

Mazwai tells me that 'very few blacks differ with the sentiments I express'. Other black journalists express irritation that he seems to be talking on their behalf. 'He comes from an era', says one, 'where there were very few black voices allowed – Qwelane, Klaaste, Thloloe, himself. And so he got into the habit of speaking for all black people, because he was one of the few who had a voice.'

Mazwai has that peculiar relationship with his readers that writers (poets laureate or publicists) often have with their clients: he does not live among them or like them. He, like them, might have a cellphone (40 percent of *Enterprise* readers do, according to the magazine's research), but his home is in Pimville rather than in Kelvin or Noordwyk and is, like its owner, utterly without the pretensions and trappings of yuppiedom. He has had a difficult life: his wife died, three years ago, after deliver-ing their fourth child; for much of his young adulthood he was an alcoholic.

Thami Mazwai has neither the brilliance nor the free-thinking iconoclasm of those Kofifi-era journalists whose glamour he so admired in the 1950s. But, unlike Can Themba or Casey Motsisi, he got over his addiction; he survived. He knows how.

Working-class hero: something to be?

Do communists and trade unionists have a different way of looking at 'black uplift-ment' and 'black economic empowerment' from people like Mazwai, Ngema, Makgoba or Shisana? I met Sam Shilowa in February 1996, at the height of the furore over the privatisation of parastatals. Two months later he led Cosatu in its high-profile and controversial national strike on the eve of the adoption of the con-stitution. Both a spokesman for workers and very much within the class of the new bosses, he embodies, sharply – and not unselfconsciously – the dilemmas facing black leaders with new power.

Sam Shilowa

One of Sam Shilowa's previous employers tells the story of meeting him across a picket line and being so impressed with his performance in negotiations that he suggested he be groomed for management. Sorry, said Shilowa's immediate boss: nice enough chap but he really doesn't have the potential.

Anybody who couldn't see that Sam Shilowa had potential must have been blind – or terrified. He is broad-faced and big-boned, exuberant and clever. His sentences, like his vast hands, go everywhere. They will climb, in spastic spirals, to the apex of an idea before crashing down into outrage; they will meander vaguely through the savannah and then take you by surprise by literally reaching out and clasping you.

On the Christmas holiday he took in Cuba, he decided to stop shaving his scalp and let his hair grow a bit. Nonetheless, the image of a shaven-haired cloth-capped giant remains: working-class hero or repossession man; I suspect he doesn't mind the ambivalence.

Journalist Phillip van Niekerk wrote in *Leadership* that Shilowa's manner 'is far more amiable than the Mephistophelean displeasure that his predecessor Jay Naidoo was able to project'. True enough: if Naidoo's persona veered towards the hood-eyed, scheming, commie intellectual, then Shilowa has the open countenance of a hammer-twirling worker who has just tripped off a piece of socialist-realist memorabilia; sort of retro, quaint and Scargillish at the same time (if such a thing is possible), an extra from the set of 'On the Waterfront'.

Well, not quite. For one, while it is true that Shilowa is the sparely educated son of impoverished Shangaan peasants and that he rose in the unions from the shop floor, he was never quite the on-the-beat security guard he has been portrayed as; he did clerical and laboratory work at Anglo-Alpha Cement, and then was a trainer at a security and cleaning firm.

And, while it is true that he had to take years off school because of his family's poverty, he finally dropped out in standard nine, not because of racial injustice or political activity, but in a fit of pique because he felt he was being unfairly punished (which he was) by a teacher who is now, in fact, an organiser for the African National Congress. 'One weakness I have', he allows, with a laugh, 'is that there are times when I'm arrogant, not willing to listen to reason.'

Certainly, Shilowa rose – meteorically – through the ranks. But, to the extent that you could separate politics and labour in the 1980s, his base was political: it was his work in the South African Communist Party underground and his primacy in Cosatu's SACP caucus, far more than his brief history as an office-bearer of the Transport and General Workers' Union, that made him Jay Naidoo's unlikely deputy in 1991 and his successor in 1993. He obliquely acknowledges this: 'Even though I grew up through the ranks, my own strong points have not always been pure trade union bread-and-butter issues. Even when I was Jay's deputy, he was involved in economic issues, while I was involved in politics. I was part of the ANC's negotiating team, I was at Codesa, and at every single large bilateral. I think it was a plus for me, as I really do understand the transition.'

It's his strong point and his weak point. Ask people about Sam Shilowa and the word you'll hear most often is 'operator'. He is, says one senior trade unionist, 'so politically canny he can hear the grass growing'. One of his best friends is Thabo Mbeki, and he is one of the few who has a direct hotline to President Nelson

Mandela. While some in labour see this as a definite boon in terms of lobbying influence, others doubt his loyalty to the sector he is paid to represent.

Let's face it: South Africa 1996 is not an easy time and place to be a union leader. After having powered the struggle for democracy, Cosatu has found itself struggling for new definition, and often seems scattershot, disparate, rudderless. Shilowa himself frames the dilemma acutely: 'We either stand accused of being a conveyor belt and in bed with the government, or we are called spoilers who just bark at all ministers and want to exercise the right of veto over government policies.' But, while he is excellent at posing the questions about the labour movement's future, he comes across as a man who does not, yet, have the answers.

Shilowa's old comrade, Jayendra Naidoo, who now runs Nedlac (National Economic Development and Labour Council), notes that union-bashing has become fashionable: 'People want the unions to be like the Amabokoboko or the Bafana Bafana ...', part of a rainbow vision where we all collaborate and win the cup. 'But the job of unions is to take up the cudgels on behalf of their membership. It is bound to be adversarial.'

In this context, it's perhaps not surprising that Shilowa's tenure has been troubled: he is often accused of not being able to supply the labour movement with the requisite vision, or to corral it behind the vision he has. Behind the scenes, though, Shilowa has in fact effected a victory in the privatisation debate: in a draft agreement with government, service delivery rather than profit generation was re-established as the primary function of state enterprises, and Cosatu has also convinced the government that, within reason, workers' jobs have to be guaranteed within restructured state enterprises. The sticking point remains, however, whether private shareholders may purchase equity: Cosatu is adamant they may not – and that is a battle it is bound to lose.

In the unions, Shilowa is known to be uncomfortable with Cosatu's hardline anti-privatisation position, and this is seen as further evidence, by some, of the claim that he has become too close to the new elite; that he is too snazzy, too high-flying, too politically ambitious: a unionist with gold hoops in his ears.

One of his favourite tricks, when making an argument, is to make of his own mother an artefact: 'My opposition to privatisation', he says, 'is not theoretical, it's personal. My mum will be 76 years old this year in May. Why should she walk five kilometres to go fetch water? Why should she only know about electricity because there are power lines runing over her property to a white farm? When talking about restructuring, we need to ask ourselves, how is my mother going to benefit?'

He insists that his bare feet remain planted in the dry earth of impoverished peasantry. But, both economically and socially, the truth is that he is no longer a member of either the peasantry or the working-class. Whatever the card he carries says, he is a member of the new elite; recently married to Wendy Luhabe, a glam and go-getter management consultant specialising in affirmative action who was previously the first black executive of BMW. He is upwardly mobile in exact proportion to the downward mobility of those middle-class leftie intellectuals who preceded him – the Bernies and Alecs and Jays. Now they have gone to Pretoria, and the unions are run by people like Shilowa: driven, ambitious, working-class men.

While Shilowa does not subject his new life to particularly rigorous self-analysis, he does observe it with a fair amount of modesty and humour. His home, in the Roodepoort neighborhood of Weltevreden Park, is comfortably suburban rather than glamorously yuppie. In a roots-nod, Shilowa has always wanted to live under thatch: he has now bought a house with a bar in the rafters ('It used to belong to an entertainer') where an SACP 'Umsebenzi' poster hangs a little sheepishly amid all the Mala-Mala action. Sure, cappuccino is on offer, but the Shilowa–Luhabe homestead is matt-finished rather than glossy, woody-African rather than slippery-Italianate. It is emphatically not, in its style or location, Northern-Suburbs.

And his criticism of the narrow 'black upliftment' mantra, the 'it's our turn now' coda he encounters at dinner parties, remains acute: 'Yes, black people are justified when they say democracy means more than the right to vote; that it means economic empowerment. But defining economic empowerment becomes a struggle, because there are those who believe it means the self-enrichment of a few, that we can produce our own black Oppenheimers. That's rubbish ...

'You have to engage with people who say, Listen, apartheid benefited a few Afrikaner businesses, so surely we're justified in doing the same thing for ourselves with privatisation? They're not looking at structural transformation, they're looking at what crumbs they'll be able to get out of the situation.'

He 'agrees to disagree' with his wife on several issues, but they generally find themselves, both say, in the same ball park. In fact, as an entrepreneur, she often challenges him, he says, with more radical positions on workplace transformation, ones that advocate blazing ahead rather than slowly building consensus around big plans.

Sam Shilowa does not balk at being sharply critical of his colleagues – and friends – now in government. But only once, in our few hours together, does he betray anger. 'If you had to ask me what is the most ridiculous sentiment, the one I hate the most, it is the one from those of our colleagues in government or Parliament who say, "You don't understand! The situation has changed!" They say, "Leave the broader picture to us, you concentrate on shop floor issues", but then they also accuse us of being narrowly focused on the interests of our own workers and not taking the development of the country as a whole into account.'

Whence does this anger spring? Despite the openness of his features, Sam Shilowa is very difficult to read. I'd venture to guess, though, that he sees himself very much as part of the team transforming this land, and that any hint to the contrary riles him. I would imagine, too, that he is prickly about still being treated, by the intelligentsia of the movement, as an uneducated workhorse from the shop floor who doesn't really have the wherewithal to run things.

Does he feel 'left out'; 'left behind'? Perhaps one could read the above outburst as defensive, but if one looks at the number of illustrious ex-unionists now languishing on the back benches of Parliament (remember Moss Mayekiso? Chris Dhlamini?), he probably thanks his stars, every now and then, that he wasn't on the list of 20 that Cosatu handed over for the African National Congress list. He remains, however, an intensely political – and clearly ambitious – man.

All he will say about his future is that he wishes there to be a choice of leadership at Cosatu's 1997 congress. But there must be times when he longs to be in the corridors of executive power. Despite the knocks to his image in the past couple of years, he'll get there yet.

BLADE NZIMANDE

Deputy Chairman, SA Communist Party

*Head of
the class
struggle*

*I interviewed Blade Nzimande – the effective leader of the SA Communist Party and
its chief ideologue – just after his election as The Party's deputy chair in April 1995.
He was one of my first profiles. He rose to prominence a year later, as chief ANC
negotiator on the controversial education clause in the constitution.*

Blade Nzimande

You respect Blade Nzimande the way you do a Jack Russell terrier: both are compact, tenacious, intelligent, scrappy when provoked, affable once they get to know you, and intensely loyal to those they trust.

At the last congress of the South African Communist Party, in 1991, he stood beside his homeboy Harry Gwala and led the vanguard cudgels against those – like Joe Slovo and Chris Hani – who would temper socialism by putting the word 'democratic' before it. At the next congress of the SACP, last weekend [April 1995], he was elected deputy-chairperson; if the Old Man, Ray Mhlaba, had stood down, he would have been chairperson.

He has another chair: that of the parliamentary standing committee on education. He is as savvy a political operator as you will find on the ANC benches: last year, he averted potential Cabinet–caucus conflict by detecting that the draft of the White Paper on education had watered down basic ANC principles. Quietly, he stopped the printing of the document and negotiated to have it rewritten.

By all accounts he is more powerful than the minister, Dr Sibusiso Bengu; some say Nelson Mandela is grooming him for the Cabinet. He is 37 years old.

And he lives through Marx, by Marx, in a way that makes you remember why the work of a 19th-century German political philosopher still provides the most powerful language there is to critique the society we live in; and thus why so many of our cleverest politicians belong to the SACP. How Marxist theory can be so right and its practical application so wrong remains one of the conundrums of our age.

Like most intelligent Marxists, Blade Nzimande embodies a difficult contradiction; one that teeters between rigour and rigidity. He is broad in his interests, deeply questioning in his approach, inherently sceptical of all systems of power and control, including the ones in which he now serves. And yet there is, ultimately, only one paradigm for looking at the world; only one language that makes sense. Only one word, really: class.

He remembers the year, nay the very month, he discovered this. September 1980. He was an honours student in industrial psychology at the University of Natal, and a lecturer suggested he read a book on Marxist ideology. 'I was immediately struck by the extent to which that text was talking about my own life experiences. I came from a depressed, poor part of Edendale, only two kilometres from where Harry [Gwala] lived. I grew up in a mud house with no water inside or outside and no electricity. When I read this, it was like Marx and Marxists were writing about our conditions in Edendale at that particular point in time. This is the main thing that continues to attract people to the SACP.'

When talking about communism, Nzimande – detached, logical – makes of his own life story an artefact: he is the model proletarian, empowered through class consciousness. Later in our discussion, once we have left the cool, stony chambers of ideology and there are the unscientific skies and fields of emotion before us, it all comes out in a far more interesting way:

When he was 13, his mother – a nursing assistant and single parent – fell ill and nearly died. 'She gave me her purse; I was responsible now; I was the oldest child. I looked inside it and saw all she had in the world: just enough to buy some canned fish and bread.'

That is how close Blade Nzimande came to being a card-carrying member of the

Lost Generation. But miraculously, his mother survived and, on a salary of R80 a month, sent him to university – borrowing herself into impossible debt through stokvels and playing the horses.

It was 1976: he and his comrades burnt the university down and lost the year. His mother borrowed some more, gambled some more. He won a bursary. He worked and worked and worked and worked. He discovered Marx and identified his class affiliation. He became a member of the intelligentsia; an African polymath of sorts in a white, leftie world, applying his theory to labour, psychology, violence, politics and – in his PhD – to the establishment of a black petty bourgeoisie. He became involved in education when he set up the Education Policy Unit at the University of Natal in 1989.

He came late to organised communism: in the same year he joined the underground structures of the SACP. What makes him so different from the previous generation of Party leaders is that he discovered his ideology not in Party schools in socialist countries, not mediated through the commissariat that ran the Angolan camps, but on his own.

In one way, this gives him an interesting idiosyncrasy – he might be rigid at times, but he confounds orthodoxies – yet in another, he typifies the new generation of South African communists: unlike people like Slovo and Hani, who had to grapple with the failures of institutionalised socialism, Nzimande has never experienced that disillusion first-hand. Even as he acknowledges that the collapse of the Soviet bloc has impacted on the policies of the SACP, he sees no need to ask, 'Has socialism failed?'; it remains an unsullied and untested ideal.

Thus, while still insisting that 'democracy' and 'equality' are cornerstones of socialism, the SACP of which Nzimande is now deputy-chairperson (and effective chief commissar) has now decided to call once more for 'the socialisation of the predominant part of the economy'.

Socialist economic policy – conveniently bumped off the SACP agenda for the past few years by the priorities of negotiation and election – is back as the central SACP concern. Ask Blade Nzimande why there is still a Communist Party and he will reply: 'We will not address poverty adequately for as long as there is wealth in private hands. That is the basis for the continuation of the SACP.'

His friend Ari Sitas, professor of sociology at the University of Natal and his PhD supervisor, notes that 'when Blade joined the SACP, he found a sort of liberal pastiche – lots of talk of *glasnost* and openness. He rebelled against it, feeling that everyone had forgotten about the basics, about class.'

One of Nzimande's more controversial stands was against the adulation of 'civil society', a category which he felt elided class differences. Likewise, he chides the ANC – correctly – for trying to be 'more Zulu than Inkatha, a battle we cannot but lose', when in fact 'we should be fighting a class battle against the IFP, which is nothing more than the party of a petty bourgeoisie that fears it will lose economic power in a democratic South Africa'.

His radicalism is, by his own admission, shaped by war. 'Blade found himself attracted to Harry Gwala', notes one ANC Natal source, 'because of a certain frustration with the concessions being made to the IFP. We were fighting on the frontlines while the negotiators were sipping tea at the World Trade Centre.'

Even as he sits in Parliament, Nzimande dogs the IFP as few others do. 'You have to remember', he says, 'that I come from this war. My wife's uncle's entire family was wiped out. I personally felt that the ANC had, for too long, been too soft on the IFP, not dealing with it firmly enough when it threw its tantrums.'

He has written that the IFP's victory in KwaZulu-Natal 'will probably go down as one of the largest frauds in the history of elections in our country'. For their part, the members of the IFP parliamentary caucus regard Nzimande as their most strident and irritating critic. IFP MP Ziba Jiyane calls Nzimande's most recent attack on the party – when he accused it of taking government funds to organise an *imbizo* – 'an abuse of parliamentary privilege and utterly unfounded'.

There was a time when Nzimande was – or was perceived to be – one of 'Harry's boys'. When Gwala's chief lieutenant, Reggie Hadebe, was murdered in 1992, Nzimande became deputy-chair of the Midlands region.

Nzimande admits now that 'I once really believed that we could defeat the IFP's onslaught upon us militarily. But then I realised how the whole force of apartheid was rallied behind it, and that our only solution was to position ourselves political-ly to defeat the apartheid regime as a way of ending the war.'

And so, as Nzimande entered the national political stage, he and Gwala drifted apart – perhaps because the old man embarrassed the young politician; perhaps because the young politician was perceived by the old man to be either a threat or a sell-out or both.

Nzimande did not stand for re-election to the deputy-chairship of the region in 1993 and, when it came to supporting a candidate for provincial leadership, he broke ranks with his region and threw his weight behind Jeff Radebe from Southern Natal.

The relationship between Nzimande and Gwala reached an all-time low last year, when the former's name appeared on a hit-list allegedly emanating from the latter, who was hence suspended from the SACP.

Nzimande will not be drawn on the issue, saying only, 'I still have a lot of respect for that old man, not only because of his sacrifice, but because he was someone from nowhere who became a formidable intellectual.' Blade Nzimande comes from the same nowhere. He could be talking about himself.

SIBONGILE ZUNGU
Chief of the Madlebe tribe

Nkosazana with a knobkerrie

As an nkosi, Dr Sibongile Zungu is custodian of the very traditional values that KwaZulu-Natal ANC leaders like Blade Nzimande claim have been abused and harnessed towards the end of illegitimate political power. But, as the only female chief in the patriarchal Zulu nation, she comes up against those values herself. Therein lie her contradictions. I spent a fascinating day with her in the beautiful – if bloodtinged – hills outside Empangeni. The following week I bumped into her at the launch of Welcome Msomi's Umabatha: *she upbraided me for referring to her, in my profile, as an 'ntombi' (maiden) when she was, in fact, a married woman. I had, of course, used the term metaphorically; her annoyance, brought home to me just how sensitive the protocols of traditional Zulu life are.*

Sibongile Zungu

Something quite miraculous happens to Dr Sibongile Zungu, *nkosi* of the Madlebe tribe, when she dons her chiefly regalia: the rather frumpish, prematurely matronlike woman, swaddled in a faux-kente caftan, transforms into the coquettish *ntombi*; flirtatious and swaggering in equal measure.

Previously, sitting inside her classically bourgeois living-room – pink leather upholstery, state-of-the-art music system – she had been grave and shy; the very model of a township medical doctor. Now, standing on a precipice overlooking her chiefdom – the sprawling rural hinterland south and west of Empangeni – she brandishes her beaded knobkerrie at the photographer when he asks her to move into the light: 'This is my territory,' she laughs. 'You're not supposed to tell me what to do. I give the orders around here.'

We're in Madonna-land; Camille Paglia territory. Dressing up clearly makes Sibongile Zungu feel fabulous. She takes the knobkerrie, a phallic symbol of male authority and belligerence if ever there was one, and plays with it, waving it about but also reappropriating it; twirling it, baton-like, and resting her cheek contemplatively against it.

It's a transformation of far more than style, for Sibongile Zungu is a Reborn Zulu. Depending on which way you look at it, she is the perfect synthesis of tradition and modernity or a mass of irreconcilable contradictions that tells you, in a nutshell, why the current position of traditional leaders is untenable.

She grew up in the starched anti-traditionalist environs of the Inanda Mission: 'My childhood was about going to church and emphatically not doing those old traditional things. That was considered to be "not civilised". We were civilised Zulus, living a civilised life.' Her mother is a nurse, her father a teacher; her grandfather, a graduate of Lovedale, is most certainly turning in his grave at the fact that she is now an *nkosi*.

How she got there is an epic tragedy of Shakespearean – or Shakan – proportions. It begins with a medical student being asked, by her boyfriend, for an urgent wedding: 'He told me he needed to marry me so he could take his position. That was the first I heard about him being a chief. So you see! Women do have power under customary law. He would not have been able to inherit without a woman at his side.'

She moved with him to his tribal lands, got a job in the local hospital, and bore him two daughters. Then, while she was pregnant with his heir, a son, they were involved in a horrific car-crash in 1989 which left them both seriously injured. She survived and lost her child; he died.

His in-laws took her in, and, in the traditional way, gave her to his half-brother to marry. She refused, and ran away from their home. 'It's a good system, the one of finding a husband for a widow. I am sure many rural women, who are not breadwinners, appreciate being looked after in that way,' she says. 'But I was independent, I was a breadwinnner, and so I left their home to make a statement.'

Certain family members sided with her, and, with the approval of the KwaZulu authorities, it was decided to make her the first female *nkosi* in patrilinear Zulu history. The half-brother, born out of wedlock, took her to the supreme court, and lost. And so, in 1991, after a two-year-long legal battle, Sibongile Zungu became the traditional leader of 70 000 people.

There is, she acknowledges, something of a cultural schizophrenia in her life. She would have friends around, 'women who would come in, wearing pants, and start playing the radio or take a CD. Then an old man would come in on his knees, cupping his hands. There'll be wine and beer on the table, and my friends will be embarrassed and leave. Meanwhile the old ones would come and tell me that I'm misbehaving and that I need to be disciplined.'

If she had to have her life all over again, she would not have taken the position. But 'after my husband's death I couldn't accept the loss, and still felt I needed something to prevent the loss. I was so committed to my husband, I thought I had to help him finish what he had started, as a way to help him live on.'

Perhaps the grieving widow, with two little girls, found solace in the ritual and enforced community that customary society provides. Now she stays because she believes in the work she does. And – in a twist of irony that undermines the very system of traditional leadership she now upholds – she has been accepted, even though she is an outsider and a woman, simply because she gets the job done.

Zungu notes that particularly the women 'originally felt they couldn't take a word from another woman'. The men were more concerned, at first, with the fact that she was single and a professional. But she has come to be seen as a 'unifier' she says, and the fact that she is unmarried is now seen as a plus 'because I devote my entire attention to the tribe'.

Alone in the trouble-torn region around Empangeni, she has managed to remain publicly non-partisan in a region with a strong ANC-supporting minority. Her car has been bombed, her house razed to the ground and she has had to send her two infant daughters away to boarding-school. But she has brokered peace in her chiefdom, between IFP and ANC factions.

She is also one of those development-minded *amakosi*: 'If the traditional system is going to be maintained, it has to be adjusted. We no longer have a society with few things to worry about. People need houses, water, electricity. An *nkosi* has to be able to provide these. He must be progressive if rural areas are going to remain rural and enjoy being rural.' Her point is this: unless traditional leaders get their act together, they will not be able to save rural values from the onslaught of the urban development juggernaut.

And here is where Dr Zungu gets controversial. The ANC would like to strip Tribal Authorities – non-elected products of apartheid – of their service-providing functions, and many traditionalists agree that the amakosi should be ceremonial and spiritual leaders rather than bureaucrats and functionaries. But Zungu believes, emphatically, that 'the chiefs are the only ones with the capacity to develop the rural areas, and this capacity has to be extended'.

She takes it further: the current House of Traditional Leaders is a lame duck, she says, 'because it is only allowed to deal with customary matters. In my view, as custodians of traditional values, they should deal with all legislation, as all legislation involves the people they lead.' She thus envisages something along the lines of the House of Lords.

But what, exactly, are these 'traditional values' that are so important? Zungu speaks of the power of ritual and ceremony, but does not go much deeper. 'Tradition should be practised for as long as it's good for the people and doesn't divide society, for as long as it brings people together at the same time to apply everyone's mind to the same task and thus make a community psychologically complete. But as soon as it becomes divisive, it loses its value.'

For this reason she is particularly perturbed by the rift in the Royal House, between the king and Chief Buthelezi. It is astonishing, listening to her, to realise just how much the uncertainty over the future of something as ritual as Shaka Day can disorient an entire community. 'People can't plan, we can't collect money. They don't know whom to listen to. In the past, the chief minister [Buthelezi] would relay the king's decisions to us. Now that that no longer happens, there is so much confusion.'

She wants, more than anything, for 'the king to speak for himself. Then people would listen. The first loyalty of the *amakosi* is to the king, and it will always be that way.' But she also says that the rift is 'a family feud that is dividing the whole nation. If the king and Buthelezi get together and resolve their differences, the people would have a big party.'

While she feels closer to the IFP 'because of the way they treat traditional leaders and traditional issues', she will not commit herself to support of any party. Observers note, however, that, particularly given that she is a woman and an outsider to her tribe, the KwaZulu authorities would not have accepted her accession if she were not 'reliable'.

She has no truck, however, with the 'warrior-nation' notion of Zuluness: 'Some leaders', she says somewhat caustically, 'use the warrior thing because they want to have a war, so warriors are what they need.'

But she does not contest the IFP's harnessing of history: 'The IFP, just like any organisation, organises identity around a certain aspect of the past that will appeal to the minds of the people they want to draw. The IFP uses Zulu history; the ANC uses the liberation struggle; the Conservative Party uses the Voortrekkers.'

The fact is, she says, 'there was someone called Shaka who did create the Zulu nation. If a Zulu nation exists, we must be proud of it. Must we discard it simply because it didn't exist before Shaka? Prior to Shaka there is no history. For me, I don't know what my family were prior to Shaka. So I'll stick to Zulu. Otherwise I might as well be !Khoisan X!'

Once more, there's a complexity to the role-playing in which Sibongile Zungu engages. When she was a child, she says, explaining why she appreciates the cultural nationalism brought in by the Inkatha movement, 'all the traditions were lost. In those days you couldn't put forward pride. There was no giving of the first crops to the king; there was no reed-dance.'

As the dusk mops light off the hills of Natal, she becomes coy, the *ntombi* again: 'I never got to dance for my king.' Who knows, she might have been queen.

WELCOME MSOMI
Creator of *Umabatha* and image-consultant
to the ANC
Ethno rehab at the Civic

In the days since I interviewed him at the time of his revival of Umabatha *in May 1995, Welcome Msomi has become celebrated more as a purveyor of kitschy patriotic spectacle than as a top-notch theatre director. It was Msomi who did the show at the CAF Africa Cup soccer finals; Msomi who did the SABC relaunch at the Waterkloof Air Base. None of this detracts, however, from the glory of his* Umabatha. *For me personally, interviewing Msomi and writing about* Umabatha *was a long-overdue return to the discipline I was initially trained in: my journalistic career started as a theatre critic.*

Welcome Msomi

The divine justice of it all. When Welcome Msomi took his 'Zulu Macbeth' to New York in 1979, he found it boycotted by the African National Congress and its supporters, who claimed that because it was 'ethnic' (Zulu costumes, Zulu language, Zulu dancing), it had to be a government plot to promote separate development and the homeland system. The man responsible for the boycott was one Sipo Mzimela.

Now Mzimela is a cabinet minister from the Inkatha Freedom Party, which has built itself through Zulu chauvinism. And Msomi, the ethnicist, receives an on-stage embrace from Nelson Mandela for bringing, to the banquet of South African democracy, a revival of *Umabatha*.

It was Welcome Msomi who stage-managed many of the public events in the ANC's election campaign. It was Welcome Msomi who mounted the 'Many Cultures, One Nation' extravaganza at Mandela's inauguration, that rather bilious parade of cultural identities that nonetheless gave South Africans their first taste of National Reconciliation.

And it is Welcome Msomi, now, who swans about the Civic Theatre on the opening night of *Umabatha*, heartily exchanging backslaps with the powerhouse assortment of 'blackoisie' and ageing white bohemia, and clad in the leopard skins of a Zulu king. 'Poetic licence!' he guffaws about his costume. But he is king tonight, triumph-antly returned.

And in his hand he clutches a trophy – the rehabilitation of ethnicity, the glory of theatrical spectacle, the neatest possible multicultural overlay, a Zulu Macbeth, with a cast of thousands and a budget of millions and a bassline insistency that will (quite literally) entrance you until, ears ringing and heart pounding after the last, mesmeric curtain-call, you will be able to wipe your brow as you leave the concrete apartheid monstrosity that is The Civic and proclaim: 'Thank God! Theatre is not dead in this country after all! *Bayete!*'

Umabatha is Shakespearean only in so far as *Macbeth* provides a story-line about betrayal and the vagaries of succession. Using the uniquely South African performance styles that have already been well encoded by Gibson Kente and Mbongeni Ngema, it is comedic rather than tragic, declarative rather than contemplative, presentational rather than naturalistic.

The soliliquies are ribald confessions, not agonised introspections. Like the masks of ritual African performance, *Umabatha* is expressionistic – it distils and freezes emotions into intensely powerful grimaces and gestures. But into his pageant of Zuluness, Msomi mixes both subversive burlesque and rigid, unassailable hierarchy. His chorus-lines of stamping, phallus-waving *amabuthi* have none of the loose humanism of the kind of boy-meets-girl-and-falls-in-love 1950s schmaltz that tribal musicals such as *Ipi Tombi* and *Meropa* appropriated from Broadway. Rather, they hark back to a kind of Busby Berkley purity, expressing social dynamics through the geometric constellations of bodies.

Thankfully, *Umabatha* has little of either *Ipi Tombi*'s legendary 'Xplosion of Joy!' or *Sarafina*'s 'raw energy!'. Energy it has, in buckets, but so refined is it that there is a powerfully alienating effect to the spectacle (an effect that many Zulu-speaking members of the audience attempt to overcome through constant interaction with the performers). In overseas reviews, critics mistook this elegance for noble savagery and tribal exuberance – the *Charleston News and Courier* declared, rather lustfully, that 'the Zulus came stomping and shuffling through the audience, pounding drums, waving spears and shields, ablaze with barbaric beauty and looking as if they were going to massacre every last one of us'.

Welcome Msomi is accommodating. He agrees to dress up in his kingly skins for a photo-shoot. And so he opens the door of his Sandton flat, ablaze with barbaric beauty. The flat is absolutely bare save inexplicably grand arrangements of blue and pink plastic flowers, and belies its occupant's repeated assertion that, 'I am home at last. I am here to stay'.

He lives here with his wife, Thuli Dumakude. They have been in the flat for a year; their lives must have been either busy or transient or both.

He played opposite her in the original Umabatha and now she is his assistant-director and chief choreographer. She has a voice that puts her in the Makeba league. When they took *Umabatha* to the States in 1979, they stayed; they came back to South Africa two-and-something years ago, leaving behind their Zulu language and dance school in Brooklyn and their teenage son, who will be joining them shortly and starting up at Michaelhouse.

Msomi's aunt was the first wife of Zulu King Cyprian, Goodwill Zwelithini's father. The young Welcome, a slick city kid raised in Umlazi and schooled in Swaziland, spent many a school holiday at the Royal Kraal, and he has always seen himself as living quite comfortably in both his western and customary worlds.

When he started *Umabatha* in the early 1970s, he remembers, 'black academics said, "You're taking us backwards. What will white people say?" They wanted to be seen only as people who have attained the white culture and didn't want to go back to themselves. They thought anything tribal was demeaning.'

Then, the territory was fraught at home by the fact that theatres were all-white and abroad by the first stirrings of the cultural boycott. Now, in the era where the battle over who owns Zulu history costs lives, and the new black elite flocks to the theatre in the fashion-modified paraphernalia of ethnicity, a revival of *Umabatha* has other implications. 'We have to demystify the whole image of the traditional Zulu garb being associated with Inkatha. Zulus are just Zulus. The richness of a culture can be so easily lost in this whole political conflict, so we have to move away from saying, This is Zulu, and these are the people who control it.'

Macbeth is the story of an ambitious prince who betrays the king, attains power, and causes chaos in the land of Scotland. 'Listen,' says Msomi defensively. 'I wrote this in the 1960s! Zulu history has always been filled with plotting – look at Shaka, Dingane, Cetshwayo. People weren't happy with the royalty so they tried to take over. And those who tried to take over ended up dying by the spear. There is a lesson to be learned for people who are after power and are not supposed to have that power.'

A four-syllabled silence, Bu-the-le-zi, hangs briefly over the air between us before Msomi banishes it by letting loose one of his characteristic eruptions of laughter. 'I know what you're thinking! Don't push it.'

If Msomi were to ask me what to put, on a visa application, as his profession, I would advise: 'Cultural Interlocutor'. Since being back in South Africa, he has been employed by the advertising industry in what cynics would call the 'black guru' post

Welcome Msomi

– telling white capital how to reach the black market.

He has just set up a public relations company, Msomi Hunt Lascaris, the main function of which is corporate image-building. One of his first clients is Basil Elk Real Estate. We erupt, together, in laughter at the image of an ageing Jewish estate agent clad in skins and surrounded by warrior-like *amabuthi* as he peers out at the reader from the property pages of the *Saturday Star*. His laughter indicates some understanding of his difficult position: exoticist, primitiviser. Need an exotic spectacle? Call Msomi!

His work at Hunt Lascaris has largely involved the below-the-line stuff, creating events with an African feel. It was Msomi, for example, who transformed the Cresta shopping centre into a mythical jungle worthy of Sol Kerzner's febrile imagination, replete with lion cubs and sangomas, for the launch of the Zulu version of Disney Studios' 'The Lion King'.

He was excoriated by my colleague, Bafana Khumalo, for his use of sangomas to sell a product, and Msomi acknowledges, easily, 'I was wrong. There are certain things that are dear to the African people, which one cannot commercialise, not only because it is in bad taste and would thus turn consumers off, but because if we don't keep those things special, we are selling our souls.'

Welcome Msomi – guru or stooge? There's a clue to the way he works, in his much-expressed irritation with 'the conferences and papers and positions about cultural policy. Let's get down to work!' His plan is to use *Umabatha* to set into motion a network of regional traditional theatre companies, 'and I'm not going to wait for the government to approve of it and pay for it – I'm just going to go ahead and do it, because I know it's right.'

Just as he did with the first *Umabatha*, when he had white authorities bellowing on one side and cultural commissars on the other. There's an unspoken bitterness towards ideologues; indeed, his primary reason for moving to the United States was not an act of political exile to join a liberation movement, but rather just the desire to be able 'to live freely'. Msomi, I suspect, will serve a ruling class (be it big business or an ANC government) if it is in the interests of his career and his art, but he will not be beholden to it. He is neither a guru nor a stooge – he makes great theatre.

SIPO MZIMELA

Minister of Correctional Services and
IFP National Deputy Chairman

Priest who takes no prisoners

In the day we spent in Newcastle in February 1996, visiting the prison and looking at his youth development project, I found Sipo Mzimela to be sympathetic. This impression clashed, however, with what I was told by people who know him much better than I do, and with what I could glean from his writings and his public utterances. Trying to make sense of these contradictions is what I find most challenging about writing political profiles: even if it means going against the grain of conventional wisdom, my project in profile-writing is to try to reflect the complexity of political consciousness.

Sipo Mzimela

If KwaZulu-Natal premier Frank Mdlalose is the bluff country doctor of Zulu ethnicist politics, then the Reverend Sipo Mzimela is its fire-breathing priest. He looks like the archetypal avuncular Anglican clergyman, right down to his clerical sideburns – a flock of lost sheep grazing down the margins of his empathetic face. But put him in front of an Inkatha meeting, and you'll see the preacher-man lurking within.

Last year, the IFP's Constitution was amended so that he could be appointed as Mdlalose's national deputy chairman, thereby elevating him above the party's moderate secretary general, Ziba Jiyane, and putting him directly in the line of succession. Given that he was an ANC loyalist until 1985, and that he only joined the IFP in 1990, he has gone far indeed. His ticket: the Hard Line.

Back from 33 years of exile (the last few as the IFP's American connection), he made his entrée into IFP consciousness when, at its 1993 national congress, he was asked to open the proceedings with a prayer.

He had just published a book, *Marching to Slavery: South Africa's Descent to Communism*, in which he prophesied that an ANC government would mean 'the end of civilisation in all of black Africa'. His thesis was that a cabal of white and Indian communists was using the ANC to further its aims, marching gullible blacks to a slavery worse than apartheid, sponsoring black-on-black violence to render the country anarchic.

Their prime stooge, since the days they set up Umkhonto weSizwe, was Nelson Mandela, 'perfect' because he was 'ambitious, power-hungry, reckless, and opportunistic', with no support base and 'no legitimate authority'; now, since his release, a senile 'buffoon', a 'laughing-stock' with a 'sick mind', 'despised, scorned, and publicly humiliated even by the youth of the organisation he leads'; 'the Father of Terrorism in South Africa'.

These passions powered his prayer at that conference in 1993: no-one in the IFP has ever forgotten the performance of the man who is without doubt the finest orator in the current Parliament. He denounced Mandela and the ANC leaders as false prophets; De Klerk he consigned, more neatly, to the seventh circle – without even the option of purgatory. He was 'born a liar, lived a liar, will die a liar, and he'll lie in Hell!'

A mere three years later, Sipo Mzimela and I are driving around Northern KwaZulu-Natal, talking about the murderers, rapists and other felons in his ministerial care. He is explaining why he is trying to move South Africa's prisons from brutal and sadistic places of punishment to humane centres for rehabilitation. 'Yes,' he says, 'some people might be lost, but they must be found. As a cleric, I have learned that no one is beyond redemption ...'

We have come from a defunct coal mine outside Newcastle, which the minister of correctional services is transforming into his first pilot youth development centre. Funded by the private sector to the tune of R45-million, it will house 600 juvenile delinquents in a nurturing and relatively free environment. It is Mzimela's passion, his legacy to South Africa. By resocialising the young offenders and teaching them skills, he hopes it will show the world that humanity can bring the 'lost generation' back from the brink. By using private sector nous to complete a 'three-year job in eleven months', he will prove his main political point too: a small decentralised government is best.

We are on our way, now, to the old Newcastle Prison, where Mzimela will do one of his renowned tours, interrogating the kitchens, inspecting the cells, and talking to the prisoners in a tone that is stern and even aggressive sometimes, but clearly concerned, and with more than a little humour: 'So you like it here in this, my hotel?' he says to a third-time offender.

He started these prison visits 'because I am not 16 years old, and when my staff in Pretoria painted a rosy picture of the prisons, I knew I needed to see things for myself. Let me tell you, things are not rosy.' Cameras that followed Mzimela on his missions caught the genuine shock and outrage on his features, particularly when he was confronted with abused children. In Transkei, he closed some facilities on the spot. 'I don't know how people could work in them, and keep other people there. Except of course that they were trained to use prisons to punish and not to rehabilitate. And when you punish, you want the inmates to sleep on the floor and eat dirt. You want to beat them up.'

At Newcastle, they've been expecting the minister for two weeks, and so things are ship-shape. Nonetheless, his face folded into characteristic disdain, he frequently expresses irritation with the warders showing us around. A boy awaiting trial complains of having been assaulted by a warder; Mzimela curtly interrogates the prison head, and orders the child off to the doctor for treatment.

The disjuncture between Sipo Mzimela the prisons boss and Sipo Mzimela the IFP leader is so severe it is shocking: his wards in the prisons are never beyond redemption, but his political opponents go straight to hell. His engagement in national politics has been absolute and extreme. He, along with Walter Felgate and Mario Ambrosini, was responsible for advising Chief Mangosuthu Buthelezi to stay out of elections and to form alliances with the right wing. He, too, is largely responsible for the fact that the IFP is not in the Constitutional Assembly. Through an arcane IFP committee he chairs called Pocola (the Portfolio on Constitutional and Legislative Affairs), he – along with Felgate, Ambrosini and other hardliners – determines the constitutional debate in KwaZulu-Natal too. On at least one occasion he has overridden an agreement between the ANC and the more moderate provincial IFP in the province.

And yet his understanding of correctional services is rational, measured and – with a few glaring exceptions, like the refusal to countenance condoms in jails as a measure against the spread of HIV – classically progressive.

Certainly, there are problems: sources in the sector say he is skittish and erratic and has alienated both the human rights lobbies and his own department. He and Carl Niehaus – the chairman of the portfolio committee on correctional services – are at present clashing over whether children should be held in prisons. On the surface Mzimela is progressive and Niehaus reactionary, for the former wants to keep children out, while the latter wants to put them back in. But Mzimela is not looking at the context – at the fact that, since thousands of children were released from prisons into places of safety last year, many have escaped because of low security and committed more crimes, and the welfare department has said it needs at least a year to jack up security. With certain reservations, the human rights lobby has backed Niehaus. Mzimela claims only he is respecting the rights of chidren.

Sipo Mzimela

If his compassion for prisoners comes from his life as a pastor (he worked in Harlem, Atlanta and Kenya) and as an intellectual (he has a PhD in ethics from New York University), then his extreme politics comes from his history as an ANC member who 'saw the light'. He is a classic dissident: embittered, unsparing of the ideology that deceived him. *Marching to Slavery* gives us a clue. In his particularly harsh chapter on how the ANC has created the 'lost generation', he writes that 'to [14-year-old] immature minds, Marxist slogans are in fact attainable goals. I thought so too, until I went to study in Czechoslovakia in 1963. That is when I discovered that communism is not just worse than apartheid; it is a thoroughly evil system.'

Mzimela, the son of an uneducated carpenter from Durban, became a teacher and a devotee of Albert Luthuli. Angered and radicalised by Sharpeville, he left the country and landed up in Czechoslovakia, where, he says, he realised he had been conned. The Czechs were unfree and miserable. One cannot fault Mzimela for his discovery, but it remains unclear why he waited two decades – during which time he actually helped set up the ANC's United Nations office – after the revelation to leave the movement.

He claims he quit the movement in 1985 when the ANC formally united with the SACP at the Kabwe Conference. As late as 1987, though, he is reported in American media campaigning for sanctions. Two years later, he was slamming sanctions. Then, shortly after the unbannings of 1990, he came home, met Buthelezi, joined the IFP, and went back to the United States a fervent convert.

Something clearly happened to Sipo Mzimela in the mid-1980s. An old comrade believes it had to do with a clash with his superior in New York, Johnny Makathini, followed by a two-year church mission he did in Kenya: 'Sipo came back a bitter man, virulent and angry.'

Mzimela says that, while in Kenya, he met 'hundreds of South Africans. I heard the stories of the torture and human rights abuse in the camps. I heard how badly things were going. I was particulaly upset by the tales of black-on-black violence.' Perhaps being back in Africa, back home in a way, threw all the painful issues of separation, loneliness and betrayal into sharp relief, forcing a crisis that could find its only resolution in a rejection of the ANC. Upon returning to the United States, say those who know him, he started talking about the ANC's domination by Xhosas.

Even today, back in South Africa, there is something about Sipo Mzimela which is unrooted. When in Pretoria, he lives out of a hotel. His only current home is his ministerial residence in Cape Town. 'There is a gap I need to fill,' he says. 'People have developed and grown. The world is different to the one I left in 1961. I don't have roots any more. So I am building a house in Umhlanga.'

Politically, too, he seems to be searching for a place to build his house. He is adamant that he joined the IFP for 'political reasons, and not because I am Zulu'. I suspect that he is right: deracinated, he is more like the white anti-communist ideologues of the party than the Zulu traditionalists. The fact that he is a black man, a Zulu speaker to boot, only adds to his potential as an ideologue leader.

There are signs, though, of Mzimela's softening. One ANC insider notes that President Mandela, with his usual acuity, has worked hard to win Mzimela's loyalty – and has succeeded, in part, with the Newcastle youth project, originally Mandela's idea, now given to Mzimela as a way to prove himself. It's interesting to note that

Sipo Mzimela

Mzimela is clearly embarrassed by his book, even though he will not go so far as to disown it, rather making excuses for it ('those were difficult political times'; 'it was written for Americans, not South Africans', etc.) He has also, for the first time, made some public noises about finding a way through the current constitutional deadlock other than international mediation.

Last year, at the height of the tension between the hardliners at Parliament and the moderates trying to run KwaZulu-Natal, Frank Mdlalose offered to resign. The man picked by Buthelezi to replace him was Mzimela. The two apparently dislike each other intensely. Country doctors use science and caution. Fiery preachers work, rather, with moral absolutes: damnation and redemption. One senses, though, that in the Newcastle district – where Mdlalose was coincidentally once a practising medic – Sipo Mzimela is discovering, through his youth centre, the country doctor in himself.

FAROUK CASSIM
Dissident IFP Member of Parliament

Ulysses in the canefields

One of the most stimulating, enriching (and delicious!) afternoons I have ever had on the job was spent with Farouk Cassim and his family at their home in Stanger in July 1995. He had just publicly challenged the IFP, which he represents in parliament, and on the very day we met, his fate was being decided in Ulundi. He intimated that if he wasn't expelled, he might well resign. Storms and teacups: nearly a year later Farouk Cassim finds himself still a loyal, if independent-minded, IFP member of parliament. After the big talk in our interview, I have to admit I'm a little disappointed.

59

Farouk Cassim

Farouk Cassim has literary aspirations for himself and his hometown. We sit in his bougainvillaea-clad, rambling flat above his father-in-law's dry-cleaning business on Stanger's main road. The muezzin from the mosque next door blares, intermittently, as we eat the exquisite bread he bakes each Saturday, and he claims for Rood Street the destiny of James Joyce's Dublin: 'I could write a novel the size of *Ulysses* about this road. All the points of my life are here – my bookshop, my home, my family's business, Zulu politics (I sleep not 50 metres from the tree under which Shaka held court), my wife's school, the mosque …'

The difference between Farouk Cassim and Kader Asmal – his wife's first cousin and another Stanger native – is not just that Cassim went tricameral and then crossed over to the Inkatha Freedom Party. It is that Asmal got out of suffocating, small-town Islam as quickly as he could (and landed up in Joyce's Dublin!) while Cassim – a man with similar aspirations – stayed put.

Asked why, Cassim compares Stanger to George Eliot's 19th-century Middlemarch: 'If you read people like Eliot, it's always in a place the size of Stanger that you can explore who you are. You can find an identity in clearer terms than if you're lost in the city. Here, wherever I go, I am myself, free to do as I choose and accepted as such …'

He compares himself to Tertius Lydgate, Eliot's idealistic but alienated doctor, who brings science and progress to backward Middlemarch. There is something literary about the persona of Farouk Cassim, but both the exterior landscape of Stanger's gentle tropical rot and the interior landscape of its muse remind me more of a V S Naipaul anti-hero than an Eliot or Joyce protagonist: the small-town intellectual with a vast vocabulary, the English teacher with ideas too big for his world, the modest man who lives in a noisy flat on the main street, rather than building a home on his 30-acre sugar farm outside town. The loner with a conscience who committed what he calls 'an act of political suicide' by taking on both the Zulu chauvinism and the iron-fist discipline of the IFP, by breaking ranks and accusing it of racism towards Indians.

Following the accusation, IFP secretary-general Ziba Jiyane publicly described Cassim – one of his moderate allies in the party – as 'unstable'; a quality, often confused with conscience, more often found in novels than in parliaments, unless those parliaments happen to be the floor-criss-crossing House of Delegates.

Here are the facts of Farouk Cassim's demise (or redemption, depending which way you look at it): after IFP whips corralled the party's Indian MPs together and gave them a tongue-lashing for laziness, Cassim held a press conference in which he accused his party of racism, citing as well Minister of Correctional Services Sipo Mzimela's ethnic slur against Mohammed Valli Moosa, whom he had told to 'go back to Bombay'.

The IFP's National Committee responded by giving Cassim an 'apologise or resign' ultimatum. Cassim says he will not apologise 'on a matter of conscience'. Talking to me on the day the committee was sitting in Ulundi (he is a member, but absented himself), he compares the silence of Indians in KwaZulu-Natal today to that of Jews in 1930s Germany: 'If you acquiesce to the little slurs now, those will confirm people in their bad habits and bad ways. We need to pick it up now and smash it before it becomes entrenched.'

Farouk Cassim

He is upset that the party lashes out at him, rather than taking the opportunity to 'look at itself and its racial problems' – the latest of which is the allegation, published in the KwaZulu-Natal press, that all the white and Indian alternates have been taken off the IFP's provincial parliamentary list and replaced with Zulus. Cassim is careful in his explanation of this impulse: 'I think that the party has been forced, by the ANC, into a position where it has to defend Zulu interests first and foremost at the expense of all else.'

One of his white colleagues, talking off the record, is far more dramatic (and deliciously Natal-colonial): 'The party is retreating into the narrowest Zulu chauvinism. It has become increasingly hardline and, for those of us non-Zulus who do not toe the line, things are tough. There's a witchhunt going on, so we have to keep our powder dry, our helmets on, and stay down in the trenches.'

At the committee meeting that decided Cassim's fate, former Nat Jurie Mentz argued against censuring Cassim. Mzimela reportedly replied, 'If you don't like it, you can also go!' To which Mentz shot back, 'If I go, the whites do too.'

The temptation is to rub one's hands with glee at the IFP – a party built on ethnicity – hoist by its own petard. An investigation into the veracity of Cassim's claims of racism leads one, inevitably, into the badlands of that very specific brand of Natal racism: 'We are not like them,' pontificates one of the IFP's other Indian MPs, explaining why the Indians in the caucus are considered laggardly: 'You see, the IFP meets in Cape Town over weekends, when we Indians come home to look after our families and see to our constituencies. The blacks, on the other hand, just stay in Cape Town. They have a gay lifestyle at the expense of all these foreign foundations. Oh yes, they live it up over there.'

Given the rag-tag bunch of white and Indian opportunists who joined the IFP, perhaps the IFP's Zulus have a point. And, unlike many of the Zulus and whites in the party, Indian involvement seems to be more about pragmatism than ideology.

Cassim acknowledges the pragmatist impulse – 'By being part of the majority party here, we non-Zulus can ameliorate our circumstances by pointing out that there are other people who live here too.' But he also carries within him the essential contradiction of Indian politics; one underscored by his announcement that, once he leaves Parliament, he will form a 'professional minority lobby that I hope will take in other minorities too, but will at the very least work to protect the interests of Indians'.

The contradiction – one to which he readily admits – is that 'the downfall of the Indian in Africa has been his insularity'. In fact, he says, 'apartheid was invented and perfected by Indians long before the Afrikaners came along. That's why it was not rejected wholesale by Indians, because it in fact gave them permission to stay out of national affairs, to stay in their own areas and do their own thing.'

He claims that the battle against this insularity is his single greatest fight: isn't setting up an Indian lobby the very worst thing he could do? He cites the experiences of Indians in East Africa and says, 'whether I like it or not, there are too many things which stamp us as a vulnerable minority. We have to be conscious of that fact and act accordingly.'

Even though 70 per cent of KwaZulu-Natal's Indians voted for the National Party, they have not found a home there the way the Western Cape's coloureds have.

Farouk Cassim

'Indians as yet have no political home,' says Cassim. Indeed, one is struck by the fact that the only credible Indian politicians are in the ANC, but most of them refuse point-blank to acknowledge that they are in the specific service of Indian interests.

Is Farouk Cassim the answer? He was, by all accounts, far and away the most able politician in the House of Delegates, that slag-heap of Indian politics, during its dying days. He now is regarded by all parties as one of the IFP's most hard-working parliamentarians – all the more reason for the offence he has taken at having been singled out, with other members of his ethnic group, for laziness.

Before the election, he was one of the IFP's most articulate spokesmen: he was often on television rationalising the IFP's withdrawal from the election. Behind the scenes, he has been at the modernising forefront of the party, and has consistently led the battle for negotiations and participation, against walkouts and boycotts.

Although he emphatically sees the IFP as 'the aggrieved party' in the KwaZulu-Natal conflict, he remains puzzled by the party's hardline attitude: 'When Mandela attacks Dr Buthelezi [yes, the honorific remains, despite Cassim's disenchantment], I just see it as political posturing, but my colleagues see it as an attack on the Zulu nation. Is it a difference in political culture? Or is it that they have been victimised in a way we non-Zulus can't understand?'

Given his liberalism and his intellectualism, wouldn't he have been more at home in the Natal Indian Congress and the ANC? He gives two reasons for having never considered the ANC: 'because I am a federalist through and through', and 'because I always found the NIC very exclusivist: they were self-appointed. How could one participate?'

Despite all, he maintains the intense loyalty to Buthelezi that the chief seems to inspire in so many people, and insists that the problems lie with the sheep of the IFP rather than its shepherd. 'Precisely where the IFP is going wrong is that there is so much deference given to Dr Buthelezi. They'd rather do nothing and not cross him than do something and upset him.' The irony, of course, is that Cassim did do something – and is out on his ear.

He wrote his master's thesis (at the University of South Africa) on the brilliant but fascist poet, Ezra Pound. While criticising the poet's anti-Semitism and passion for Mussolini, he argues that Ezra Pound's fascism has been misunderstood and over-exaggerated, and attempts to explain that Pound used fascism as a metaphor for perfection and completeness, rather than as an ideology. His thesis is called, 'Ezra Pound: Poet or Propagandist', and he concludes that the two functions were, in Pound's work, interdependent.

Farouk Cassim is only just this side of wacky. He spends his spare time writing a school textbook of word games called the 'Turbo Word Booster' and is obsessive about futurism: he adores Ray Bradbury and Alvin Toffler, and once tried to start a school with Toffleresque Third Wave 'infospheres' rather than classrooms.

As I left his Middlemarch-in-the-canefields, he gave me a copy of a poem he had recently written about Buthelezi: 'He was polite or he was brusque/ As the occasion found him/ But he had magic and that is his truth ...' Unlike Farouk Cassim's bread (a recipe passed down from his grandmother) or his thesis (erudite and complex) the poem is devoid of creativity; pure doggerel. Buthelezi has been his Mussolini. But Cassim, unlike Pound, has been unable to turn autocracy into poetry.

FATIMA MEER
University of Natal sociologist and
SABC Board member

Whirlwind in a sari

When the organised Muslim community was up in arms at the SABC for screening the anti-fundamentalist documentary 'Jihad in America' in November 1995, I went to see Fatima Meer, the outspoken SABC Board member who, not for the first time in her life, was supporting the censorship of something perceived to be offensive to Muslims. As with Sipo Mzimela, I found myself faced with a dilemma. Despite her problematic public positions on a whole range of contentious issues, I liked her enormously, and felt real empathy for her after a tragic few months in which she had lost her son – a colleague of mine whom I knew fairly well – and undergone serious heart surgery.

Fatima Meer

Fatima Meer takes something of a perverse delight in her reputation as a nuisance. She remembers an account, in the Inkatha mouthpiece *Ilanga*, of an event she organised for her great friend Winnie Mandela upon her unbannning. 'The general gist of it was: "What's that meddling coolie doing here?"' It's a feeling she gets, too, on the South African Broadcasting Corporation board, where she has served diligently and cantankerously for over a year: 'Often I find that the African members of the board are not being assertive enough. But I'll always speak up! I can almost hear the old guard muttering under their breath: "These blacks are all right, but *her!*"'

Sure enough, one senior SABC manager tells me: 'We can handle Dr Ivy [Matsepe-Casaburri, the chair] fine. But when we catch sight of that little, stooped figure in the sari clumping down the corridor, we grown men quiver in our suits!' She is the hard-liner on the board: respected for her moral line, she drives her colleagues to distraction by asking, always: 'But is it the right thing to do?'

Like all true eccentrics, Meer holds to a wide range of beliefs with passionate conviction. Among them: Winnie Mandela is the innocent victim of both apartheid and dirty politics within the African National Congress; the Ayatollah's revolution in Iran was a 'great success'; Salman Rushdie is a blasphemer; and 'Jihad in America' should not have been shown on the SABC. Like most true eccentrics, too, she is far more enjoyable company than the hackishly correct.

Her career has been, well, restless. Despite crippling banning orders, she has built up a reputation as a prolific, if quirky, academic. Her books have included the compelling *Trial of Andrew Zondo*, which should be on every school curriculum, and *Higher Than Hope*, a propaganda exercise masquerading as the biography of Nelson Mandela. She was principal of one of the braver – and more ill-fated – social experiments of the 1980s, the Phambili School, where she found herself at the centre of a row over mismanagement.

At Natal University, she founded her Institute for Black Research – among other things it raised the blood pressure of her old friend Mangosuthu Buthelezi (they studied Native Administration together) by publishing the first research to conclude that Inkatha was destabilising Natal – and set up a publishing house, Madiba Press, which has moved from social research into Gandhibilia and children's literature. Most recently, she has branched into script-writing: her account of Gandhi in South Africa, funded by the Indian government and bought by the SABC, has thrown her into new controversy: is it ethical for a board member to sell her wares to the corporation?

She made no money off it, she says, and besides, the deal was sealed before she was appointed to the board. She motivates her positions with vigour and charm. Even after the worst few months of her life (she had serious heart surgery and lost her son, Rashid – a highly regarded radio journalist – in a car crash), she is immensely engaging.

The home she has made, like her mind, is not suburban, even if it nestles in the heart of Durban's Indian bourgeoisie. It was built in the 1950s by activist-architect Alan Lipman – to its implacably mod nautical lines she has agglomerated, over the years, the whimsy of bamboo latticework and antique carpets; of wooden, stained-glass Victoriana that she has spirited off demolition sites. Like its occupants, the house is at ease with its locality (Meer, sharp-witted and well-travelled, nonetheless peppers her discourse with Durbanisms like 'flim' – as in '"Jihad in America" is a propagandistic flim that is antagonistic and hostile to Muslims').

Her husband Ismail is a famed lawyer/activist who, despite his age (76) is one of the most energetic members of the KwaZulu-Natal provincial legislature. In South Africa they are Gujerati aristocracy; colleagues and contemporaries of the grand old gentlemen of struggle – Mandela, Sisulu, Marks, Dadoo. Although she will not say it, perhaps her loyalty to Winnie comes from the space the two women had to find as ambitious and articulate wives of more famous men. Like her friend, Meer does not hold her peace.

She maintains, correctly, that 'Jihad in America' is prejudiced against Muslims. But there are two problems with the support she gave to the Muslim groups who wished to get it spiked: firstly, that she believes that censorship is in some instances justified and, secondly, that she supported, at least at first, the board's intervention in a management issue. 'Jihad's' screening is, for her, a critical moment in the balance that needs to be maintained between the rights of minorities and the rights to free speech. The supreme court ruled in favour of the latter, and the programme was aired.

'If the SABC had a track record for showing films about Islam, and some of these were positive,' Meer says, 'I might have said: "Oh well, this is propaganda, but it's a different perspective, so show it!" But I asked the SABC to furnish me with a list of films they have shown in the past two years, and it is pathetic.'

Fair enough. But here the analysis begins to teeter. Those opposed to the screening of 'Jihad' become characterised as the downtrodden masses, while those in favour of it are the oppressing elites. How can she, an intellectual, challenge the faith of ordinary people when 'that's all they have! Do we now go roughshod over their lives and say: "Stand aside! you are a bunch of fanatics! You are ritualistic and superstitious and there's no room for this stuff in my world and, because I have no respect for it, you're not going to have it either!" '

She used exactly the same argument to justify her decision to boycott Salman Rushdie's abortive tour to South Africa in 1988. It is spurious, for it does not take into account the power that imams and rabbis and priests have in shaping the consciousness of ordinary folk: Iranian villagers didn't know that such a thing as *The Satanic Verses* existed before their *ayatollahs* distributed its saucy bits and put a death *fatwa* on its author's head.

She rationalises the fundamentalist revolutions of the Middle East as a movement 'of people trying to reclaim themselves and their lives in terms of their own ideologies and their own indigenous cultures'. 'Jihad in America' must be seen within the political context of 'those who won't give their oil to the West versus those who will'. Any excesses that have occurred – in Iran, in Sudan, in Algeria – are teething problems that have come about because 'they are in the infant stage of articulating themselves'.

There is, Meer writes in her riveting account of a 1984 trip to Iran, entitled 'Towards Understanding Iran Today', 'a Shi'ite heart beating inside each Sunni Muslim'. On this trip, she found that heart. She arrived in Iran sceptical, and left, if not a convert, then at least a passionate apologist for a revolution that, she concludes, is 'real [and] a continuing process. It benefits most Iranians, it hurt some – but democracy is about the greatest good of the greatest majority and the present government passes that test'.

Say what? What about the executions of opponents, the senseless ten-year war with Iraq, the brutal repression of dissent, the subjugation of women? Meer says she would gladly take up a chair at Tehran University, despite the fact that the women are veiled in public. 'All the evidence I saw was of a free flow between men and women, and as much gender equality as I've seen anywhere else in the world.'

She does write that even though her newspaperman father had taught her to view religious leaders with caution, 'Iran's *ayatollahs* were different: they gave the impression of Plato's super elite. Still, I wouldn't leave my destiny in their hands. I would insist on a share in it. How could they be trusted, for instance, to protect my rights as a woman, to interpret the Qur'an to serve my interests and not usurp these to pursue the claims of men over women?'

And therein lies the essential contradiction in Fatima Meer. She is devout, but she prefers finding her own God to collective faith. Even though fellow Muslims stop her in airports and exhort her not to wear the sari, she chooses its secular sexiness over the more austere *hijab*. She revels in the unconventionality of her own upbringing – although her father had two wives, one of them, her mother, was white; she did not even send her children to *madressah* ('we were very modern!' she laughs). She is one of this country's wildest women and one of its most powerful advocates for gender equality. Yet she feels compelled to defend a movement which has at its core the reshackling of women. Her Islamism, perhaps, is motivated by militant anti-West politics rather than religion.

And yet she clashed with the Black Consciousness movement in South Africa in the 1970s, because 'the liberal inside me found it difficult to go along with their hard line on race'. Her world – while rooted in patrician Gujerati society – is intensely non-racial. Her own cows are not sacred: 'Yes!' she says, 'the criticism that *Higher Than Hope* was hagiographic is well earned! You must remember, the man was in prison! I hadn't seen him since 1970. I was totally in love with the man. He was a hero, incarcerated, and no way would I say anything nasty about him.'

In many eyes, she has lost most credibility through her public support for Winnie Mandela. As in the furious letters she wrote to the media during the trial, she believes that all Mrs Mandela's enemies 'cannot cope with a Winnie who talks. She can be very demure. She comes across almost like Princess Di. And all the world saw this aspect of her. But once she decided to use her voice, they couldn't cope with it. They wanted her to be the reconciler before it was time for reconciliation.'

There is a characteristically self-deprecating story that Meer tells of her friendship with Winnie from the time they were detained together in 1976: 'I used to be in my cell in my sari, not the best of garments in a confined space. So a friend brought me some dresses. One day Winnie and I met on the way to a meeting, me in my long dress. Winnie said: "You make that look like something you bought from OK Bazaars for two shillings! Give it to me and I'll show you how it should be worn." I obliged, and she made it look like a designer outfit.' What purports to be a story about her friend is, in fact, about herself: her sensibility, like her style, is *prêt-à-porter*.

CAWE MAHLATI
Acting Chief Executive of Bop Broadcasting

Queen of her own soapie

When I interviewed Cawe Mahlati in March 1996, she was leading the Bop Broadcasting Corporation to a future in violation of all previous agreements and decisions made by the SABC, the North West government, and the Independent Broadcasting Authority. She seems, at the time of writing, to have got away with it, and after having spent a day with the fastest-talkin' woman in the west, I'm not surprised.

Cawe Mahlati

Night has fallen over dirty-grey veld around Mmabatho; the sun has set behind the hulking Rhino Recording Studios, built by Bop Broadcasting during the height of the bantustan's deluded grandeur. Cawe Mahlati and I wander through the boma and along a water feature, back to her Executively Thatched Bungalow, where we happen upon Martin Mabiletsa, senior adviser to North West Premier Popo Molefe.

'Martin!' she effervesces, rushing into his arms before introducing the journalist at her side as 'someone who wants to expose me as a vapid *nouvelle riche!*'

'No, no,' the old man responds, a mirthful baritone to Mahlati's shreiks, 'not a vapid *nouvelle riche!* A *brilliant nouvelle riche!*'

Cawe Mahlati hit the scene, with big hair and a big mouth, as M-Net's frontperson in the Independent Broadcasting Authority's public hearings in 1994, chanting the mantra 'Let The Market Decide!' I joked in print, at the time, that her hairdo could catch more signals than a satellite dish. After spending a day with her I can safely report that her brain is even more receptive. She might look like an Afro-accessorised kugel, but she is anything but vapid. Bold and beautiful, she is the star of her own soapie: peripatetic (she has lived in at least six countries), brilliant, iconoclastic, hyper-verbal, ambitious, brazen and aggressive.

Who else but a soapie queen would leave a powerful job as the senior black person in the fastest-growing pay-TV company in the world for a six-month contract at an ailing Rhino in the yonder that, to all intents and purposes, had already been consigned to the culling-pen? Mahlati saw the gap and took it.

When Mahlati arrived, it was a foregone conclusion – ratified by the IBA – that Bop Broadcasting was going to be subsumed, wholesale, into the SABC. But she has wheeled and dealed, lobbied and loopholed. When she took over the reins, her predecessor Solly Kotane had retrenched almost everyone there – to the tune of R400-million, an amount that would have merrily bankrupted North West province. Unblinking, she stared the unions down to R150-million. She fired all the managers, and rehired those she needed on month-to-month contracts. She reduced the staff from 715 to 260. She got the province to give her R54-million for the upcoming year (down from R93-million, but a good deal more than zero, which is what was initially expected). She sent out a flutter of press releases declaring Bop back in business.

And it is. Mahlati believes she has found a loophole in the IBA's report on public broadcasting: while it states that all the ex-homeland networks are to be incorporated into the SABC, it does not stipulate what should happen to Bop-TV, the flagship of the network. And it says quite clearly, says Mahlati, that 'any assets not nessessary to the formation of a new national Public Broadcasting Service must be disposed of'.

Clearly, given the three channels it has been allocated already, SABC does not need Bop-TV. Compound that with the fact that the IBA has not yet licensed a commercial broadcaster, and you begin to see how clever Mahlati is. She is currently sketching 'several scenarios' on Bop's future: her clearlyfavoured one is a partnership between the private sector and North West, with commercial services subsidising provincial public broadcasting. Pushy pushy gets the ball rolling. At a meeting in early March, a committee led by SABC chair Ivy Matsepe-Casaburri agreed to have a *bosberaad* soon to sort things out once and for all.

Is she involved in any of the consortia that might bid for a slice of the pie? She throws her head back and lets out a guffaw. 'No!!! Not yet. I haven't been invited.'

Mahlati's riches might be *nouvelles*, but she comes from a line of Transkei missionary-class intelligentsia, literate for five generations. Her father, a Latin and Greek scholar, ran the famed Osborne Mission at Mount Frere. Her brother is a kidney transplant surgeon at Groote Schuur. 'To all intents and purposes,' she says, 'I ought to have been a yuppie. Had my parents not been black, I would have come out of Sandton. Directly.'

The picture she paints of her youth is of tweedy eccentricity in the 'Little England' of the Transkei, all pies at the Central Hotel, piano lessons and catechisms (her father allowed them to choose their own religions; she, the perennial drama queen, went for Catholicism). She calls her parents 'Mother' and 'Daddy': ex-Healdtown and Fort Hare, they were Unity Movement stalwarts who rejected the trappings of the material world.

How, I ask her, is it possible that a land with such a powerful elite could become as destitute as the Transkei is now? She answers by telling me about the Mount Frere public swimming baths: 'After Matanzima and his crew took over, everything went to the dogs. They even closed the pool, because they were scared their children would drown. The barbarians didn't even think about teaching their children to swim.'

Shrieking with laughter at the subversiveness of it all, Mahlati chooses to describe herself, to me, as a fusion of the *amaqaba* and the *amagqoboka*. The former are her mother's people, the 'people who smear their faces', the 'blanket people' – fierce anticolonial warriors or country bumpkins, depending on which side of the blanket you lie. The latter are her father's people, the Christian converts – the 'pierced' people. 'They were the first quislings, really,' she says, 'those who forsook their tradition and cultures as soon as they realised there was superior gunpower, and, for their own survival, aligned themselves with the British.'

Here's the subversiveness of Mahlati: eschewing the 'sellout' connotations of *gqoboka*, she says that 'for me, the ethos of the *amagqoboka* is very important. Whoever imposes a particular superiority to me, I've gone out to learn it so I can beat them at their own game.' This is how she explains her rigid adherence to the market, her *laissez-faire* time at M-Net: 'The reality of conquest, for me, is that you submit. The old African tradition is that once you've been conquered, you submit yourself to the norms and the rules of your conqueror, and you master those rules so that you can conquer again.'

Deep down, she confides, 'I'm a *qaba*, totally! It's just the outside that's *gqoboka*!' Mahlati would not agree with the crunchy old Audre Lorde feminists of the 1970s that 'you can't use the master's tools to pull down the master's house'. It makes sense that the book that changed her life was Camille Paglia's *Sexual Personae*. She will not only live in the Master's house – she'll throw huge, fabulous parties there. She *will* show her cleavage; she *will* play with all that is pagan about her sexuality and her racial identity.

It also makes sense that, during her time abroad, her two mentors were Brigitte Mabandla and Lindiwe Mabuza. Both women challenge the categories of acceptable female behaviour even as applied by the gender-sensitive ANC. Mahlati is the wild woman, the outsider. Although she claims to be comfortable in all worlds, she often speaks of her own – that of Buppiedom – as if she doesn't quite belong. As if she is a wisecracking observer who sees it all from the margins.

In her late thirties, she has neither children nor husband. Her understanding of sexuality is libertarian: 'In South Africa, I'm not sure whether it's better to be a wife or a mistress'; 'monogamy is a Christian imposition, an 18th-century ideal that has lost its time and will not survive'; 'I don't believe you can police a penis. If it wants to, it will.'

Nothing irritates her more than the sanctimonious white left. The 'nanny class', she calls them, intellectuals who think they know best. Citing the Wits 13, Tony Leon, and Dennis Davis's attack on the credentials of Human Rights Commission chair Barney Pityana, she makes the point that 'white liberals do not have the humility of saying, "Perhaps I'm wrong, let me listen to you." No. They go into the intellectual defence of a position they have taken, and they back themselves into a corner.' Like many in the new black elite, she believes that 'in five years' time, Afrikaners and Africans will have made up, and the problem will be with the English liberals'.

What is refreshing about her is that she doesn't articulate these ideas from a perspective of Africanist essentialism. Listen, for example, for some classic Cawe rant on the idea that African society is communalist and egalitarian: 'Nonsense! Bullshit! This idea from white feminists that there's a sisterhood of black women together is absolute crap ... There are deep class divisions. Those relatives of mine who are indigent and need to come home so that I can feed them, I treat them as servants. They clean and cook for me, I give them food in return. It's not like we live together as one big happy family. Strictures and distinctions exist, particularly in African society, which is extremely hierarchical!'

Her particular take on the race-politics of broadcasting goes something like this: the white left conned black South Africans into believing they should be socialists, thus keeping them poor. Now they're trying to con black people into believing they should have public broadcasting, 'educational TV', when in fact 'all the people want from TV is to be entertained'. The very idea that you can have popular public broadcasting is 'a fantasy'.

Her instincts here might be right – no one is denying that the masses would rather watch The Cawe Show than The Ivy Show – but her facts don't neccessarily add up to her passions. Making a point about how a commercial Bop-TV could subsidise a public broadcasting station, she threw several examples at me of how this happens, including Britain, 'where Channel Four funds the BBC'. In fact, Channel Four's excess goes to ITV, and and the BBC draws its revenue from licence fees.

She also gave me a list of countries – France, Canada, Australia, Germany – where there is no local content quota, but where there is much local production because of government subsidy. She is dead right about the government subsidies, dead wrong about there being no local content quotas. The thing about Mahlati is that she – an experienced lawyer who has done time with IBM – thinks on her feet. There are thus bound to be factual casualties along the way.

There are also bound to be enemies. While there's no doubt she did wonders for M-Net – a clever, politically connected black woman praise-singing the market – one television source feels 'she might have been more effective if she weren't so damn abrasive'. That's the way many of her staffers feel about her at Bop-TV too.

Cawe Mahlati

She is, says one broadcasting player, 'ten steps ahead of anyone else in the sector, always strategising. This means she is a smoke and mirrors person.' An example: pick up some Bop publicity bumf and you'll read that she is the corporation's 'New CEO'. Ask her what her salary is, and she'll refuse to disclose it on the basis that she is a 'consultant' on a short-term contract, and 'not a public official'.

One way or the other, her decision to move to Bop was masterful. She has relaunched her career. It could land anywhere. For the moment, though, Mahlati is in Mmabatho. Her hair is back down to scale, and she professes to not wanting to be anywhere else. It's a Sunday night, she and Martin go looking for a drink. Everything is closed, even the O'Hagans that has become the Popo-generation's drinking hole of choice. 'Mmabatho!' she cries, in mock exasperation, out of Mabiletsa's white Mercedes.

No longer His Master's Voice?

I interviewed Zwelakhe Sisulu in February 1996, at the time of SABC-TV's contro-versial relaunch, during which Sisulu presided, uncomfortably, at a high-budget, ill-conceived and kitschy spectacle that took place in a hangar of the Waterkloof Air Base beneath a Jumbo Jet. Sisulu has had a hard time at Auckland Park and so, once more, that dilemma: how to write, critically, about one of the nicest, most straight-forward people I know? There are few profiles I have agonised over as much as this one: I hope the result helps explain Zwelakhe Sisulu more than it judges him.

Zwelakhe Sisulu

When he was a reporter at the *Rand Daily Mail* in the late 1970s, Zwelakhe Sisulu led a group of black colleagues from the publication on a protest march to John Vorster Square, where they were summarily arrested. Upon release, they were summoned into a senior editor's office, who bawled them out: 'How could you do this? It's a discredit to the paper!.'

Sisulu challenged the editor: 'I'm baffled. What we did was a concrete expression of the *Mail*'s editorial policy.'

'Ah, you don't get it,' the editor responded. 'You don't march. You *write!*'

Sitting now in an office on the top floor of a perpetual controversy about the relationship between the public broadcaster and government, Sisulu remembers that earlier confrontation as a watershed: 'For me, it showed the thin line that, in a sense, was beginning to define me out of South African journalism; that I was now, in a sense, a black activist.'

Cleaving a branch for his own personal destiny apart from that of his legendary family, Sisulu insists that 'I did not set out to be an activist. My activism began with my journalism.'

He spent two years in devastating detention; he set up and edited the *New Nation*, the ANC's functional internal mouthpiece; his political profile has propelled him to the most powerful media position in the country. And yet Zwelakhe Sisulu's professional identity solidified in those five years, from 1975 to 1980, when he was a working journo in the newsrooms at the South African Association of Newspapers.

And he carries with him, even now, the psychology of the journalist; a psychology captured most pithily by that doyen of post-war British journalism, James Cameron, who said something along the lines of: 'Every day, when I sit down at the typewriter, I think: This time they will find me out.'

Zwelakhe Sisulu is high on the charm. He is clever, articulate, charismatic, and blessed with those *gemutlische* Sisulu features that radiate hospitality and dependability; cheeks you could settle into with a cup of tea. But, like most good journalists, he is palpably insecure; one senses, lurking beneath the bluster, a man who feels he's a little bit of an impostor.

An example from the SABC gossip mill: For months, Sisulu took his lunches at the Johannesburg Country Club across the road from the SABC. Then, one day, his secretary called to make a reservation, and was told that if Sisulu wanted to continue dining there, he had to become a member. He has not been back since.

The story says much about Sisulu's diffidence. A government official, who has known him for years, says, 'He is one of the shyest people I know. When I looked at him at that launch, I saw an expression on his face which seemed to me to be saying, "I just want to sit in my office and do my job! I don't want to be on stage in front of a Jumbo Jet." Zwelakhe is a low-profile person with a high-profile name.'

His dilemma is that he carries with him not only the name but the chromosomes of his parents. He was propelled into leadership by those around him who saw this. Thus was he pushed, by fellow black journalists, into leading the Writers' Association of South Africa (WASA) in 1977. Thus was he pushed into setting up the *New Nation* in 1986; into becoming heir apparent at SABC in 1994. There is as much duty (filial or national) as drive in his upward mobility.

His contract at SABC expires in October next year. Will he make himself available for re-appointment? He will not say. He believes, however, that he will eventually go back to newsprint: 'There's no doubt in my mind that TV is the medium of the present and the future. But I do still think, if one wants to engage intellectually, that print is the best way.'

One of his senior staff, with much experience in television, says that 'he has been here for two years, and I still don't get a sense that he has any passion for television. TV just doesn't seem to be in his blood; he doesn't have an instinct for it.'

He agonised over his appointment and took it, say those close to him, with extreme caution and anxiety. These emotions, unfortunately, were writ large on his features every time he spoke. He had a hard time fostering confidence or providing vision. His greatest error, once he became chief executive in 1994, was to announce far-reaching reforms and objectives, and then not implement them speedily: employees feared retrenchment and rapid transformation, and then, when it didn't happen, the air at the SABC became poisonous.

It has been, for the past three years, a nightmarish place: rudderless, chaotic, back-biting, anguished. Last year, as more people 'took the package' and got out, Sisulu and his senior staff found themselves concentrating on strategic planning rather than on the more immediate crises in management.

His detractors in the sector – of whom there are many – feel that Sisulu, lacking confidence, has been overly reliant on bad advisers and that he has shielded himself from the corporation with a ring of yes-men (he is obsessed with 'loyalty to leadership'). They point, too, to the appalling way that the *New Nation* was managed, and to Sisulu's very poor relationship with journalists there.

But the SABC, and the South African broadcasting sector, have often proved themselves to be better producers of bile and gossip than programming. How fair is the flak Sisulu gets?

Certainly, I have found myself riveted to the screen almost every single night since the relaunch. I've seen some brilliant documentaries (mainly from Britain); some great old movies; some inspired magazine programmes; and more than a little lunacy masquerading as language policy – like the debate between Jacob Zuma and Frank Mdlalose, where the two native Zulu speakers, after having been introduced in Setswana, spoke English to each other.

Never mind the Babelish proportions of it all and the fact that non-Tswanas mightn't even think to tune in – thereby missing a critical debate. Far more worrying is the dishonesty of it all: that programme was as Setswana-speaking as I am.

Then there's the local-content issue: a cursory glance at Wednesday's schedules reveals that, out of 24 hours of viewing on SABC1, only two and three-quarters are locally produced: of that, only one and a half were produced externally, outside the SABC. Much the same is the case on SABC3, and the ratios on SABC2 are only slightly better. Sisulu answers these and other criticisms of the schedule with the rote – but not unacceptable – response that 'we are building capacity'.

As to the criticism that the launch sent the wrong message in having both President Mandela and broadcasting minister Pallo Jordan offering perorations, he is unswayed: 'We couldn't do better tactically than getting the President and Pallo to say, in their own words, that the independence of the public broadcaster is inviolate.'

But Mandela said something else too: he called Sisulu 'Comrade Zwelakhe'. It was more likely the collegial greeting to the son of his oldest friend than the deliberate attempt to make a political point, but the effect was nonetheless the same. Which brings us back to marching versus writing, or, in this case, broadcasting.

Sisulu's record – as party loyalist or free-expression warrior – is ambivalent. Speaking at a WASA conference in 1980, he maintained that all journalists were 'propagandists' – the question was simply whether 'one is a collaborationist propagandist or a revolutionary propagandist ... if expressing the aspirations of the people is propagandist ... then surely we are propagandists.'

His role at the *New Nation* was unmistakably one of publicising the ANC; not inappropriate, given the ANC's banning. But, says one senior journalist who worked with him there, 'as soon as things started getting more complicated, and there were a number of conflicting ANC positions, he found himself in trouble'. The paper, for example, steered well clear of the Winnie Mandela controversy – another instance of Sisulu's life being complicated by his family connections.

Certainly, at the moment of the ANC's unbanning, Sisulu – also unbanned – connected immediately with his mother-movement; working as Mandela's first press attaché. Later, though, he stalled when offered the editorship of the ANC's ill-fated daily newspaper: he was apparently uncomfortable with the control that would be wielded from Shell House.

Now, at the SABC, he is under constant pressure from government. A revealing incident took place at the time of Joe Slovo's death. TV news had, ill-advisedly, decided to broadcast only an hour of the state funeral. Sisulu received calls from dozens of parliamentarians demanding that the whole event be screened. According to sources at Auckland Park, Mandela even phoned, and Sisulu – knowing that he would not be able to say 'no' to the Old Man – told his secretary to say he was unavailable. The eventual decision, taken by the chief executive himself, was based entirely on 'newsworthiness': the proceedings were screened for only two hours.

Zwelakhe Sisulu feels that the TV relaunch was yet another watershed for him: he confesses to having been terrified that 'it might not happen', but, now that it has, he clearly feels more confident. One of his senior managers feels that 'he is growing in confidence, now that he believes this job isn't beyond him after all'.

One senses, too, that he has also grown weary of marching, and desperately wants to start writing again. Whatever his future trajectory – first black editor of the *Sunday Times*, member of Parliament, political columnist – he is unmistakably part of the new ruling elite, tied by the umbilical cord to South Africa's destiny. Two of his siblings, Max and Lindiwe, chair committees in Parliament; his sister-in-law, Sheila, is special adviser to the Minister of Education and a member of the SABC board.

Pippa Green wrote about the Sisulus in *Leadership* in 1990 that you could 'measure the political climate' of apartheid South Africa by the Sisulu family's 'suffering, its fears, and its hopes'. That was at the moment when the family was reunited after 30 years of exile, imprisonment and perpetual harassment.

Now, perhaps, you can measure this land's reconstruction, and the vagaries of black upward mobility, by the Sisulu family's current achievements. Unlike that lift that takes you to Zwelakhe Sisulu's 28th floor office, things are going up quickly. It's kind of hard to get off, even if deep down you think you might want to.

JILL CHISHOLM
Chief Executive: Television, SABC

A Lois Lane in tweeds

I interviewed Jill Chisholm only days after she had assumed her position as head of SABC's Television News Productions (TNP), in August 1995. Eight months later, she was promoted to Chief Executive: Television, making her the second most powerful person in the vast corporation after Zwelakhe Sisulu. Her legacy to all of us is the relaunched SABC TV with its new schedules: make your own decision as to whether she should be praised or condemned.

Jill Chisholm

When Jill Chisholm – a Lois Lane in tweeds – was sent off to cover Parliament for the *Rand Daily Mail* in 1969, a certain Cabinet minister would hiss at her, every time they crossed paths: '*Gif in klein botteltjies.*' [Poison in small bottles.]

She was the first-ever female political correspondent in the land. At first, she remembers, 'there'd be the patronising stuff of "here's this girl and she's coming to do this job, ha ha ha". But if your work is decent enough, you'll show them up sooner or later, and then they start reacting to you in an entirely different way: they become hostile to you. And that's where all good journalists should end up.'

Where Chisholm has ended up is running the SABC's Television News Productions. She is the real thing: she comes from an illustrious two-decade career at Independent Television News in London.

She jokes that she should hang a sign saying '*Gif in Klein Botteltjies*' on her door at the TV Centre. It might be more appropriate to drape a huge banner warning '*Gif* in Large Canisters' between the Brixton Tower and the Piet Meyer Bulding. From the rotting carcasses of propagandistic times past to the anarchic, backbiting, desperate, disillusioned moodswings of today, the SABC has become one of the toxic dumps of this transition.

Zwelakhe Sisulu might be finding his feet; SAfm might have stabilised; African-language soapies might be topping the ratings. But things are still dismal over at TV news and current affairs. When did you last watch 'Agenda'? And how many journalists attending press conferences now seem like old friends to you because of those long, slow pans over scrawling hacks that TV news editors seem to be so inexplicably fond of?

Once Television News Productions was released from the iron grip of Johan Pretorius and Christo Kritzinger, it went haywire. Democratisation became anarchy: Ameen Akhalwaya lasted weeks, Nico van Burick left after allegations of links with Military Intelligence, and poor old Bob Kearsley was sent squealing back to the torpid antipodes. Staffers spent so much time tearing each other's eyes out over 'The Way Forward', it's a wonder the news got out at all every night.

Chisholm is utterly unfazed. When I offer my condolences and ask her if she is surviving, she cocks her head and looks at me as if she doesn't understand the question. 'I'm loving this job,' she says. 'How could anyone not?' She is completely in control; precise and clipped, friendly in a distant sort of way, and very clear about boundaries. Leading me into her office, she puts between us the widest possible expanse of table.

At the first meeting she had with the TNP staff, one of them recalls, 'she gave us a chance to express all our frustrations, and then, without even saying much, made us feel like we should stop whingeing and start working. A number of us left the meeting feeling quite stupid.' I know the feeling: I felt the same way when I asked a question she didn't like. She'd very politely dispute its premise and that would be that.

She wears no makeup, and her tweeds are not power-suits; she eschews the dominatrix drag of stilettos and pencil-skirts in favour of an image of dependability. That, after all, is what managed to move her from the *Rand Daily Mail*'s women's page into politics: 'It took me a long time to get away from writing gossip at opening nights.

And the way I did it was to become reliable. There's nothing as good at getting a woman into places as becoming reliable. I could cover anything, and I wasn't going to make a mess of it.'

Chisholm was brought up by a single mother, a nurse, in Parktown boarding houses. She did not go to university. When she left South Africa with her husband (fellow *RDM* journo Sean Stiles) in 1971, she arrived cold in Britain. Within a decade she – a colonial, a woman – was executive producer of the ITN Ten O'Clock News, one of the most-watched broadcasts in the country.

She is, by her own admission, ambitious. 'We do have to address gender issues in our programming,' she says at one point in our conversation. 'And heaven forfend, as a woman, that I wouldn't have that view, because I think my whole life is an illustration of the problems women have.' When asked to elaborate, she says: 'Women get places slower than men.' She is in her 50s.

When she took direct responsibility for the merging of 'Agenda' and 'Newsline', things which had not been sorted out in six months were decided in a day. 'She walked in,' says journalist Callie Long, 'took the current affairs issue up, and brought it to a point. She managed to focus a staff that was demoralised, worried and panicking. It's a rare quality.'

The new-look 'Agenda Newsline' was launched three days before our meeting. In her assessment of the first few bulletins, Chisholm is perhaps a little too upbeat, even though she feels that on Tuesday night Max du Preez did not intervene enough in the 'crossfire' debate between pro-lifer Claude Newbury and pro-choicer Marj Dyer, and she was disappointed in the way that Leslie Mashokwe's panel discussion on health issues 'just failed to get going'.

Du Preez did withdraw, rather uncharacteristically, while Dyer and Newbury carried on like an old married couple who had been through the same fight one too many times before. And Mashokwe's debut on TV1 was dreadful – nine parts bluster to one part articulacy. In contrast, new girl Sylvia Vollenhoven's Sunday night documentary was an innovative and compelling treatment of a subject – women's upliftment – that can be worthy but dull.

The problem with the 'Agenda Newsline' merger, says one senior TNP staffer, 'is that it's still the same people just being shuffled around. Things will only improve if we get an injection of new people. But where we are going to find them, God alone knows.' When Chisholm first addressed her staff two weeks ago, she said, quite firmly, that mistakes were understandable, but that they could only happen once. Her mettle will thus be proven, in a month or so's time, when she is forced to do away with people who are simply not up to scratch.

In the meantime, she is beginning to make her presence felt. Her major intervention, says one source, has been to dilute the influence of Freek Robinson and Mashokwe – who have been the effective managers of current affairs – by putting more people on air: 'It was tactically very sound,' the source says, 'to empower more people and create a balance so that she is not dependent on any one individual or group.' Chief of cameras Robby Klarenberg has received more than one call at home when Chisholm was dissatisfied with camerawork; she correctly reversed a decision to can CNN; and she has at last started a 'beat' system for reporters. Perhaps her most difficult and unpopular decision was to pull a programme on violence against women, in which ANC MP Thandi Modise accuses her husband of abuse.

At last, though, there is someone up there who is engaged in news and the issues around it. For the first time ever, says Long, 'we are actually interacting with the editor-in-chief. She'll just wander in and talk to you. She'll ask you what you think. There was a whole year, in the old days, when I didn't even see Johan Pretorius!'

Snuki Zikalala, a news reporter, says that Chisholm 'is concerned about the product rather than the politics of this place. She wants accuracy and quality.' Other staffers worry, however, that her concentration on programming and quality will lead her into difficulty. 'She doesn't understand the intricate transition politics here,' one says, 'and unless she picks it up quickly, she'll be undone.' At the moment, that's the only negative thing anyone has to say about her. She can rest assured, however, that the scratching sound amid the applause is that of knives being sharpened.

She responds that she understands how 'immense' the upheaval is in the lives of her staffers, as in the lives of all South Africans. 'They're finding and defining themselves. So you have to be sensitive to where they are at. But that doesn't mean you compromise, ever, on professionalism.'

She is candid in her critique of SABC TV news: it is 'introspective' –'but for a statutory nod at Bosnia, we only acknowledge the rest of the world when it forces us to' – and 'event-driven': 'our diaries are heavy with photo opportunities and events, and I'd like to see much more of putting those events into context rather than just saying: "this happened today" or "so-and-so went there today".' She has, to her immense credit, already declared war on rote press-conference coverage, and is trying to move TV news toward appropriate graphics when the live picture just isn't interesting enough.

Chisholm left South Africa in its darkest days, in 1971, after two years in Parliament, 'in the most positively depressing place I have ever been in my life. Working in an institution dedicated to constantly passing new laws to suppress something or close down something. There are no limits to my admiration for Helen Suzman. I think people dramatically underestimate what she went through to be what she was.'

It figures that she would have Suzman as a mentor: they both manage to present unassailable integrity without sounding self-righteous. How easy it would have been for Chisholm to return the triumphant exile. But she does not wear, as a badge of any kind of honour, the fact that she was regularly interrogated by security police in the early 1960s before leaving the country. In fact, she does not even mention it.

And she didn't vote in last year's election. 'I didn't know if I was coming home yet. To have voted and sat out there would have been dishonest ... And I was not going to become a "Sunshine Settler" – back here because the weather's good and the trouble's over. I've only come back because there's something here for me to do.' Scrubbed, unsentimental and canny, Jill Chisholm conforms to her own definition of a good journalist: a sceptic rather than a cynic.

RIANI DE WET

Former MEC for Public Media,
North West Province

Klerksdorp Icarus

At the time I interviewed her in April 1995, Riani de Wet, as the North West minister responsible for Bop Broadcasting, had grand plans. These failed, and she has to be held somewhat responsible that for the chaos Cawe Mahlati found upon arrival almost a year later. I love this photograph, because De Wet is clearly having, as she puts it in the profile, a 'fat jol' in one of Lucas Mangope's executive jets. Well, a little bit too much of a fat jol: a few weeks later, the 27-year-old was removed from her office. Among the allegations against her was the mishandling of her portfolio and a jaunt, to Sun City, with her mother on the jet.

Riani de Wet

There is a popular European TV-ad for hair-spray that features a female executive and a Learjet: 'Hamburg 7 a.m.; conditions: windy', the text reads, and you see the woman descending from the plane, hair a perfect blonde helmet above her head. 'Paris 8 a.m.; conditions: rain' – and the woman's hair is still in place; 'Rome, 11a.m.; conditions: sun' – not a strand out of place.

Mmabatho International Airport, 8.30 a.m.; conditions: torpid. Twenty-seven-year-old Riani de Wet, North West Province's Minister for Public Media, strides into the airport, looking not quite as impermeable as Learjet Lady but certainly zippy in green, subtly tie-dyed ethnogarb that, it later transpires, was made by her mother back in Klerksdorp.

She will be flying, today, to the Free State and the Northern Cape in one of the fleet of compact executive jets that Lucas Mangope left behind. The mission: to rally support for a provincial broadcasting plan that, if successful, will keep the lavish Bophuthatswana Broadcasting Corporation from the clutches of the SABC juggernaut and turn it into the hub of a provincial network.

Bloemfontein, 10 a.m.; conditions: torpid. Kimberley, 3 p.m.; conditions: torpid. Doesn't quite have the same zing as a little gallivant around Europe. No matter: this is a state visit in its own right. 'We're gonna have a fat jol on the way back to Mmabatho,' says MEC De Wet as she leads her team of older men across the tarmac, referring to the drinks cabinet stashed under one of the seats in the jet.

Riani de Wet is very down-home; a sharp, working-class Klerksdorp girl (father, miner; mother, doctor's assistant) who refers to her hometown as a 'big city', wants to visit the drive-in pub in Kimberley, and does not look at home in a Learjet. Which is not to say that she does not enjoy it: she has a home-girl's appreciation for the finer things in life.

Being a provincial cabinet minister is, in fact, De Wet's first real job. She dropped out of Rand Afrikaans University, and worked, before the election, as a hotel receptionist and a hostess on the Greyhound Citiliner.

Her detractors – of whom there are many in the broadcasting business – like to joke about how her only prior experience of broadcasting is over the Greyhound PA-system. She knew nothing about broadcasting, or provincial government, when she was elected.

Nothing has changed, say her detractors. They are wrong. She might still be new to the field, but De Wet has done her homework. She does not possess a sparkling intellect, but she has a solid diligence and an instinct for common sense.

North West premier Popo Molefe apparently earmarked her for the job before the election – when he was the African National Congress's national election organiser and she the region's Department of Information and Publicity official.

Local insiders say that the symbolic significance of having a white ANC Afrikaner in his cabinet was top priority for Molefe. Others say that De Wet, in the words of one, 'came from nowhere, and just happened to be the first vaguely appropriate woman and white person on the list'.

One way or the other, the Citiliner hostess has become one of the more influential and effective politicians in North West. She finds power 'hilarious. Sometimes I'm frustrated. I think here I am and I'm the whole MEC and I told them to do something and they ignored me! How dare they! I say to myself, Riani, you think you've got power but you've got none. Then another time I'll say something quite innocently, really, just thinking out aloud, and people will jump to it. They'll just move and I think, Wow!'

As we get onto the plane in Mmabatho, Bop Broadcasting head Solly Kotane calls to his minister, 'Riani, you're sitting in our ex-president's seat.'

'Yes, Solly,' she retorts, quick as a whip. 'But at least I don't phone you at six in the morning to complain about the music you're playing on my radio station!'

Once we are airborne, she confides: 'You see, Mangope tried to buy the airwaves by pumping in more and more money. But it didn't work. I'm trying the opposite approach. I've just cut the budget of Bop Broadcasting by thirty per cent. Now they don't have the money to buy American programmes any more, so they'll be desperate. That's where I come in, with my four-hour weekly special, the Riani de Wet Show!'

She plays with power the way you would expect a woman in her mid-twenties to. She likes to fool around – but she takes herself very seriously too. If she wasn't responsible for a budget of R150-million, you could mistake her for exactly what she used to be: an eager young student who enjoys a 'fat jol' but also has had the intense revelation of truth. She has the earnestness – and occasional sentimentality – of a young Afrikaner who has seen the light.

Chris Landsberg, the black student leader at RAU when De Wet was there, says that 'she was the last person we thought would go into active politics. She was utterly committed, really diligent, but not the kind of person with aspirations.'

Nonetheless, she was 'one of the committed few Afrikaans-speaking whites who would stick out their necks against apartheid and racism on campus. It made them very unpopular. People like Riani established progressive organisations at Afrikaans universities, and that was no small feat.'

She remembers clearly her fall from innocence. As a member of the National Party Student Movement, she participated in a conference that decided to send a message to the Cabinet that the ANC should be unbanned and Nelson Mandela released.

'We had been asked to consider this question, but when we came up with our answers, the leader of the conference – a senior NP leader still very prominent – told us that our answer was unacceptable because the ANC was a terrorist group. That was it. The hypocrisy! My belief that the National Party was interested in democracy was shattered.'

And so she drifted, via the Progs, into organisations like Jodac (the Johannesburg Democratic Action Committee). Her formulations of anti-apartheid Afrikanerdom are heartfelt and emotional: 'Anybody with half a brain should have seen that apartheid was wrong! Wrong! Wrong! And we progressives, not them, are the real Afrikaners. I mean, guerrilla warfare was founded by General de Wet!'

Her family is 'strongly NP' – but, she says, 'my mom is one of Popo Molefe's greatest fans. She has even written him letters of support when the going has got rough.'

Perhaps there is a key to De Wet's success in the fact that she is not viewed, in her hometown, as a *verraier*, but rather as the person who could introduce the good burghers of Klerksdorp to their new leader, and vice versa.

Perhaps she has been lost for a while: 'What people like Riani went through was such a shift,' says Landsberg. 'It gave concrete meaning to their lives, but it also disturbed their lives – where they fit into society, about themselves as individuals.'

But she has now found herself, clearly, in politics. And she is passionate about her work: 'People say that I'm too close to Bop Broadcasting,' she says, 'but how can I not be? I'm the minister and they want answers from me. Who, ultimately, is accountable to people? Not the SABC board. Not the IBA. Not Bop Broadcasting. I am. I am an elected official.'

All this means that 'while the concept of no government control over the media is one I support, it's an intellectual one that means little on the ground. Maybe it would be different in Gauteng, but this is the *platteland*. People know each other. People talk to each other. There's that communality. And if they have problems, they come to Riani – and they want answers.'

Proud of her working-class roots, she likes to see herself as a woman of the people: one of the most significant changes in her life since her new status, she says, is that 'for the first time in my life I can afford to go to the hairdressers twice a week if I want to. But of course I don't have the time for that – and if I do, then it's with colleagues for a meeting.'

One of her pet peeves at the moment is the sense of entitlement she finds among former Bop civil servants. She remembers watching the protest outside parliament on the day it opened last year: 'There was a woman toyi-toying, shouting "*Mali! Mali!*" in a leather jacket. Now I mean, fuck off! You wear a leather jacket and you're toyi-toying for money and there are people in this province who can't even afford to feed themselves! That's the legacy of Bop.'

Here's the thing about Riani de Wet: she is open, honest, unguarded. Easy to make fun of. Her bluster – the broad gesture, the sometimes salty language, the jaunty over-confidence that is so clearly a consequence of being uncomfortable with authority – makes her look brash sometimes, and easy to disdain. Perhaps she is too young for her job, but that is not her fault: her earthiness is a symptom of her realness.

The junket is over. Now, back in a rather anodyne suburban mansion provided by Bop Broadcasting, it's time for De Wet to kick off her pumps and relax. She puts on Tchaikovsky's 1812 Overture.

As the martial music begins to build, she talks of her loneliness: 'Sometimes I worry about how young I am – not because I think I'm too young to be making decisions, but because I'm too young for the life I'm living. I have no personal life. I don't have time for it.'

The cannons start to boom. She is conscious of the fact that she is unpopular in some quarters: 'Many treat me with contempt – here's a little girl, what does she know? People seem to underestimate me, and baby, that's their problem, because sooner or later they're going to suffer for it … not because I'll launch a vendetta against them, but because they think they are stronger than they really are.'

There's a tough side to De Wet; the side that chooses to relax to the 1812 Overture.

ROELF MEYER
National Party Secretary-General
and Chief Negotiator
Too damn straight to leave the laager

I interviewed Roelf Meyer in February 1996, in the week FW de Klerk announced Meyer was quitting cabinet and becoming the National Party's secretary-general. He has always been a moderate, and in our interview he spoke at length of the importance of keeping the party in the Government of National Unity. Even though Meyer was largely responsible for persuading the NP to vote for the constitution in May 1996, the fact that the NP left the GNU must be seen as a defeat for him. The qualities that make him a good politician make him an inscrutable, if amiable, interview subject. He gives nothing away. So while I'm confident that I have a clear understanding of his politics, his personality remains an enigma to me.

Roelf Meyer

Driving to Pretoria to meet the New Face of the National Party on Monday morning, I heard FW de Klerk giving an interview about his party's new direction on SAfm's 'AM Live' show. He affably said how happy he was to be 'back on Radio Today once more'.

Unlike De Klerk – who sometimes seems still to have his Yesterdays and Todays a bit muddled, whose frownlines habitually betray an irritability lurking behind the forced *bonhomie* – the National Party's new secretary-general is blessed with a deceptive 'gee-golly-shucks' countenance. A vision of perpetual youth that makes him seem as if he is in permanent awe of the democratic miracle he has helped fashion: Roelfie in Wonderland. History literally slides off his features. Age cannot wither him, nor the National Party's history stale his infinite variety.

And that, says one senior National Party tactician, is one of the major reasons why he has been made custodian of the party's future; why he was given the job of expanding the party beyond an Afrikaner special interest lobby. 'Man, he looks good! He's the media's blue-eyed boy. A good, honest-looking *boereseun*. Even if he has enemies within the party, outside he can make no mistake. He's a bit like Nelson Mandela. He doesn't even have a good pronunciation of English!'

True enough, Meyer's English – fluent but heavily accented – connotes wide-eyed farmboy rather than repressive military patriarch. He struggles tremulously for the right accent rather than blustering, Vorster-style, his way through a pronunciation slip. But Roelf Meyer is no *ingénue* Alice drinking bottles of growing potion (or youth elixir) he happens to find strewn in his path. He is the teller of his own story, he places the bottles there himself, he is one of the sharpest and subtlest operators on the South African political scene. He has apparently always known that his Cabinet influence would wane once the constitution was written, and has long been angling for a new platform.

Certainly, by dropping him from the Cabinet and giving him the nigh-impossible task of bringing black people to the party, De Klerk may be consigning him – as Stoffel van der Merwe was previously – to oblivion. But the opinion of *Beeld*'s Tim du Plessis is far more likely: 'De Klerk's order in 1992 to Mr Meyer was: "Just negotiate, and I'll bring the NP along." Four years later, Mr De Klerk is speaking in almost the same vein to him: "Do what you need to do to the NP, and I'll protect you." Which Mr Meyer will certainly need.'

Roelf Meyer is one of the most likeable personalities you will ever meet. But although he is affable and informal, he remains enigmatic. Unlike Pik Botha or Leon Wessels – over-emotional repudiators of the past – he offers no articulation of his transformation. And always conventional and never a rebel, he has never considered the option of dissent, in the way a Breytenbach or a Fischer – or even a Slabbert or Wynand Malan – did. Now close to 50, he is still, ultimately, the good *boereseun*. Although he comes from a very ordinary farming family that was on the margins of Afrikaans society (his father seldom went to church, and was not politically involved), he has built his own profile through an almost-textbook rise through Afrikaans institutions: the church, the Afrikanse Studentebond, the Rapportryers, the Ruiterwag, the Broederbond, and – of course – the National Party. He doesn't swear, he doesn't drink (much), he doesn't fool around: he's too damn straight to leave the NP.

Roelf Meyer

He often talks about how, when he entered Parliament aged 32, in 1979, he was hit by how 'unreal' and 'unacceptable' it was, and how it gave him 'no satisfaction'. He certainly gave no hint of it at the time. *Vaderland* parliamentary correspondent Dries van Heerden took to calling him 'klein FW'. A decade apart, their political careers followed very similar routes through Afrikaner institutions.

In Parliament Meyer gravitated naturally towards De Klerk and Adriaan Vlok, then Chief Broeder on the benches, firmly in the Transvaal centre-right axis of the party. Like De Klerk, he took care not to trumpet his precocity: he kept his head down, making strategic interventions where they would be noticed. By 1986, he was handpicked from the back benches by PW Botha to be deputy minister of law and order under Vlok. This threw him right into the heart of the Botha-era repression. In February 1987, he told Parliament that 'the detentions over the past year were "worth it" because it was better to have more freedom for millions of people than to have a few disrupting normal daily life'.

He was also appointed chairman of Botha's Joint Management System, which co-ordinated security forces and service-providers with the aim of eliminating 'trouble-makers' through detention and winning the hearts and minds of black people by improving township infrastructures. Meyer neither acknowledges nor repudiates his role at the epicentre of evil, save to say that he was 'frustrated' at the time because he realised a 'political solution' was neccessary and that he would be happy to go to the Truth and Reconciliation Commission to talk about it.

Whatever his involvement in the repressive securocracy, one thing is certain: he is more comfortable in the new, ANC-led South Africa than any of his party colleagues. He receives frequent plaudits from a (perhaps trouble-making) Nelson Mandela. In 1989, after being appointed deputy minister of constitutional development, he announced publicly that he would resign if there was no move towards change within two years. That vow, he says now, 'drove me'. After Codesa collapsed in 1992, he became minister and the government's chief negotiator, following a brief and unhappy stint as minister of defence, when he was known by the generals as 'The Canary' because his only prior experience in defence had been as a choirboy at the Air Force Gymnasium in the late 1960s.

As chief negotiator, Meyer 'surprised all of us', says one journalist close to the NP: 'He seemed to develop both personally and politically at Kempton Park.' His first move was jettisoning the Inkatha Freedom Party, the darling of most of his colleagues. Suddenly the good little prefect found himself having terrible fights with the teachers, with powerful people like Hernus Kriel, Tertius Delport, Kobie Coetzee and Rina Venter, all of whom regularly accused him of selling the party – and white folk – out. He had to defend himself, because he knew he was right. Unlike them, he understood that you could not outmanoeuvre the ANC, and that conceding certain points was the only way forward. And so, says the journalist, 'He developed a self-confidence, a toughness. He fought back.'

Even now, he is loathed by people like Kriel – whom he further antagonised with his technically correct support of Mandela's stand during the Cape Town demarcation dispute last year. Once more, the hawks in the party accused him of 'betrayal' and of 'ANC lackeyism'. His supporters counter by explaining that his very 'pragmatism' is the reason why the National Party has any influence at all. And true enough, the famed 'Roelf–Cyril channel' that kept negotiations going during the desperate days following the Boipatong massacre in 1992 brought South Africa back from the brink of civil war. Meyer – to his immense credit – was often more interested in saving the situation than in fighting for party interests.

Perhaps De Klerk gave Meyer the job of secretary-general to make Meyer accountable to him and no longer to Mandela, and to tie his only really viable successor more directly to the party's fortunes. Now, perhaps, what distinguishes Roelf Meyer from his colleagues is the understanding that the NP cannot win black support through an offensive on the ANC. He understands, says one senior ANC leader who knows him well, 'that if you say, The ANC doesn't deliver!, it sounds like you're saying, Blacks can't do the job; that these attacks translate, in the minds of black people, into racist attacks from people bitter about losing power'.

While people like Hernus Kriel and Pieter Marais go out of their way to set up the ANC as the communist Anti-Christ, Roelf Meyer goes out of his way to emphasise the fact that there's very little separating the two at all. The 'overall objectives' of the NP and the ANC, he says, 'are very much the same, because we both want to uplift people and ensure we close the gap between the haves and the have-nots'.

He speaks like a social democrat rather than a 'Christian democrat' conservative. Unlike even De Klerk, he will not push a conservative moral agenda around bringing back the death penalty and outlawing abortion. His approach seems to be to woo people from their traditional support of the ANC, not by emphasising difference, but rather by saying, 'Hey, we're just like the ANC!' Why black people would vote for a De Klerk-led ANC rather than a Mandela- or Mbeki-led ANC is beyond me: perhaps the Meyer approach is the only one, but it seems more like a political cul-de-sac than a route to future power.

During most of the battles between Meyer and the NP 'hawks' last year, De Klerk stayed on the fence. This, according to insiders, caused more than a little tension between the NP leader and his new crown prince. It seems more than likely that Meyer extracted from De Klerk a commitment to his vision for the future before accepting the job. De Klerk, for his part, must have extracted a commitment from Meyer that he would be prepared to work as an opposition leader rather than as a member of the executive. It remains to be seen whose definition of 'opposition' prevails.

The wisdom of De Klerk in appointing a conciliator rather than a combatant as party organiser also remains to be seen. It surely goes against the grain of the combative and restive Nat ranks. In our interview he acknowledged that the NP rebirth before the 1994 elections was a dismal failure: 'There is still the perception that the NP is a white party, because its leadership is white. Certainly, that kind of thing will have to change.'

Is Danie Schutte's blood boiling yet? Has Hernus had a hernia? Wait for this: 'We have to become sensitive to the aspirations and needs of black people. Traditional supporters of the NP are interested in things – like the preservation of Afrikaans – which are obviously not in the minds of black people ... As long as this prevails, people in the black community will have difficulty with the NP. Understandably so.'

The hawks can rest easy, though. This is not the thin edge of the wedge. Meyer remains a strong advocate of the National Party's interests. In a closed bilateral between the ANC and the NP at the World Trade Centre, for example, he led the NP's campaign to extend the Government of National Unity beyond 1999. Cyril Ramaphosa rejected this out of hand. Now, Meyer says, 'Frankly, it might be difficult for us to find each other on this, but I'm still looking for a solution. I have something in the back of my mind that I'm sure will get us through this …'

Waves of nostalgia: fly-hooked fingers, late-night sessions, taking to the dance floor together. It sounds like the Roelf–Cyril channel all over again. With one significant difference: the ANC no longer needs the channel. It is in power. It will get its way. The extent to which Roelf Meyer understands this will determine his political longevity.

BRIGADIER ROLAND DE VRIES
& COLONEL SOLLY MOLLO

SANDF's new brothers in arms

When I started scratching around for someone to profile in the military, I heard about a unique friendship that had developed between these two senior officers, from the SA Defence Force and uMkhonto weSizwe respectively. And so I broke form to interview them together. When I met them in September 1995, both had already become key players in integrating the new defence force. Since then, Mollo has replaced De Vries as Officer Commanding 7 Division, and De Vries has been appointed Director of Transformation at Military Headquarters.

Brigadier Roland de Vries & Colonel Solly Mollo

Colonel Rocky Williams, an uMkhonto weSizwe commander now at the Defence secretariat, remembers how officers from MK and the SA Defence Force bonded, courtesy of Charles Glass, round the braaivleis fire. An MK guy would look at his watch and say, 'My God! It's 23h00! I better get moving – my wife's gonna *moer* me!' It would be a revelation, says Williams, for the SADF officers: Wow! These *ouens* have wives too and they also need to get home! Forget ideology! Bury the past! A soldier is a soldier; a man is a man; the hearth is the hearth and we'd better get back to it quickly or we're all gonna be in bigtime *kak*!

It happened in the army workgroup of the Joint Military Co-ordinating Council, responsible for planning the integration of the new defence force last year. That April – just days before the election – group leaders Roland de Vries (an SADF brigadier) and Solly Mollo (an MK instructor now a colonel in the SA National Defence Force), succumbed to one of those Roelf-and-Cyril moments in Plettenberg Bay, whereto De Vries had commandeered the troops for some R & R and a sail on his Hobie Cat.

As I sit with them over beers at Voortrekkerhoogte's Army College, De Vries tells the story: 'The locals said there had not been wind for a month. But God smiled on us. The wind blew! The guys from Robben Island were terrified of the seas. I took them all out, one by one, out past Robberg – I counted 40 sharks there once in half an hour – and when I was with Solly he slipped and the boat capsized. Rough seas, that day.

'Me and Solly were talking so much! It was while we were sailing that we arrived at the concept that this "Unity is Strength" is nonsense. We decided that the New South Africa's motto should rather be, "Diversity is Strength!"'

I have this image of two men, both highly-respected military commanders, bobbing around in the rough seas off Robberg, surrounded by 40 sharks, brainstorming a new motto for the South African National Defence Force. Although Mollo was studying to become a lawyer when he was called in to negotiate for MK last year, both men believe in the brightness of the SANDF's future with such fervour that they are sometimes quite blinding. Perhaps because they found each other, white and black South African, through it.

De Vries was, until recently, Officer Commanding the vast 7th Division, responsible for 50 000 civilian force troops. Now the SANDF's Director of Transformation, he is one of the army's authorities on mobile warfare, and he commanded a mechanised infantry brigade during Operation Modular, the SADF's successful incursion into south-east Angola in 1987. Mollo was recruited by De Vries last year to be the Senior Staff Officer (Personnel) of 7 Div. Both are headed – at each other's side – to very high places indeed.

They have become colleagues and friends: their kids play together, their wives are *huisvriende*, the families holiday together where, while Oom Roland makes a *potjie*, Oom Solly and his mother, a matron at the Dennilton Hospital, sing Afrikaans hymns.

Says Mollo: 'I am an African child ('*Ek ook!*' interjects his boisterous friend). He is my brigadier. To me he's my father. A revelation to me. At first I said to myself, I don't understand this one. You wouldn't believe he's a *boereseun*.'

Sure, there's rank – even as we drink beers, De Vries calls Mollo 'Solly' while Mollo calls him 'Brigadier' – but they most certainly don't behave the way I expect from soldiers. I dodged the draft, but not, at first, for political reasons: I was just too damn terrified. As a white boy in Total Onslaught South Africa, the army was telling me what it was to be a man: men killed, men protected. Men were strong, silent and sure. Women existed so that men could have something to protect; something to kill other men over. The army was the place that broke your spirit: it shaved your hair off and kicked the shit out of you. It was certainly no place to be if you were a Jew, a klutz, a four-eyes or a *moffie*. (I only learned later, from friends, how wrong I was on that last score.)

I could only listen with wonder, then, as De Vries – sentimental and psychopop in equal measure – told me how he and Mollo got people talking in the army work-group: 'We had what I call tribal stories, sitting around the fire and telling each other our most intimate things. I get goosebumps thinking about it. By using high group interaction we really built trust. If you have trust, you have a high level of interaction based on the win-win situation.'

Forget the Truth and Reconciliation Commission. Brigadier Roland de Vries has another idea: 'We want to arrange campfire evenings where we get a whole lot of civilians together sharing tribal stories.' I have absolutely no doubt that, after a campfire evening with De Vries, the Azasm heavies would be embracing their white teachers and calling them 'Ma'. I have one piece of advice for Dr Zuma: get the Bara nurses and the Gauteng government off to the brigadier immediately.

A few months ago, De Vries and Mollo took a team from 7 Div off to see the battlefields of Natal. Now they want to do the same in Angola so that, De Vries says, 'we can appreciate each other's tactics.' This is one reason why he, the military theorist, is so thrilled by integration: he has long urged the army, in his writings and in his training courses, to merge guerrilla tactics in with conventional methods. 'To me, integration was a great opportunity to put this into practice and learn from each other!' He loves Shaka, Rommel, Napoleon, Mao, De La Rey, Giap – not because of what they individually fought for, but because they were such brilliant proponents of mobile warfare. What makes him unique as an SADF-trained theorist, says Mollo, is that he will look at Shaka or Mao in the first place.

When asked about his ideology, De Vries answers, 'I am a Christian,' and, cryptically, tells a story about how he would never stay put in his church's Sunday school as a child, but rather ran 'all around Vanderbijlpark visiting all the other Sunday Schools'. The message is clear, and underscores what people involved in the military transformation process have told me: he is an experimenter, a maverick who has risen in the ranks because, despite the fact that he goes his own way, he is an inspirational commander and brilliant strategist.

But he begins his book on mobile warfare, published in 1987, with the statement that 'there is no doubt about the profane aims of the RSA's communist-inspired enemies', and quotes, approvingly, from a right-wing American journal, that 'the Soviet strategy is … to foment internal revolution to overthrow the existing power structure … and establish their surrogate, the African National Congress, as the new government …'

He would say that he is a military professional, serving the needs of whichever government was in power; I tend to agree with General Colin Powell, however, when he says there is no such thing as an 'apolitical' military commander. My guess is that

Brigadier Roland de Vries & Colonel Solly Mollo

De Vries, like many other Afrikaners, has undergone not so much a Damascene conversion as an awakening: he says, quite frankly, that those times with the army subgroup were 'the best times of my life'; he is one of those Afrikaners who love the New South Africa for the freedom it has brought them from narrow-minded control.

He tells the story of how he refused to allow a Rhodesian task force to work out of his base in that country in 1979 because they were gunning down children. But still, he was a Brigadier in the SADF in the Total Onslaught days. He fought in Angola and he killed. Then again, so did Mollo. Perhaps, the ex-MK instructor ventures, that's why some soldiers from MK and the SADF have found it easy to connect: 'When you talk about the defence community, you talk about people who know what life is and know what death is. We know what it means to build trust. We all have the same kind of tribal stories.'

Rocky Williams claims that no part of South African society has transformed as rapidly as the military, and says that part of this is due to 'the myth that we're a unique breed, perpetuated through ritual, with all its paraphernalia and mystique. Although the ideologies might be different for MK or the SADF, the mystique is the same.' But there's also a reality, he adds: 'there's a very pragmatic side to soldiering – about getting a job done in relation to a certain order.'

But Mollo is the first to say that 'not everyone will be like Solly Mollo and land up in 7 Div working under Brigadier de Vries. You have MK officers in many units sitting around doing nothing, because their commanders are ignoring them or feel threatened by them.' And there is still much racism: Mollo tells the story of a group of former-MK officers who went on a training course: a rifleman, a little boy, called them *kafferkoppe* to their faces.

And these are officers' issues; for ordinary soldiers things are much tougher. The mutiny at Wallmannstal last year – in which both SADF and MK share blame – shows that while De Vries and Mollo might be models for integration, they are certainly not archetypal. Now integration has swollen the SANDF to such an extent that 40 000 troops are going to lose their commissions over the next four years. Already, the demobilisation process has begun, and while Mollo circumspectly says that 'transition is tough', military analysts have slammed the Defence Force for throwing cash in the faces of unwanted soldiers: those who take the cash will spend it, and then at least some of them will turn to banditry.

Then there is that word, 'integration'. Spend an evening with Roland de Vries and Solly Mollo at Voortrekkerhoogte and it's clear, from the very outset, that the culture they share is not one that integrates MK and the SADF. Solly Mollo – like the MK he comes from – has been absorbed rather than integrated into a phenomenally powerful culture and tradition: that of South African militarism.

Sure enough, there has been – in the case of Roland de Vries at least – some magical counter-absorption. But despite the *scathamiya* songs that drift over from the training fields, despite the way Mollo greets an old comrade with an *'Eita Da'* as well as a salute, this is still Voortrekkerhoogte, a fortress of conformity and hierarchy and control. If I had to do the *pro patria mori* routine and was given a choice of commander to follow into battle, it would be Roland de Vries. But if I were 18 again, and there were still conscription, I'd be outta here.

GENERAL TIENIE GROENEWALD

KwaMakhutha murder accused
and Freedom Front senator

Onward, Christian soldier ...

In November 1995, murder charges were laid against General Magnus Malan and 14 other senior apartheid military personnel for the massacre of 13 innocent women and children at KwaMakhutha, because they had authorised and supervised the training of Inkatha hit-squads. It was alleged that the strategic mastermind was General Tienie Groenewald – although he was acquitted of all charges six months later, due to a document proving that he had asked to be transferred off the project. I interviewed Groenewald on the day before he first appeared in court. I was under no illusion about his complicity in apartheid atrocities. I felt, however, that what often gets elided in moral outrage – and lost in the rote reporting of courtroom pro-ceedings – is the chillingly clinical credo by which people like Groenewald live. I wanted to understand Groenewald's relationship to his own morality.

Tienie Groenewald

Forgive us our sins as we forgive others. The day after Major-General Tienie Groenewald was charged with murder, his wife underwent chemotherapy. The Groenewalds are devout Christians, and the general has been trying to save his wife's life through prayer. Eight months ago, when she was given only weeks to live, they decided that they needed to forgive their own enemies if they were to be forgiven by God; if she was to be saved.

And so, he tells me, 'we got together and drew up a little hate sheet, of all the people who have done us wrong and whom we needed to forgive'. Groenewald, now a Freedom Front senator, was very close to the heart of PW Botha's securocratic regime: he was the South African Defence Force's head of propaganda from 1980 to 1982, he set up and ran the State Security Council's intelligence subcommittee from 1982 to 1984, and he was a chief director in Military Intelligence from 1984 to 1986. He is one of the prime exponents of the Total Onslaught, the destabilisation of Southern Africa, and the internal repression of the States of Emergency.

But Joe Slovo was not on his hate sheet; neither was Ronnie Kasrils nor Samora Machel. In fact, only one politician was: FW de Klerk, 'because of the way he let down the Defence Force. Mandela saw to it that every single one of his members got amnesty, but De Klerk just dumped his people.' So did he forgive De Klerk? The general pauses, for a long while. 'I do think I've forgiven him,' he says, unconvincingly. 'But I certainly will never trust him again.'

Forgive us our sins as we forgive others. With murder charges and terminal illness, the Groenewalds are going through trying times. They have subjected themselves to their own personal Truth and Reconciliation Commission. Does the general think South African military leaders, or any white South Africans, have anything to apologise for? 'Yes, but I see this in a Christian way. I apologise to God. I don't see why I need to apologise to Bishop Tutu.'

He sees his arrest in a Christian way too: 'I've lived according to Christian norms. So to be arrested for murder is the most humiliating experience I've ever been through. I've always thought of myself as clean. I've never been involved in anything illegal, immoral or irregular. I maintained my Christian principles in my married life – I've never played around. I really do consider myself to be a person of principle. Now to be arrested for murder! That's something!'

If Magnus Malan has responded to being arrested for the murder of 13 innocent women and children at KwaMakhutha with outrage and apocalyptic doomsaying, Groenewald is more considered. He is the quintessential backroom boy: shadowy, low profile, unknown outside his own world. He attained public prominence as one of the generals who broke with De Klerk, founded the Afrikaner Volksfront, and then set up the Freedom Front. He spoke rebellion and then he spoke peace.

It was Groenewald who put the committee of generals together that spearheaded the call for self-determination and, later, the Concerned South Africans Group alliance with Lucas Mangope and Mangosuthu Buthelezi. Constand Viljoen might be the charismatic new leader of the Afrikaner right wing, but Groenewald is its master strategist: both the Volksfront and the Freedom Front were, by and large, his inventions, and his major coup was getting Viljoen involved.

The two generals first connected in 1978 when Viljoen was head of the army and Groenewald head of air force intelligence. Groenewald had identified a Swapo camp at Kasinge, far behind enemy lines in Angola. He managed to convince Viljoen to attack it by lying to him that if the army didn't do it, the air force would, and thus shame him. Viljoen went ahead, and the operation was, says Groenewald, 'beautiful, just bloody well done. Only two or three dead, five wounded.'

I have to ask about the other side before I am told, 'Seven hundred dead.' Swapo asserts that Kasinge was a refugee camp and that the dead were largely women and children. An account by one of the South African soldiers sent in to execute the wounded, published in the local media a few years ago, confirms this, as do reports by United Nations organisations. Groenewald insists, however, that 'only a few civilians were killed. Our intelligence picture was complete, we knew everything.'

One way or the other, over seven hundred people were killed; it was the worst massacre of the war.

One of the most perplexing things about military men is their unassailable sense of morality. Groenewald is no exception. He contradicts his anger with De Klerk by asking, 'Why would I go to the truth commission? What would I apply for indemnity from? I've committed no crimes!' The only time he ever questioned South Africa's morality, he says, was when it sold G5s to Iraq. He has no shame about his role in implementing the State of Emergency, nor in sponsoring counter-revolution in Angola and Mozambique.

He is affable, articulate and intelligent, the sole mark of severity a moustache, white now, cut in a straight line above his lip. Talking to him, though, I felt I was experiencing a throwback to another era. The condition of my interview was that we would not discuss any matters directly relating to his murder charge. In describing the political context around the charge, however, he retreated into the offensive defence of Total Onslaught: the arrest of the generals is, in his opinion, clear-cut evidence that the commies in the ANC are beginning the second phase of their revolution.

Commissar Tim McNally? Comrade Frank Dutton? 'You cannot have a Marxist state if there's opposition. Look at revolutions all over the world: the first thing they do is neutralise and immobilise the opposition.' This ties in completely with what he has seen in Parliament, 'where socialism is slowly being introduced into the system', through things like Jay Naidoo's 'centralised planning'. The free marketeers in the ANC are losing the battle; in fact, 'very prominent members of the ANC have come to us [to help them] counter the communists, who are putting all the papers on the table in the [ANC's] National Executive Committee.'

The era of reconciliation is over, he says. The era of retribution has begun. He feels personally hurt, 'because of the role I've played getting the Afrikaner to play a constructive role in the new South Africa and preventing an armed uprising'. Fair comment. Whether it represents contrition or self-interest, however, is a moot point.

Perhaps there is no contrition because there is still precisely that unassailable belief that he was on the side of the just. Is it true that the securocrats ruled South Africa in the 1980s? 'If only it were!' he exclaims, telling me about how effectively the security forces upgraded Alexandra after having 'isolated' (read: detained) all United Democratic Front operatives there.

As chief of 'Comops' (Communications Operations), he was responsible for training Unita and Renamo in propaganda and political work. The 'most exciting' period of his career , he says, was setting up a co-ordinated intelligence network for PW Botha's State Security Council. Every morning, for two years, the heads of all South Africa's intelligence services would meet under his chairmanship; he would then prepare a daily (yes, daily) briefing for the cabinet.

He is frank about the state's sponsorship of Inkatha: 'I said at the time that it was imperative to boost organisations like the IFP if we were to have a multiparty system. The aim of supporting the IFP was to oppose the ANC, there's no doubt about it.' He believes the support should have been overt rather than covert, but says that 'the stigma would have embarrassed Buthelezi'.

Once more, though, there is that thin line of morality, separating the acceptable from the unacceptable. While he says he was not involved in the SADF's dirty tricks in the Namibian elections, he feels that 'it could be justified, within certain parameters, to manipulate an election outside South Africa's borders if it's in the interests of this country. But for the SADF to meddle internally, no! I could never justify that! It would be manipulating a democratic process.' I have struggled with this distinction: as with all the moral lines that Groenewald draws in the shifting sands of South African history, as with the border that he and his cronies erected between us and the world and impelled us to defend, this border too I find invisible.

During the course of our discussion, General Tienie Groenewald compared FW de Klerk to Neville Chamberlain, pussyfooting around Hitler; and Piet Retief, leaving his weapons outside the kraal. Retief, like De Klerk, wasn't wrong to negotiate with the enemy, but he was 'just plain stupid' to surrender arms before doing so. Groenewald also told me about his father, the son of a Cape rebel who served with Jan Smuts in World War I, but joined the Ossewa Brandwag 20 years later: 'The most humiliating moment in my father's life was when Smuts came and took his rifles away.'

The most humiliating moment in Tienie Groenewald's life was last week's murder charge. As with his father, he too has been disarmed, immobilised, emasculated by the state. He is no sentimental idealist, no Boer visionary. 'We live', he tells me, 'in a world of violence and corruption, and it's very difficult for individuals to find their way through it.' That's as close to an admission of guilt or sin as Tienie Groenewald is going to get.

KLAUS VON LIERES UND WILKAU
Former Witwatersrand Attorney-General

The Prussian of Pritchard Street

The controversial former attorney-general of the Witwatersrand took early retire-
ment on the grounds of 'ill health' in mid-1995, and then reappeared in the public
eye, six months later, as defence counsel for five Inkatha Freedom Party accused in
the KwaMakutha trial, which began in November of that year. I interviewed him
shortly thereafter.

Klaus von Lieres

'I'm glad', said one particularly laconic senior counsel after the opening of the Trial of the Generals in Durban last week, 'to see that Klaus is feeling a little better.'

The comment was a reference to the fact that on of the advocates defending the accused is none other than Klaus Peter Constantin Otto von Lieres und Wilkau, the former attorney-general of the Witwatersrand who took early retirement, aged 55, in May because of ill-health. Now, six months later, he finds himself, boisterously, at the centre of the grandest show-trial of our time – representing, interestingly enough, not the generals themselves (his former commanders: he is a Citizen Force brigadier), but those Inkatha Freedom Party members accused of actually pulling the triggers of the guns that killed 13 people at KwaMakhutha.

KwaZulu-Natal Attorney General Tim McNally told the media that his courtroom clash with Von Lieres would be a 'battle of the giants'. The shadow of O J Simpson falls long indeed: just swop the bloody glove for a note reading 'Chapter 1, verse 1' and the Bronco for a white Combi, then throw in a slaughtered goat for that African feel. Von Lieres as Johnnie Cochran and NcNally as Marcia Clark – if nothing else, there is a vocal congruence: Klaus, like Johnnie, is booming and bluff; Tim, like Marcia, is reedy and shrill.

Von Lieres says he barely ever watched the O J trial: he doesn't approve of tele-vised courtrooms – 'it's the modern version of a Roman circus', turning legal proce-dure into mass entertainment. He does, however, understand the enormous signifi-cance of the KwaMakhutha trial. 'There is a critical issue at stake: may the govern-ment act outside the bounds of the law when it finds itself in a situation of crisis?'

Given who his clients are, he will not venture to answer this question. Klaus von Lieres remains something of an enigma in South African law. This is the man who fought the battle to have the AWB election bombers denied bail – and won it. This is the man who made the decision to prosecute Winnie Mandela; who was the first prosecutor to charge a security policeman with the death of a detainee; who got Janusz Waluz and Clive Derby-Lewis convicted of murder for the death of Chris Hani. He was that rare thing indeed in the ranks of the state advocates: not only a sharp lawyer, but a showman.

But to many of the lawyers who have found themselves pitted against him during his 30-year tenure as a state prosecutor, Von Lieres's not-unexpected spurt of activi-ty so soon after his May retirement is further proof of his ideological bias. Von Lieres disputes the characterisation: 'I retired my post for one reason only. I was diagnosed as having a vascular occlusion in my legs, and the stress of managing a team of 300 prosecutors was dangerous to my health.' Now, as an advocate at the bar, he can work at an easier pace. And he took on the KwaMakhutha case for one reason only: he was briefed, and he couldn't refuse. That was that.

Most of his colleagues acknowledge that he is a good prosecutor and a very clever man. But they also describe him as 'brash', 'bullying', 'of obtrusive temperament', 'rude, difficult and unhelpful'. I sit with Von Lieres in his temporary office in Schreiner Chambers, where he's not quite at home yet. He is a large-boned man, but there is, today, none of his legendary fury. If he is the Bismarck of Pritchard Street I see none of it. In fact, if there is any vestige of Prussian aristocracy in his demeanour (his father, a German nobleman, emigrated to South Africa in the 1920s), it is extreme courtliness. He answers my questions, talking to a point four paces behind my left ear. When pleased with himself, he allows the quickest of snake-lick smiles to flash across his features. He is opinionated and self-assured, yes, but in a most bland and evasive way.

Except for the knuckles. Garlanded with chunky gold rings inlaid with stones – upmarket knuckledusters – I catch them cracking against each other as he makes a point about conflict. From that moment on, I cannot take my eyes off them. They move with a deliberation that borders on menace. They remind me that my subject is containing himself for the purposes of a media interview. They are involuntary signifiers that their owner is, in another context, a fighter.

He answers the charges against him ably. As a prosecutor he was, he insists, utterly independent. Was he not the first to lay charges against a security policeman for the murder of a detainee? Did he not bring policemen to book and get them the noose for killing suspects in drug investigations? If he was an apparatchik, why did Chris Heunis once accuse him of 'undermining' government policy by refusing to prosecute squatters? He even prosecuted a National Party MP for electoral fraud, for God's sake!

He certainly does not speak like a discarded apparatchik. He believes we are reaping the harvest of the past, because 'the state used legislation to try to enforce its political policies and once you misuse law, the citizenry loses its respect for it ... That is why we are in such a total mess today.'

His only complaint about the transition to democracy, he says, is that 'it didn't happen 18 years earlier, when PW Botha first started speaking about it. Eighteen lost years!'

Why, if this is what he thinks, do so many people consider him to have been an agent of the state during those 18 years? He answers with a rare surge of extremity: 'The revolutionary alliance's propaganda machine, with all its international support, was absolutely brilliant. It even outdid Goebbels. It was so good the government itself began to believe it. The biggest propaganda trick of the 1980s was [to claim] that South Africa was a police state. This was done by concentrating on so-called security offences. Sure we had lots of people in the security branch; but no way was South Africa a police state. If it was, we would never have had so high a crime rate!'

He is particularly proud of the fact that he made a point never to prosecute anyone under security legislation if he could get them under common law. Others counter that by using common law rather than security laws he was refusing to acknowledge that the people he was prosecuting were not common criminals, but rather individuals committing criminal acts for a political cause.

One senior legal source, who clashed often with Von Lieres in court, feels that the attorney-general was neither corrupt nor a state hack, but rather that he was just unable – or unwilling – to see dissent as anything other than criminality.

The source points to the fact that Von Lieres sued Minister of Justice Kobie Coetzee for reneging on a promise to appoint him director-general of justice (he lost the case). 'This man is no lackey. He is his own boss; he doesn't toady to anyone. But it just so happens that his belief in "law and order", in defending South Africa from the forces of darkness, coincided perfectly with the political aspirations of those in government. There was no improper interference; there didn't need to be.'

Klaus von Lieres

Another senior counsel, who knows Von Lieres well, feels that even his tough prosecution of 'bad cops' fits this profile well. 'They were the bad apples that were contaminating the whole cart and thus had to be made an example of. But the cart, in his eyes, was good and proper; it was never questioned.'

Perhaps the problem, ventures an advocate who does much criminal work, 'is that Klaus as prosecutor was not just a man representing the state's side of an argument. He was a missionary, a crusader. He was right, and if you represented the "criminal", you were wrong. You were not just doing your job, you were an evil and dirty person, and he had no time for you.'

Another advocate laughs, remembering how he was once invited to a function in the attorney-general's office. 'I had to leave, as there were just too many generals there whom I had cross-examined in one case or another!' Von Lieres is as much a military man as he is a legal crusader. Much decorated, he is in fact one of only three brigadiers in the Citizen Force (another is Roy Andersen, head of the Johannesburg Stock Exchange). He sees no conflict of interest in being an independent attorney general and an SANDF senior official. 'Look at Andersen! Does the fact that he's a brigadier affect his business on the JSE?'

It is a spurious argument. Klaus von Lieres, unlike Roy Andersen, was a public official appointed to be the public's representative in court. He represented our interests. Certainly, he prosecuted generals accused of fraud, but how could he have been entrusted to keep a check on the often-illegal military activities of the state when he was deeply implicated in the military hierarchy himself?

Von Lieres insists that he had 'nothing to do with Military Intelligence or covert action'. There is no reason to doubt him. But there is evidence that he was deeply involved in the repression of dissent. He served on the Steyn commission of inquiry into legislation affecting the security forces, was chief investigator in Judge Eloff's commission of inquiry into the South African Council of Churches, and was Judge Steyn's deputy in the notorious commision of inquiry into mass media, which ruled, in 1982, that the media be controlled through a state-established council and register.

His relations with the media have always been strained. In 1993, he made the decision to prosecute rookie *Beeld* journalist Andries Corniellesen for refusing to testify against Peter Mokaba in the 'Kill the Boer' brouhaha. It was a capricious and irrational action, and Corniellesen's 12-month sentence was overturned on appeal.

Previously, he locked horns with the *Vrye Weekblad*, suing Max du Preez for accusing him of wearing grey shoes and of conducting a vendetta against the paper, and for persistently calling him, in its satire column, 'Herr Klaus Peter Constantin Otto von Lieres und Wilkau (*wasgoed ingesluit*)' – the last an idiomatic expression roughly approximating 'everything including the kitchen sink'. Perhaps it wasn't a vendetta (he won), but, according to Du Preez, the *Weekblad* was charged 12 times in two months – once for paraphrasing Joe Slovo before he was unbanned.

The cynics would say that by taking on the KwaMakhutha case, Von Lieres is betraying his political sympathies. Or that he is desperate, in that nowhere called 'retirement', for the limelight once more. Perhaps, like Johnnie Cochran, he has found a perfect way to merge political zeal with a love of glamour. Glamour? We'll have to wait till March, but my instinct is there's not going to be much of that commodity hanging around the KwaMakhutha trial.

ARCHBISHOP DESMOND TUTU
Chairman, Truth and Reconciliation Commission

The ultimate test of faith

If the Magnus Malan/KwaMakutha trial shows us one way of dealing with the atrocities of our past, the Truth and Reconciliation Commission gives us another. The commission began sitting in April 1996; on its eve, in the midst of a gathering storm about it, I interviewed its increasingly embattled chair. Three high-profile families had lodged a suit at the Constitutional Court in an attempt to stop the commission because, they said, it denied them their rights to justice. Tutu weathered the storm and conducted the first round of hearings skilfully. On the second day, he wept when an old man broke down describing his torture: 'I thought I was strong enough [for this job] but I am not.' All indications are that he is.

Desmond Tutu

Wonderful! Wonderful! Wonderful! Ever since I spent time with Desmond Tutu a few weeks ago, I have caught myself, repeatedly, doing The Arch whenever something has pleased me. Head thrown back, arms extended upwards in an angelic 'V', spasms of praise oscillating through outstretched fingers, exaltant voice asqueal with wonderfuls. Over the course of 24 hours, I must have seen him perform this ritual more times than he prayed (which is a lot: he even called for divine assistance before I turned the tape recorder on, 'so that at least I can have someone on my side'. His prayers were heard: my tapes remained blank.)

If the grave and plodding Mandela is our reliable father, then that hyperactive little figure in ermine at his side is our naughty uncle; the one who carries all the family's emotional baggage, weeping for us when we grieve, dancing when we celebrate. Ready for retirement, he neither sought nor wanted the chairmanship of the Truth and Reconciliation Commission. What better man, though, to play the lead in the drama of Truth and Reconciliation, manifesting externally all the emotions of restitution and contrition – and ultimate catharsis – that we, black and white alike, are expected to feel?

Tutu has minted our political discourse: it is he who appropriated the term 'rainbow' from Jesse Jackson and imported it into our New South African vernacular. It is he, in fact, who coined the term 'New South Africa' years before FW de Klerk started chucking it around. And it was he who first started speaking about reconciliation. When he was appointed first black Anglican Dean of Johannesburg in 1975, he wrote an open letter to John Vorster in which he said: 'I am deeply committed to real reconciliation with justice for all, and to peaceful change to a more just and open society ...'

The Desmond Tutu who will chair the first hearings of the Truth and Reconciliation Commission in East London should thus be even more exuberant than usual. He is presiding over the realisation of his very own dream. And yet the Tutu who has appeared in public in recent weeks has seemed subdued, introverted, even slightly depressed.

On the TV programme 'Two-Way', the man who spoke about reconciliation at Steve Biko's funeral had to sit and listen while Biko's widow said, bitterly: 'I don't see the Truth and Reconciliation Commission solving my problem ...' He had to sit and listen while Griffiths Mxenge's brother said: 'What is really annoying us is that we understand that the previous government [did nothing]. But the present government, for which my brother and sister-in-law died, they sit back and do nothing ... Bishop Tutu delivered the ceremony at my brother's funeral. He was witness to the fact that people said that when this government took over, justice will be done.'

Here he was, Nobel Laureate of Underdogs, accused of being a sellout for presiding over a process that will grant perpetrators amnesty rather than meting tough justice out to them. And his accusers were the very people he put his life on the line for. Tutu, a little man, often uses his animated hands to make himself seem bigger. Wrapped tight in a black jacket, the ermine just peeping through, he seemed here, however, to shrivel into dimunition.

In the cool chambers of his own space he is compelling, setting 'justice with ashes' against 'amnesty with the possibility of continuing survival for all of us': 'It's *realpolitik*, this forgiveness thing. It's not just something in the realm of religion or the spiritual. If justice is your last word, you've had it. You've got to go beyond it.'

'Beyond justice' is a peculiarly Tutuesque combination of Christian faith – 'which is ultimately a faith of grace' – and African communalism: '*Ubuntu* says I am human only because you are human. If I undermine your humanity, I dehumanise myself. You must do what you can to maintain this great harmony, which is perpetually undermined by resentment, anger, desire for vengeance. That's why African jurisprudence is restorative rather than retributive.'

In the 'Two-Way' studio, though, faced with the wrath of a few high-profile victims, he retreated to churchy sentimentality – to the comfort zone of religiosity – and sanctimoniously reminded viewers of Christ's words on the cross, 'Forgive them, for they do not know what they do.'

With scant resources, an enormous task to fulfil, a wrenching moral conundrum to resolve, and 16 wilful commissioners to lead, his job is nigh impossible. And though he doesn't admit it, he is having a rough time. When he talks of the need for political compromise, he is told to stop being a politician and to behave like a clergyman; when he talks like a clergyman, Marius Schoon writes, with righteous indignation, that he has no right to use public television to impose his 'Christian views [on forgiveness] on all of us'.

Certainly, the very notion of a truth commission comes from Christian ideas of confession and absolution (even if Tutu does say it's about *realpolitik*). But sometimes it sounds just a little too easy. It's one thing for Tutu to jump up at a Dutch Reformed Church synod, as he did in 1990 after NGK clergymen apologised profusely for the sin of apartheid and proclaim: 'I cannot, when somebody says, Forgive me, say, I do not.' It's quite another, however, to grant forgiveness to monsters who simply list their atrocities and expect amnesty without contrition, as the Truth and Reconciliation Act allows.

Tutu's faith, says a source in the commission, is 'his greatest asset, but also his greatest blind spot. It allows him to be a visionary leader, a symbol of reconciliation, beloved to all. But it also imbues him with the theological fatalism that, at the end of the day, a force higher than us will make things happen. At times this leads to a lack of managerial rigour and attention to detail.'

It's not just clerical thought that is hampering Desmond Tutu in his current assignment, it's clerical style too. He comes from the Anglican Church, one of the most rigid hierarchies imaginable. Here Father is father, and Arch is king. Tutu led both the South African Council of Churches and the Anglicans from the front. He would pronounce, often brilliantly, and the rest would have to come panting up behind.

But the last thing the 16 very assertive members of the Truth and Reconciliation Commission want is a Father. They are politicans, they are lawyers, they are on the move. They are tough as nails. Many of them, even those who have a deep affection for him, see his clerical paternalism as offensively patronising – and they have told him so. 'He would try', says one source in the commission, 'to be the big father with his little chicks. And the little chicks told him to get lost. That astonished him – in the church, you don't answer back!'

The result had, according to this source, a profound effect on the work of the commission: 'He found himself lost, not knowing what to fall back on. This made him sad and unsure of himself, and he became defensive – threatening to leave – or ineffectual. It would take ages to reach decisions, because he wasn't able to move them forward and he didn't want to let go of something if he disagreed with it. We'd never finish an agenda because he responded to criticism with long-winded anecdotes.'

That, say the commission's critics, is one reason why it has taken four months to set up a body that is only going to last for one-and-a-half years. There is still – shamefully – almost no communication and public education coming out of the commission, and there remains much fuzziness about how reparation will work, or even about how much money will be available. Tutu, of course, cannot shoulder all the blame for these problems: given that the TRC is itself a political compromise, every decision it makes becomes a mini-Codesa. The largest amount of its time, for example, has gone into haggling over affirmative action appointments. One commissioner notes that: 'We are an impossibly diverse bunch. And in fact, to the extent that we have any coherence, Bishop Tutu takes the credit. He has this amazing capacity to get people talking.'

Perhaps, too, The Arch will begin to shine from Monday onwards, once the backroom stuff is over and the dancing and weeping can begin. For one of his greatest assets – and it is an asset – is that he loves the limelight; it burnishes rather than diminishes him. If there's action, he's in it.

He really is an international superstar. Hang out with him and you'll feel it immediately. He has handlers, he has whims, he needs his space. I spent a good deal of time waiting to speak to him – following him as he moved from engagements, observing silence as I chased him on a brisk trot through Orlando West, hanging out in his comfy and stylish Soweto home – while he performed his inviolate daily rituals. It was worth it, though, for when he engages with you, he is *there*. He manages to combine folksiness and dazzling intellect like no one I've ever met.

It's an intellect which can be cold and brutal. I heard him on a talk show a few months ago, defending his position that gay people should be ordained into the church. His arguments were righteous and heartening, but when ordinary folk phoned in to rant about Sodom and Gomorrah, there was none of his usual paternal indulgence – these are lost sheep, let me help them see the truth. Rather, he was sharp and dismissive, and dealt with them like the blinkered fools they are.

Those who know him say that he is like this when he is unsure of his ground. Perhaps that's why he is having a hard time negotiating, publicly, the truth and reconciliation domain. One thing about him that is worth cherishing, even if it does sometimes cause problems in its wake, is that he says what he believes is right, and damn everyone else. Thus he defends gay clerics, advocates abortion reform. Thus he lambasts his friends in the new government for boarding the gravy train.

But the same impulse leads him, at a meeting of violence victims in Guguletu this week, to describe the 'political trials' of Eugene de Kock and Magnus Malan as 'taking up the courts' time and costing millions of rands that could be spent in more productive ways'. This is clearly a counter-attack on those opponents of the TRC baying for 'justice'. Tutu may be right, but it's not the politic thing to say if the intention is to bring high-profile malcontents like the Bikos and the Mxenges on board.

Back in Orlando West, it's after breakfast, and The Arch At Home performs the Eucharist in the magnificent little chapel behind his house. I'm reminded of something he once said in the bad old days, that South Africans have an hour of sanity a week, when people of all colours drink the blood of Christ out of the same glass. Today it's nothing so grand, just his wife Leah, his assistant and his bodyguard taking the wafers. Still it's an event, and in liturgical fervour, the archbishop breaks his bejewelled crucifix. After the service, he says to Leah: 'I dropped my cross. I'm such a *bleddy domkop.*'

'Yes,' she replies, embracing him, 'you're a *bleddy domkop.*' And she kisses him. It's hard not to love these people, even if you hardly know them.

The Desmond Tutu of SA Jewry

I interviewed Rabbi Harris in September 1995. If part of my project is to understand South African public figures within the context of their ethnicities – of where they come from – then perhaps it goes without saying that, because I am a Jew, my profile of Rabbi Harris is the most personal I have written. Of course, when you engage in the politics of your own ethnicity, when you are perceived as 'turning' on your own people, the response is often very angry indeed: one rabbi wrote to the paper that I had clearly betrayed the fact that I was brought up badly; others were hurt or upset that I had not acknowledged their own roles in the anti-apartheid struggle. Many other Jews, though, have written in appreciation of my sentiments.

Cyril Harris

This week, during Rosh Hashanah, two strange things happened to Rabbi Cyril Harris. They are not unconnected. On Tuesday morning at 6a.m. he received a personal call from Nelson Mandela, wishing the Jewish People a Happy New Year (his awestruck maid had to explain to the President that he didn't take calls on holy days, but promised to pass the message on anyway).

The previous night he was heckled, for only the second time in his life, as he gave a sermon to the Yeoville Synagogue congregation. He had begun by softening up his audience, in his timbrous and melodic Glasgow lilt, with a Jackie Mason joke, much kitchen-Yiddish, a line from Janis Joplin ('Oh Lord, won't you buy me a Mercedes-Benz?'). Then things started to get heavy: The New South Africa, he said, was 'not coming on too well'. It was 'moving too slowly'. And Jews had an obligation to help speed things up.

'Some of you might say, why should we help these *schvartzes* when they are killing us with all the violence, all the car-jackings and muggings and murders. Well, that's equivalent to anti-Semitism. It's like the Christian who was swindled once by a Jew and now says all Jews are *ganovim* (crooks)!' The gist: there are bad and good blacks, like there are bad and good Jews. Most blacks are good, decent people.

Most of the few hundred Orthodox rabbis whom Harris leads wag their fingers at the future, accuse Yitzhak Rabin of 'shaking the bloodstained hands of terrorism' (a direct quote from one rabbi on the first night of Rosh Hashanah this year), and scuttle into the obscure netherworld – the ghetto, really – of biblical injunctions and ethnic chauvinism in the face of this new South Africa.

They have retreated beneath the broad-brimmed black hats of right-wing fundamentalism, while Harris appears to all the world like a dapper and elegant professional who just happens to have a mauve silk yarmulke perched atop his coiffed silver hair. In counterpoint to their wild and unruly beards, he clips his close to the jaw.

At this point in his Rosh Hashanah sermon, however, his eyes blazed; his beard quivered. He became a biblical prophet; his favourite Isaiah, perhaps, he of the swords into ploughshares. 'There are those Jews', he said, 'who say that the Bible tells us Judaism is only for the Jews, and that we should put Jews first and not worry about the *goyim* [gentiles]. Well that is nonsense!' He bellowed, he shook his fist, 'Nonsense!,' and proceded to quote chapter and verse from the Old Testament, where Abraham helped the Sodomites even though they were the most evil people on earth.

It was at that point that the Rabbi was heckled, for precisely the same reason that Mandela phoned him. Finally, the Jewish community has a religious leader battling insularity, providing moral leadership from the front – a Hurley, a Tutu, a Storey.

This is the Chief Rabbi who marched with the Muslims for Bosnia, who has launched a Jewish RDP project called 'Tikkun' (making things right). This is the Chief Rabbi who spoke first at Chris Hani's funeral and then at Joe Slovo's, implying that the atheist, communist Slovo was more of a Jew than those devout hypocrites who supported apartheid ever were. This is the orthodox Chief Rabbi who tells me, as we sit in the study of his Upper Houghton residence, that 'I'm a great believer that God judges us on fact. Not on whether we serve him and pray three times a day, but on what we did as human beings with respect to our other human beings. I think Joe Slovo comes out very very high according to those criteria.'

Cyril Harris

Perhaps the ultras are irritated with him, but the Jewish Board of Deputies, which runs secular Jewish affairs for the 90 000-odd Jews of this country, are, in the words of chair Marlene Bethlehem, 'thrilled and delighted with the role he has taken. He has played an important and valuable role bringing the community into the new political agenda.'

Whether or not other Jews approve of Harris's left-wing politics, they know that they have to make a compact with this new South Africa, and he is their agent.

South African Jewry has never had so high a profile. Harris read at Mandela's inauguration; he has introduced, into the South African political discourse, an institutional voice of Jewish conscience. Taking the lead from his mentor – retired British Chief Rabbi Lord Jakobovits – he has carved a public moral role for himself, pronouncing on matters the way South African Jewish leaders never have before.

Many in the Jewish community think he is playing this suit to bolster a candidacy for the British chief rabbinate. He is clearly ambitious: he notes, however, that – at 59 – he is now too old to be considered.

While he might be doing wonders for the profile of Jewry in South Africa, and while he might be helping his congregations find a way into democracy, his moderate orthodoxy is not succeeding, yet, in bringing secular Jews back to the faith. If you want to see a robust, muscular Judaism at work, go to the *Or Sameach* ('Joyous Light') congregation in Glenhazel. Here are services filled with young people, singing the ecstasy of rebirth; nothing at all like the mumbling old men you'll see in other, shrinking congregations, left behind by children now in Sydney or Toronto.

'If Rabbi Harris has failed,' says one of his supporters, 'it's that he has not provided an appealing enough alternative to these fundamentalists. They provide the bodies when it's time to count the faithful. So even though he might disagree profoundly with them, he cannot clash too publicly with them.'

He will clash with them, though, on Israel. He is almost alone, in this country's rabbinate, in supporting the relinquishing of land on the West Bank in favour of peace. Here, unlike in the United States or in Israel itself, there has never been a dissenting Jewish voice, which he thinks is 'a great pity'. If you want the angry Harris response to the 'bloodstained handshake' genre of pulpitry, find out where he is speaking on Yom Kippur next week: peace in Israel will be his subject.

Harris, an outsider (he arrived here in 1988), notes – sometimes with approval and sometimes with concern – how insular and tightly knit the South African Jewish community is: 'Nowhere else in the diaspora', he says, 'is there a lower marrying-out rate. Nowhere else do so many Jews go to Jewish schools.' But, on the other hand, 'there's a kind of ethnicity in South Africa which has a totally negative impact on bridge-building. It's not just the Jews – Hindus, Zulus, everyone's keeping to themselves. It allows Jews to strait-jacket themselves and make no room for the wider issues of the society they live in.'

I know what he means. I went to a Jewish school, and I still resent it bitterly, for when I asked questions – why do we pray? why do we have to keep sabbath? why do we need to keep kosher? – I was given answers that had nothing to do with faith, or with spirit, or with history, or with metaphysics, but that were either mechanistic ('because this is what makes you a Jew!') or, worse yet, chauvinisitic ('because this is what makes you different from – and better than – the *goyim*').

Cyril Harris

Not only did it make me cynical about faith, but it gave me no clue about how to be a South African. And so there is something quite revolutionary in Harris's injunction, during his Rosh Hashanah sermon, that his flock must 'answer the challenge of what it means to be a South African Jew'.

Cyril Harris is an open-minded man: he loves Wagner, he loves to read history, he is cricket-mad. His wife, Ann, is a lawyer; she runs the Law Clinic at Wits University, and is a fierce advocate for the rights of orthodox Jewish women, a campaign that often puts her in direct confrontation with her husband.

Nonetheless, there is still something insular about life around the rabbi; something that comes, perhaps, with the territory. I get into his car and his bodyguard turns round to ask me, 'So, where do you *daven* (pray)?' Teaching a Jewish Studies class at Wits, Harris breaks a piece of chalk as he is writing. 'Anti-Semitic chalk!' he exclaims. Ann Harris proclaims that her labrador, Blackberry, is Jewish: 'Good *Shabbes*, Blackberry!' she says, and the dog lifts his paw for her to shake it. The Yiddish interjections; the self-referentiality: it's all a bit cloying.

One person's ghetto wall is another's fortress of pride. We all choose our own sites to erect the boundaries around our identities. I suppose what I respect, ultimately, about Cyril Harris is that his walls are porous – they let ideas pass through. But why do Jews need their 'own' way of becoming involved in the RDP? Why not just participate, wherever you are, whoever you are, just because you are South African?

During Harris's Rosh Hashanah sermon, he asked the congregation why Jews often only 'feared' or 'despised' *goyim*. Why not 'help' them instead? I listened to him in the congregation my family has belonged to since my birth – that of the Great Synagogue. But now, for the first Rosh Hashanah of my life, the Great Synagogue is empty, looming domed over Wolmarans Street just east of Joubert Park like a grumpy dowager, abandoned.

Now, outside the Great Synagogue, the streets reek of urine and grilled fatty meat. The community is now too small to fill the vast shul; too scared to come into these badlands for services. And so it squats in a function-room at the Transvaal Automobile Club until a new plan can be made.

As I sat listening to the Rabbi's sermon, in a room still redolent of the mock crayfish and kola-tonic functions of my childhood, I remembered, with the nostalgia that is so central to ethnic identity, how I recited my Bar Mitzvah portion to the filled, burnished pews of Wolmarans Street; how I called my blessings to the response of the choir up beneath the vaulted central dome; how I imagined swinging from the vast chandelier during the doleful liturgy as the ritual pomp of my history paraded before me in a never-ending blur of rabbis, torahs and song; mystical, awesome, utterly incomprehensible except as an indicator that I came from somewhere.

Pity the poor 13-year-olds denied the opportunity of trying out their newly cracked voices in such a chamber! Perhaps, though, the engagement of the current Chief Rabbi makes up for it. Perhaps Jewish faith will make more sense to them, now, than it ever did to me.

But why, I asked myself as I listened to his sermon, are there still only those options – to fear the *goyim*, to despise them, or to 'help', patronisingly, with our superior skills and values? As I struggled with the nostalgia of my own Jewish childhood, I felt that Harris was asking the right questions, yet not quite answering them.

The taxpayers' bouncer

Once Gill Marcus agreed to be profiled, it took a while before we could find a time. It was April 1996: she had just been appointed deputy minister of finance, the rand had just collapsed. We finally did meet, late one Sunday night, after she had spent the day in a crisis meeting convened by President Mandela between labour, business and government.

Gill Marcus

There's a story Molly Marcus likes to tell about how her daughter, all of 5 years old, announced one day that she would not be going back to school because of how nasty the teacher was. When Mrs Marcus went to investigate, the teacher was perplexed: 'I don't understand,' she said. 'Gill is the best-behaved girl in the class. I never shout at her!'

Little Gill retorted that that wasn't the point: 'It's not that you shout at me. It's that you shout at everyone else!' The deputy minister of finance remembers, with a classically self-deprecating laugh, that this might have been the dawn of her political consciousness: 'I've never been able to do something if it isn't for someone else. If the motivation is not to do it for others, it doesn't turn me on. And so I suppose if the teacher is shouting at the class, even if not at me, it's not on. I'm leaving school and going home. That's that.'

One of the remarkable things about Gill Marcus is that such sentiments sound neither maudlin nor self-righteous in her mouth. Speak to anyone who has known her over the course of her twenty-year commitment to the ANC, and you'll get an image of selflessness that sometimes seems a little perverse: 'Gill's strength', says her former boss Pallo Jordan, is that 'she is the sort of person who can put her nose to the grindstone and do work that others would consider to be drudgery. She is utterly reliable.'

If she has one weakness, he adds, 'it is her impatience. She puts huge demands on herself; she's at it from an unearthly hour in the morning until the moment she goes to sleep, and so she can be very impatient with people who don't work as hard: this can put her on the very bad side of people. She sometimes doesn't see that we are all made differently and lead different lives.'

Certainly, as anyone who has worked on her parliamentary Joint Standing Committee on Finance will tell you, she does not suffer fools, laziness or political expediency gladly. This is something we journalists – who often are all three of the above and then some – know well from the days, between 1990 and 1994, when she effectively ran the ANC's Department of Information and Publicity from Shell House. She was curt, efficient, and sometimes extremely unpleasant. We used to call her 'The Head Girl', indulging in that masochistic fantasy of someone we knew we could rely on and had a grudging respect for even if she often made us feel like lifeforms so primitive we should be squelched underfoot if we weren't so damn neccessary.

But something is different now. After spending some time with her a few weeks after her appointment as deputy finance minister, following two celebrated years as one of our most sucessful new parliamentarians, I think I can safely report that, even if she is as committed a workhorse as ever, this sister is finally doing it for herself. She'd never admit it of course, but there is a glint to her eye, an exuberance to her gait, a gentle Yiddish lilting humour to her voice that says, I've arrived! I love what I'm doing, I'm good at it, and yes, I have power. These days Gill Marcus schmoozes; she throws her head back and laughs, freely, easily; she even flirts.

She insists that she has not changed a bit. Perhaps journalists now fetichise her because she does to others – cabinet ministers, captains of industry and now senior bureaucrats – what she used to do to us: she demands they do their job properly. But there is no doubt, too, that she has found her vocation: 'I'm absolutely fascinated by money, how it works, what it's dynamics are and how you get it. It's got its rules and you need to understand them. It's like a detective story. Often I'll come home and pick up a document and say, "God! Do I really have to read this?" And then I find that I can't put it down.'

Her engagement with finance is an intellectual one. She is obviously quite brilliant and yet her political strength comes from the fact that is entirely unencumbered by jargon or rhetoric. Her father and uncles, the Marcus boys, were renowned, in the 1930 and '40s, as the hefty practical wing of the Communist Party. They were dirt-poor *boerejode* (platteland Jews) from Kroonstad who came to town and trained as accountants. They weren't the ones who sat around and debated theories of revolution. They were the ones called in to move piles of literature when you heard there was going to be a raid; the ones who did the Party books. And they were the bouncers who stood on the steps of City Hall when Party meetings were taking place, and beat up the blackshirts who tried to disrupt things.

'If my dad and his brothers were on the steps,' says Marcus, 'people would look at them and say, "Those boys are there. We're safe. They're tough!" ' Does she like the image? 'Absolutely! Good for them! They were prepared to stand up and be counted!'

The next generation of Marcuses are perhaps more critical of party dogma and more formally educated. But in one respect they are the same: 'We are not', says Marcus, 'armchair people. We're a practical lot. Sure I analyse and make strategic inputs. But activism and politics are very practical for me. How do I make things happen?' She might not be a bouncer, but she clearly likes the idea of people feeling safe when she's around.

Gill Marcus, Miss Practicality, did not get involved in student politics when she was at Wits in the late '60s 'because it didn't seem real; it didn't seem like it could achieve anything.' Her family had not gone into exile in the early '60s, partly because they weren't Party leadership and partly because, unlike with the more famous Slovos, there was no tension between politics and family: family came first.

And so they all moved to London together in 1969. As is well known, Gill ran the family salad-bar in Knightsbridge. She joined the Communist Party, she started clipping newspapers for the ANC. She allowed her Party membership to lapse upon re-entering the country. She signals that this was because she was appointed an ANC spokesperson, and so she had to emphasise that role. The real reason, however, is clearly that the practical Marcus gene had overpowered ailing Marxist ideology.

From being a backroom workhorse, Marcus has become a serious leader of the ANC. She is one of only three women (along with Nkosazana Zuma and Frene Ginwala) on the 18-member National Working Committee. Does she ever have to 'unsex' herself, I ask, to rule the waves of finance? 'I'm aware', she responds, 'that women in power have created an androgynous zone where they are gender-neutral. Or conversely, they play up the dolly-bird image. To me, they are both totally unacceptable.' She pauses, laughs. 'I mean, it'd be a bit difficult for me to play the dolly bird or to be androgynous!'

She has proven herself in finance, a very male world, and she has managed to do so in caftans rather than stiletto heels and power-suits. Yes, she says, 'there are problems. It is automatically a golf-course and locker-room approach. If you're not on the golf-course or in the locker-room, where do you talk to them? But I play it to my advantage that I'm not one of them. It's up to them to make the effort. I'm totally available, but not in the locker-room. So yes, they have to think about how they change their style.'

There is no doubt that her role, as a woman at the helm of the finance committee, was perhaps one of the major blows for gender equality in the first two years of South African democracy. The fact that there were three very efficient and powerful women on this committee – herself, Preggs Govender and Barbara Hogan – has been one of the most tangible and striking instances of the consequences of the ANC's gender equity principle: the committee, powered by women, was anything but a locker-room.

But although Marcus was a member of the Women's League, and although she clearly is committed to the principle of gender equity, she is not one of the ANC's gender warriors. Certainly, she has been supportive of the Women's Budget – an initiative of the finance committee to track how much women benefit from state expenditure – but she does not integrate gender issues into her work the way colleagues like Nkosazana Zuma, Sankie Nkondo, Frene Ginwala, Brigitte Mabandla or Geraldine Fraser do. She was not actively involved, for example, in the National Women's Coalition or the Beijing conference. Perhaps this is because her ethos, here as everywhere, is that she 'gets on with it': she is not comfortable in talking-shops.

'Just let me get on with it' is her response to any question about her role, along with Trevor Manuel, as custodian of our ailing economy. Rather than muddy the waters, she wants to leave it to Manuel to deal, publicly, with the currency crisis; behind the scenes, though, she is already hard at work in the area of economic planning; an area, she says, which needs 'constant evaluation and a lot of planning right now'.

Even though she will not talk further about her current portfolio, there is much evidence, as to how she will play it, from her chairship of the finance committee. Her committee was open, accessible, and immensely powerful. She was forthright in her criticisms – particularly of the ineffectiveness of parliamentary procedure, the way the executive used parliament as a rubber-stamp, the way the RDP was negatively affecting budgetary procedures, and the hopelessly inefficient way the state collected revenues. She insisted that no new taxes should be levied until the state beefed up its collection services, and she was firm about sending budgets back to departments if they were not properly prepared or motivated.

The most sensational example of this was when she sent the Post Office budget back to her ex-boss, Pallo Jordan. It was, says a colleague, 'an act of great courage'. There is one school of thought that says she was moved to a deputy-ministership – often a nowhere-zone – precisely because she was performing the watchdog role of parliament a little too well; because she was a little too independent of the executive.

In the unlikely event that this is true, it is a misguided perception. If the fiscus is a Party meeting in City Hall, we the taxpayers can feel secure with Natie Marcus's daughter on the steps. Like her dad, she has proven you can be tough and a mensch simultaneously.

TREVOR MANUEL
Minister of Finance

*Minister
of
common
cents*

I met Trevor Manuel just after the announcement that he would replace Chris Liebenberg as finance minister in March 1996. His attempts to staunch the 'rand-slide' following his appointment have received mixed reviews, and he has had a difficult time asserting himself against the sentiments of the market as the ANC's first inhouse finance minister.

Trevor Manuel

Ask any Western Cape activist the secret of Trevor Manuel's success and you'll be told, '*Hy't gejob innie area.*' He's a homeboy; he worked his own 'hood. In the worlds of Davos and Brussels, he might be the smoothest South African product to have emerged in the pipe-fragrant wake of Thabo Mbeki. In that inexplicable place that rules us all, The Market, he might be the reason why our rand buys more or less. But in the working-folk townships of Kensington and Factreton, he's that hard-working young fellow who used to go door-to-door selling *Grassroots*; who built a civics movement around whether you could build *hokkies* in your yard and hang washing-lines between your tenements.

He's the one who, in the rough-and-tumble world of Cape Flats politics, once even punched out current Western Cape Nat MEC Peter Marais at a public meeting; the long-haired biker who used to cruise around in tight Lee jeans, studded shoes and leather jacket. He's the one who used to lead the klaberjas sessions in Victor Verster prison, where he spent three years in detention during the states of emergency.

What is truly astonishing about our new minister of finance is not that he is the country's first black captain of the economy. Nor is it that he has only just celebrated his 40th birthday, or that he is not a professional businessman. It's that, only a decade ago, he was a rough-hewn United Democratic Front street-activist. It's that he has no tertiary education but for a technical diploma in civil engineering. It's that this solid workhorse of the UDF – a man who made sure the folks were on board rather than one who soared into high-falutin' policy – has emerged as one of the sharpest managers of the new government.

Manuel loves to sing and dance *goema*-style and remains a raver in that uniquely Western Cape way. But he has trimmed his trademark Castro-beard down to a discreet little moustache. He is to be seen, now, in power-suits rather than fishermen's sweaters. He still loves his Flight of the Fish Eagle brandy, though, and he still loves a fight, as Anglo's Michael Spicer discovered when he challenged Manuel's competition policy. There remains something homey in his slate eyes, something rough in his features that not even a lifetime of transatlantic Concorde travel could smooth out. It's a commodity that The Market, 'jittery' about his appointment, doesn't unfortunately measure: it's called realness, and Manuel's got it in buckets.

Despite his worker roots, Manuel's elevation to perhaps the most important Cabinet post after those of Nelson Mandela and Thabo Mbeki is not a bolt from the blue. Following a short spell in the private sector when he worked for the Mobil Foundation, the ANC made him head of its Department of Economic Planning in 1990. He was responsible for fiscal policy while Tito Mboweni handled trade and industry. Mboweni was preparing for the Trade and Industry post that Manuel got, and Manuel was expecting to be deputy minister of finance under Derek Keys.

Very much under the tutelage of Mbeki (an economist by training), Manuel played a critical role in guiding the ANC away from its traditional adherence to centralised planning and towards the market economy it was to espouse. At the side of the ANC's consummate diplomat, Manuel was introduced into the world of international finance. Some in the ANC believe his rapid rise to be the result not only of his managerial competence, but of the fact that he has been one of the few people comfortable in both the ex-UDF nexus around Cyril Ramaphosa – his natural home – and the exile nexus around Mbeki. Even in his early days as a UDF activist in the treacherous Western Cape, he showed a remarkable acuity for staying out of faction fights.

His victory, in Trade and Industry, was to take a department whose sole *raison d'être* was to stifle competition, and make it the vanguard of a 'liberalised' market economy. Convinced that South Africa's introspective economy – a function of apartheid isolation – was fatal, he embraced the General Agreement on Tariffs and Trade (Gatt) in a way that few other developing countries did, and set about slashing tariffs and threatening monopolies.

He made few friends, either in big business – whom he baited with tough anti-monopoly talk – or among comrades in the labour movement: the lifting of industrial protections inevitably means job-loss. 'I'm talking to a trade unionist,' he says with trademark laconic Bogart-from-Bonteheuwel narrative style (as if the South African transition were a Chandler novel), 'and he is explaining to me what he calls the view of the left on issues like jobs, international trade, etcetera. So I say to him, "Hold on," and I go off to find an old *Newsweek* that has an article on Pat Buchanan in it. And I read it to him and say, "You're saying what Buchanan's saying, and you're telling me it's a left view?"'

He remains deeply unpopular among both unions and management in the motor and textile and clothing industries, which have borne the brunt of tariff liberalisation. Given his own roots (his mother is a textile worker), the symbolism was intense when his ex-UDF comrade Ebrahim Patel led a march of the South African Clothing and Textile Workers' Union to Parliament to present him with a withered bouquet of flowers. The implication: he had betrayed his own.

As we sit in the kitchen of Kader Asmal's ministerial residence in Pretoria (where Manuel 'squats' when in town), I ask him how he feels about his Department of Trade and Industry's reputation as the swashbuckling New Thatcherites of our time.

Suddenly, before my eyes, the remains of our Nando's meal becomes a micro-economy. With two empty Coke cans, a roll of paper towels, a cold chicken breast and a steadily emptying pack of Gauloises, the industrial drama of tariff reduction is played out on Asmal's table, replete with misled workers, misguided unions and mollycoddled industrialists who claim to want market policies while not wanting to lose any of their privileges.

With passion now, he outlines his pragmatism: 'Africa is dying!'; African countries have either resisted the World Bank and the International Monetary Fund or prostrated themselves before it – either way they are 'feeble, that's the real world we live in … Rather than seeing these institutions as God or the Devil Incarnate, my view is the agnostic one that says, Shit! This thing is here! It's alive … Let's rather work out how to deal with it, let's study the countries who have worked the system because they dared to understand it.'

Likewise, Gatt 'is not a decision taken by comrades around the world. So you say, Don't like it! Don't like it! But it's out there. It's real. We gotta understand what it's about, and work it.'

Many on the left of the ANC are deeply suspicious of this pragmatism, which they see as a Trojan Horse for the interests of global capital. 'Trevor', says one senior player, 'has been overeager to show the West that we're on board. So he has concentrated too heavily on trade policy and on external perceptions rather than industrial policy and internal requirements. There's this naive liberal belief that free competition will solve all our ills.'

Remembering his beginnings in the civics movement, Manuel tells a story that seems, to me, to be a perfect guide to his philosophy of pragmatism. He recalls that, in Factreton, there was a group of tenants who wanted to buy their homes from the council. This was resisted, strenuously, by a Trotskyist segment of the civic 'who opposed the view that people should buy their houses because property was evil and workers shouldn't have it'. Manuel, on the other hand, suggested that the civic take its lead from what the people themselves wanted, and conducted a survey which revealed that over 60 per cent wanted to buy their houses. 'Watching what happened to the other leaders, how they just shrivelled up and lost their support base, was an object lesson in how intellectuals become alienated from their constituencies.'

His close comrade Cheryl Carolus talks about the 'organic' relationship to policy-formulation that grassroots activists like she and Manuel had: 'Trevor, particularly, had a remarkable ability to listen, to figure out what he needed to achieve, and then to go for it without ideological baggage. He was thorough and conservative, always the voice of reason.'

Manuel has nothing but disdain for the doctrinaire left, perhaps because he went to the elite Harold Cressy High School, where he – the child of ordinary workers – was exposed to the Unity Movement cant of the children of teachers and professionals.

Now, as finance minister, he remains as committed to pragmatism as ever. The private sector will be happy to hear that he is open-minded about exchange control. But if The Market expects another arch-conservative in the Liebenberg mould, it is in for a bit of a surprise: 'I don't think,' he says, 'that fiscal discipline is an end in itself … It's about what you spend it on. If your deficit is funding an infrastructure which is creating jobs and will have a kickstart effect, then go borrow for it. You're borrowing to invest. But if it's merely to pay salaries, buy toilet-rolls and fund holiday flats for retired generals, you obviously can't use the deficit to finance that.'

Which doesn't mean he's going to chuck money mindlessly at social welfare. He tells the cautionary tale of Zimbabwe, where 'for the first 10 years, investment in health and education was phenomenal. But today Zimbabwe sits with a deficit of 16 per cent [of the Gross National Product, as opposed to South Africa's 5,9]. They had to borrow from the IMF to get the most rudimentary stuff.' So Manuel's first question, when faced with his colleagues all wanting finance, will be 'is it sustainable? There's nothing worse than the tragedy of developing countries where you build hospitals but don't plan to staff or equip them.'

His mantra, like that of his new deputy, Gill Marcus, is efficiency. He thus puts much faith in the new Revenue Service, and in Marcus's pet project, the Expenditure Evaluation Unit, which will, he says, 'tag each rand as if it were a fish, and follow it through, to see what it buys'.

Manuel is clearly – and openly – having a stressful time coming to terms with the fact that he has, overnight, become a commodity whose mere existence determines the value of the rand: 'We've had Liebenberg and Keys, and before that a series of Nats who were all established businesspeople and perceived to be fairly pliable in this thing called The Market. Now you've got something different: he's young, he's black, he's uppity, he's given other people shit.'

It's an image, you can tell, that he quite enjoys struggling against.

GERALDINE FRASER-MOLEKETI
Minister of Welfare

Cinderella-in-waiting

By one of those coincidences, I happened to interview Geraldine Fraser-Moleketi, then deputy minister of welfare, in the very week, in February 1996, that her minister, Abie Williams, was forced to resign after allegations of fraud. I thus published the profile amidst speculation that she was about to be promoted. It only happened three months later, when the National Party walked out of the Government of National Unity, making her one of the youngest members of Nelson Mandela's cabinet. More than any of her fellow-communists, I feel, Fraser-Moleketi and her husband Jabu Moleketi embody the South African 'new left'.

Geraldine Fraser-Moleketi

When Geraldine Fraser was 6, her younger sister Debbie was cast, in the school play, as Little Bo Peep. Anywhere else, the older sister might have felt some sibling rivalry and left it at that; but this being the Cape Flats, with all its pathologies of race and taxonomies of skin-tone, the issue came down to a curl. Debbie, you see, had fairer skin than Geraldine and straighter hair – set, for the play, in a bo-peepish cascade of curls.

The deputy minister of welfare remembers 'going into the bathroom and just weeping. My dad came in, and when I told him what was wrong, he said, "It's not the curls that are important, it's what you do with your life."'

Her parents found a compromise to suit her kinky hair – 'they gave me little plaits, with a little *krulletjie* at the bottom' – and Fraser-Moleketi remembers the event as a watershed: 'I grew up from that moment thinking, I'm going to lick them all. It's not important what I look like, it's important what inputs I make.'

After spending time with Geraldine Fraser-Moleketi it is quite possible to imagine her, all of 6 years old, 'making inputs'. Her single-minded focus and her tendency to stress every syllable have sometimes led people to believe that she is a Communist Party hack, a pedantic ideologue. They are wrong: hers is rather the lingo of development-speak ('We must unpack the issues around multi-sectoral collaboration if we are to mainstream them' is a sentence she might say), but it is uttered with such fervour that it undergoes that all-too-rare alchemic conversion from jargon into passion.

A few days after we met, her National Party minister, Abie Williams, resigned after being raided by the Office for Serious Economic Offences, following allegations that he had accepted bribes from a company awarded the tender to issue pensions in the Western Cape. The consequences of this may yet see her in Cabinet – or may see her working beneath a less erratic, but also less pliable, National Party superior: Williams pretty much let her run things. One way or the other, the issue of graft in pension funds is going to be squarely on her desk from now on.

Let's go back, though, to a bucolic suburban Sunday afternoon at the home she has just bought with her husband, Gauteng MEC for Finance and Economic Affairs Jabu Moleketi, in Observatory; well within the catchment-zone of Sacred Heart College, which their three kids attend. Today, both grannies are in attendance, but Fraser-Moleketi does not spirit me away into a quiet little study for the interview: she steers me down to sit at the pool, in which the children are noisily splashing. She then performs, perfectly, that feat of modern motherhood – giving me her undivided attention while catering to her kids' needs simultaenously. I think I can safely say that neither I nor 4-year-old Selomzi felt neglected.

There are stories of how visitors to the SACP offices – where she worked as Chris Hani's assistant for two years – would be greeted by Fraser-Moleketi suckling Selomzi; of how, when she was a technical advisor to Joe Slovo at the World Trade Centre, some of her colleagues objected to breast-feeding at the negotiating table.

She stood her ground. She made her inputs. She prevailed. That is how Geraldine Fraser-Moleketi gets ahead. She and her husband are fast developing as one of the power-couples of the new political order. Despite their new suburbanity, they are decidedly down-home, with none of the jazzy affectations of upward mobility: they are intense, verbal, argumentative, workaholic and untrendy. Controlling the budget of the largest province, he is, by all accounts, the star of the Gauteng Cabinet: superbright, pragmatic in that Alec Erwinish sort of way. She has taken a Cinderella of a ministry, stagnating beneath the bluster of Williams (and suffering, even within the ANC, from a dearth of substance and interest due largely to the fact that Winnie Mandela ran the desk before the elections), and begun – with the help of new director-general Leila Patel – to transform it into a powerhouse of new ideas.

He is secretary-general of the Communist Party in Gauteng; she sits on both its Central Committee and Politburo. He preaches fiscal restraint as the only path towards economic growth; she wants to turn her ministry from being a dole-provider to 'encouraging self-reliance'. They embody the shift that is already taking place from Old Red to New Left in this country, bringing it into line with Western social-ism: their communism seems to have less to do with centralised planning and the other rigid dogmas of the failed socialist experiment than with a faith in long-term vision, a commitment to close-to-the-ground politics and – most refreshing – a train-ing in critical thinking. In Marx they – unlike so many of our new leaders – have a tool for complex social analysis.

Speaking to both of them – '76-ers who went into exile and met in Angola while waiting to go on an advanced course in urban insurrection in Moscow – one is struck, again, by the validity of the thesis that the Party expanded its influence within the ANC ranks by seeking out the intellectual cream in exile and rendering it an elite through specialised training programmes.

Certainly, there is in Geraldine Fraser-Moleketi a certain 'hard-coreness', but this probably has as much to do with her upbringing in the treacherous politics of the Western Cape as with any Stalinist training she received in exile. The daughter of a teacher and a factory worker, she managed to get into the elite Livingstone High School, one of the fulcra of the far-left Unity Movement, which was as much an intel-lectual outlet for the coloured middle class as it was a liberation movement.

Trotskyist reading groups, Marxist–Leninist revolutionary cells, quislings under every bush: awash in the Western Cape politics of the mid-1970s, Geraldine Fraser came of age. About racial identity she is still hardcore. Returning to the country before her husband in 1990, she decided – characteristically – to go and live in Soweto with her unknown in-laws rather than in the Yeoville area with her friends.

One day, her oldest child, Thando, came back from school and asked, 'Mommy, what am I?' The children had been taunting her, because of her coloured mother, on the school bus. 'Just tell them you're a South African,' her mother shot back. 'It's not an issue.'

It takes a long time to get Geraldine Fraser-Moleketi to acknowledge that in present-day South Africa, race is in fact an issue. Since her appointment, she is aware that she runs the risk of being fetishised as a 'top coloured' in the ANC. 'But I'm not', she says with characteristic firmness, 'going to go back to the Western Cape and say, Look! I'm coloured and I'm in the ANC, so you've got nothing to fear. No. What I'll go there to deal with is the issue; to say, What is the problem? Is it a lack of self-esteem or what? Why do you have these insecurities? If I allow myself to become a "coloured leader" in the narrow sense, how will I relate to my kids? What do they call themselves? I don't want to create such a crisis of identity.'

She acknowledges that her 'rigidity' can sometimes be a bit of a problem; perhaps it is an overcompensation for her smallness of stature (she can't be much more than

1,5m) and her feminine physicality. She claims the opposite: that her femininity serves as a useful cover, precisely because it is deceptive. One way or the other, 'I did once say to Jabu, in jest, that maybe I should put on a lot of weight and start wearing those large dresses, then I'll be taken seriously!'

Anyone who does not take Geraldine Fraser-Moleketi seriously does so at their peril. A parliamentarian who knows her well describes her as 'tough as nails'. But, says Leila Patel, 'her impact on the welfare sector has been amazing. Everyone respects her, from the traditional Afrikaner organisations through to the NGO sector. She has shown herself to be very committed, and very passionate. People know they can depend on her.'

Even Abie Williams liked her – and one of her skills is that she has proven adept at working with him; unfazed even by his perpetual sexual banter. There was, for example, a political problem with the White Paper: Williams got cold feet over the fact that the change in emphasis from service-delivery to development would mean that largely white old-age homes would have to close shop. Fraser-Moleketi brokered a compromise and, unblinking, evoked the parliamentary majority to put her own and Patel's vision back on the table.

If Welfare is indeed a Cinderella, then the deputy minister's growing profile cannot but help its status. She chairs an inter-ministerial committee looking at 'children at risk' (children who need state assistance of any kind) and, perhaps most importantly, leads the organised gender-equality movement in government, running the Beijing Secretariat from her office: she recently convened a 'conference of commitment' at the World Trade Centre, to ensure that the platform of commitments to gender equality agreed upon at Beijing are entrenched throughout government.

Jabu Moleketi remembers how, when he moved into the residence she occupied in Angola, he asked for some food. She said, 'There's the kitchen'. There was none of that, 'Here's someone who's just moved in, so let's be hospitable and prepare him some food!' The retraining of Jabu Moleketi had begun (and by all accounts, was very successful).

Now, fifteen years later, the deputy minister of Welfare has decided that President Nelson Mandela's 'New Patriotism' needs some retraining too. And so she used it to make a point in the presidential debate two weeks ago:

'I said that if you look at the victories of our sportsmen, it's all taken a very macho slant; it's boys' stuff. I think it's great we've had victories, but we need to make the girl child feel part of it. So I said, "When I look at the victory of Bafana Bafana, I see it as a victory for all the youth of this country." We need to move away from the exclusively macho image of patriotism.'

Indeed, Fraser-Moleketi's leadership of the South African delegation to Beijing (along with Health Minister Nkosazana Zuma) struck a blow for South Africa's international reputation perhaps more profound than that of the Bafana Bafana. The South Africans played the critical role in leading the progressive agenda. They led the charge to include sexual orientation on the platform, and Fraser-Moleketi – through nimble footwork and a crash-course in Islamic theology – won even Iran over to the concept that girl-children should be allowed to inherit directly.

Geraldeeeeeen! It doesn't quite have the same ring as Feeeesh or Shoooes. But Fraser-Moleketi's Banyana Banyana were hot in Beijing.

PETER MARAIS
MEC for Local Government, Western Cape

The Nats' blackface Elvis

I interviewed Peter Marais in June 1995, at the height of his confrontation with the African National Congress – and his own national minister, Roelf Meyer – over the demarcation of Cape Town for local government elections. As a result of an application to the Constitutional Court filed by Marais and Cape Premier Hernus Kriel, elections were postponed in Cape Town until May 1996. Marais lost the bid, and – although the tone reflected in this profile is one of supreme confidence in the fact that his approach was winning over coloured voters to the National Party – the true effect of his politics of coloured nationalism remains to be seen.

Peter Marais

I will testify, before a court of law, that Western Cape MEC for Local Government Peter Marais was stone-cold sober when, at the end of our interview, he launched into a serenade that included a hip-rotating Elvis impersonation, some Johnny Mathis crooning and a pitch-perfect rendition of The Platters' 'Twilight Time'.

The pinnacle of his political career might be his current standoff with central government over the demarcation of the Cape Peninsula metropole but, in another life, his greatest glory was singing with the Big Beats when they opened for Cliff Richard and the Shadows at the Luxurama. These days, his songmaking is confined to composing and singing doggerel to the jaunty rhythms of *Kaapse Lied*.

During last year's election he recorded eleven such hits, including the following (sung to an obscure Presley tune): '*Joe Slovo is/ 'n kommunis/ Allan Boesak is sy grootste pêl/ Hy lei ons kinders na die hel/ Almal na die hel.*' (Roughly translated: Boesak is leading our children to hell because his big buddy is Joe Slovo the communist.)

His sobriety notwithstanding, meeting Marais was, at times, like revisiting an old racist stereotype from my childhood: the 'coon carnival' image of Cape coloureds that white Vaalies encountered when they went down to Cape Town for the Christmas holidays. It was like watching the stereotype bite back, for Marais – blustering, buffoonish, folksy, but nobody's fool – is the voice and face of a robust coloured chauvinism all the more remarkable because it is buttressed by precisely the process of caricature for which it claims to be seeking redress.

Marais's voluble discourse is replete with proclamations about The Coloured Man ('The coloured man has found a home in the National Party'; 'The coloured man will never support things like prostitution and pornography and abortion'; 'The coloured man is an Afrikaner') that is, at times, wilful in its racism. While Nats in the rest of the country go out of their way to insist that theirs is a party for all races, something different is happening in the one province they actually rule.

'There has never',' says Marais, 'been a real close affinity between blacks and coloureds down here in the Cape. Right now fear still channels most of the decisions that people make. Fear of the unknown. And what we see happening all around us – the murders, the assaults, the disrespect for authority and conventions – that doesn't help bring us any closer. We also have our skollie elements, but we frown on them. We never carry them on our shoulders like heroes. When you see a man dying in the street with a tyre around his neck while the people around him are dancing, that's foreign, man! It's foreign to us! It's got nothing to do with race. It has to do with behavioural patterns. With norms. With standards. With preferences.'

Sounds familiar, doesn't it? When the demarcation board paired African Khayelitsha with white/coloured Tygerberg, the plan had to be approved by the Western Cape Provincial Committee. Marais stands accused of dropping two ANC-supporting members from the committee, replacing them with NP sympathisers, and pushing through a new plan that gave Tygerberg more coloured townships and dumped Khayelitsha with a now excessively large Cape Town that would have over two million people. Defying even the NP minister responsible for local government, Roelf Meyer, Marais stuck to his guns. President Mandela issued a proclamation declaring the newly configured provincial committee invalid, and Marais now plans to take central government to court for violating the Constitution.

He is adamant that his decision to excise African Khayelitsha from white and coloured Tygerberg also has 'nothing to do with race' and insists that it is all a question of financial viability. The gerrymandering, he insists, was done by the demarcation board in the first place, which is a lackey of an ANC that is 'trying to destroy anything that is Afrikaner or Afrikaans. They cannot stand an enclave like Tygerberg, which is all-Afrikaner and where they have no say and so they have to dilute it.'

Possibly Marais is right about the unviability of a Tygerberg/Khayelitsha substructure and about the ANC's machinations. But so clouded is his speech in racial pathology that sense often eludes it. What I found so fascinating about his language is that he has taken a group of people who could serve as a role-model for the rest of this country due to their hybridity – their very lack of racial purity – and claimed, for them, the cultural and linguistic purity of Afrikanerdom; one which must now be fortified against dilution.

Marais's colleague, Health MEC Ebrahim Rassool, is one of the ANC's more lucid thinkers when it comes to an understanding of coloured ethnicity. He notes that everyone – including his own party – has become so tied up in the technical battle over Tygerberg and Khayelitsha that they have lost sight of the real import of the battle, which is about a hollow 'coloured jingoism' that is appealing precisely because it papers over all the very real cracks in coloured identity.

Rasool's point is that Peter Marais is no unguided missile, no loose cannon. 'The support I'm getting for the stand I have taken is enormous,' says Marais, correctly. Not surprisingly, he is a local hero in the precincts of white Durbanville (where he lives now) and in the Bishop Lavis and Elsies River townships (whence he hails). And his party is reporting back that his stand is swelling both its support and its coffers. Through a battle over Tygerberg, his home town, Marais is showing coloured people that he can deliver the goods: entry into the laager.

He celebrates his heritage as part Griqua and part white Afrikaner, and is absolutely adamant, from the evidence of the past four generations, that he has no black African blood in him whatsoever: 'People think that the coloured is a cross between a black and a white, which is a ridiculous simplification. There is a minuscule amount of black blood among coloureds.'

But the articulation of a difference from black people is only one part of Marais's narrative of coloured pride. The other is an aggressive assertion of equality with white people. About his much-publicised dispute with Meyer, he responds testily: 'I don't think Meyer occupies a higher position in the party than I do.'

In fact, the NP has become a coloured party: 'I think that white Nats are not used to being in an opposition role. They don't know how to handle it. Coloured Nats, on the other hand, have been in opposition politics ever since we were taken off the common voters' roll, and so our white colleagues have got a lot to learn from us.'

There's something exquisitely patronising about it all; something quite cheeky too, given the fact that Marais was never even elected to office in the tricameral parliament. After losing Bishop Lavis to a popular Labour Party candidate, he was appointed to the President's Council, where he stayed until its dissolution, crossing the floor several times before becoming one of the first Labour parliamentarians to move over to the Nats.

Marais first realised the plight of his people when, aged 12, he watched his father – a 'great man' who wrote very popular morality plays about the dissolution and redemption of the coloureds – being humiliated by his white foreman. 'I asked my dad, How can you let him speak to you like that? Why don't you bugger him up? And he replied, Because he's a white man.' From that moment on, the young Marais hated The White Man.

It festered for a couple of years, until he organised a gang 'to go beat up the white schoolchildren in Maitland, because they had a swimming pool and we didn't. We gave them a good working over. I came back and I sort of had a feeling of achievement: Hell, I've hit a white child! I hit him pow-wow! I'm stronger than you. We talked for days about it. Did you see how I smacked that *boertjie, jislaaik,* man!'

He went into tricameral politics with the same intention – 'I wanted to give the *boere* hell from here to kingdom come' – but found, to his surprise, that The White Man was 'a lonely, scared person who surrounded himself with laws to protect himself; who feared that his standards would be destroyed because he couldn't compete on the open market with the masses. And so he devised all sorts of plans how he could give me equality, without giving me power over him, because he couldn't trust me and my motives.'

But once The Coloured Man realised that all The White Man wanted was to be his friend, he – in the persona of Peter Marais – magnanimously extended a hand of friendship and camaraderie. And saved him – by ensuring his political longevity through the infusion of coloureds into the NP. By giving him Kraaifontein and Blue Downs and Brackenfell (coloured areas that Marais included with Tygerberg when he redrew the boundaries) so that he wouldn't have to take Khayelitsha.

So now that The Coloured Man has real power – rather than the Pyrrhic victory of a brawl at the Maitland swimming pool – he is flexing his muscles. 'The ANC', says Marais, 'could drive the Western Cape to adopt a far more accommodating stance towards the position of the Inkatha Freedom Party in KwaZulu-Natal. If they keep whittling away our powers, perhaps we too will seek international mediation.'

He rises to his theme, proclaiming that Chief Buthelezi is becoming 'more and more popular' among coloureds. People, he says, 'are getting tired of wishy-washy politics in which everyone is clapping each other on the back and congratulating each other. People don't feel safe if there's no real opposition. If everyone's complimenting everyone else all the time, people get suspicious. They feel much safer if there's confrontation.'

Earlier on, I was subject to a romantic vision of coloured people as 'jovial, friendly, *laissez-faire*'. The wonderful thing about The Coloured Man (or The Zulu Man) is that he is so entirely a construct that you can write your own script for him: he can be the jolly minstrel transformed, by one stroke, into the belligerent warrior. But his malleability in the hands of his author becomes utter intransigence in the face of his opponents. Peter Marais knows he's on to a winning thing, and he knows that, given who votes for the National Party these days, there's very little that a simpering Roelfie or a pedantic Valli can do about it.

TOKYO SEXWALE
Premier of Gauteng

The Tina Turner of the provinces

In April 1995, Pallo Jordan was dropped from the cabinet and Cyril Ramaphosa had announced that he was leaving parliament for the world of big business. It was in the context of heightened speculation over future ANC leadership –and specifically whether anyone would challenge Thabo Mbeki for the mantle of Mandela– that I profiled Tokyo Sexwale. I spent a lot of time chasing him around. He is renowned for his rather exasperating impulsiveness but also for his generosity of spirit: once he had made time for me, we spoke freely and at considerable length.

126

Tokyo Sexwale

South Africa is just like Tina Turner. So says Tokyo Sexwale the morning after he has been to both her concert and the Freedom Day celebrations: 'When Tina came off stage I heard she was upset. The lighting didn't work; the sound was bad. But meanwhile I in the audience thought it was 101 per cent. It's just like South Africa! I sat with international leaders in Pretoria [at Freedom Day] yesterday and they just gasped ... The world has got more confidence in us than we do in ourselves, perhaps because we are the players, like Tina on stage. As Shakespeare says, "All the world's a stage," but when you're a player on that stage, you are uncertain, as an actor, do people get the message? Your mannerisms, your gestures, are they coming through? The anxiety as to whether people will accept you, it's just enormous.'

A classic Tokyo torrent. Creative, iconoclastic, just this side of loopy; masterful metaphor swimming against the current of linguistic anarchy. And it contains within it a fascinating conflation: the nation and the man become one – as they often do in his mouth – and it is the Gauteng premier's own performance-anxiety he lands up talking about.

He is obsessed with the relationship between form and content; questing perpetually, to use one of his favourite terms, to 'manage the tension' between them. There is no South African politician as self-conscious about leadership and public image. He is, after all, our first post-modern leader, media-made at the moment of Chris Hani's assassination. Hani pops up, in his conversation, almost as a nervous tic. This is not just expediency talking: the death of his great friend, and the way he handled it, has imprinted itself deeply upon his psyche – as a model moment of how to fuse the form of politicking and the content of changing society, and as his political coming of age.

But it is also a legacy against which he is constantly struggling. Those close to him say that he is desperate to show the world that he does have innate substance; that he *was* somebody before Chris Hani died. Many national ANC politicians either dismiss him or view him with contempt. For years, on Robben Island, he was secretary of the General Recreation Committee, but he was far more than a games-mistress: because he managed to use the the position to create space, on the island, for comrades to meet and organize, he became a key leader.

He was renowned for his inventiveness, persuading the authorities to let 'Roots' be shown by telling them it would show those slave-driving Americans up to be 'worse than South Africa', and getting Judy, then a para-legal and now his wife, to conceal communist literature into the back of a TV-set. A young and uneducated man when he went in, he found the life of the mind through interaction with the old-timers, particularly Govan Mbeki and Joe Gqabi.

When I first interviewed Sexwale in his capacity as an MK commander in 1991, shortly after his release, he made a big fuss of not speaking to me because, he said, it was common cause among 'comrades' that the *Mail & Guardian* was a state intelligence front to discredit the ANC.

He is, thankfully, no longer that kind of 'heavy'. He has studied Nelson Mandela so thoroughly he can distil him to 'five key words, nothing more: *however, but, notwithstanding, nevertheless* and the phrase, *having said that.* Mandela has for the first time really unenveloped the essence of life for me. Life is average! It's not the tallest, not the shortest, it's average! It's not black, not white, it's grey! It's metaphysics, it's

Tokyo Sexwale

philosophy. Life is bipolar!'

He has learnt, through Mandela's perpetual qualifiers, that every statement has a counterstatement. The difference between the two, though, is not simply that Mandela finds the average through carefully balanced syntax while Sexwale finds it by holding fifteen contradictory opinions with equal passion. It's that Mandela (the consummate insider) leads with effortless ease, while Sexwale (the perpetual outsider) shows the strain. You see the veins bulging, the heart pulsing energy and humanity, as he mediates a dispute or leads a group of unarmed ANC supporters into a hostel or answers your question. If we feel comfortable with Mandela, it's because our aspirations are safe with him. If we feel charged by Sexwale, it's because he carries, onto the battlefield that is our future, all our passions and fears. He lives dangerously.

His dilemma is that you cannot study to be Mandela. He tries just a little too hard. He has enough epigrams on leadership to write his own Little Red Book: 'A true leader is a leader of the opposition – you don't just lead those who chose you, you must lead your enemies too'; 'The art of leadership is to claim failure'; 'Leadership is not simply about being so far ahead of your people that you can see the precipice – it's about being able to come back and persuade them to change direction.'

And he does live by these. On leading the opposition, Democratic Party Gauteng leader Peter Leon, a stern critic of his premier, notes that 'despite his problems, Sexwale is a real democrat. He is non-partisan in his leadership of the province, and in fact he often berates his caucus for coming down too heavily on the opposition.' On persuading people to change direction, there is substantial truth in Sexwale's oft-made claim that he turned Gauteng around by leading the campaign to stop political violence on the East Rand.

Ask him to claim some failures though, and he falters. His weakness is his ego; the fact that he refers to himself as 'the prime minister' rather than 'the premier', that he places himself, godfatherlike – a Cuomo, a Chirac – over a province that just doesn't have the powers of New York or Paris. One critic notes that 'unlike other premiers, who are modest about their powers and capabilities, he clothes himself in imperial grandeur – he makes claims that he is absolutely unable to fulfil. Like that he will stop crime, or build 150 000 houses in a year. And so, with him, it's often the case of the Emperor not having any clothes.'

A source close to him acknowledges that he does not admit failure or wrong-headedness easily, if at all (he still swears by his 150 000 houses in one year plan), but makes the point that, 'unlike other politicians who will retreat into silence when burned, he comes back and overcompensates. He'll say he was misquoted or misunderstood, and then work really hard to make things right.' There are many examples of this: his comment about a referendum on the death penalty, for example, followed by a passionate defence of the Constitutional Court ruling or homophobic statements reported in a Sunday paper, followed by a meeting with gay groups in which he went further than any other senior ANC leader has in affirming sexual equality.

If you really want to understand Tokyo Sexwale, read *Primary Colours*, the brilliant anonymous *roman à clef* that uses fiction to expose the true nature of Bill Clinton. Henry Burton, the narrator in *Primary Colours*, writes that Jack Stanton (Clinton's stand-in in the book) 'taught me everything, told me nothing. Gradually I came to see how he devoured every aspect of public life – nuances, and hints of nuance, that only he knew existed. It was, I imagine, something like the way a hawk sees the ground – every insect, every blade of grass seems distinct, yet kept in perspective ... He was incredibly undisciplined about time, and making decisions, and figuring out who should do what on staff, but there was a strict precision about self-revelation. He was always in control.'

Like Stanton/Clinton, Sexwale has a way with ordinary people that is quite breathtaking. Like the character in *Primary Colours*, he 'puts his big ears on' when he listens to you, making you feel that you're the most important person in the room. Like Clinton, he is a man of substance, a man with more policies and ideas than his head has room for; but like Clinton too, though, he is inconsistent and capricious. He is more White House than Shell House; a snazzy, jazzy American politician trapped in the body of a comrade who must at all times be accountable and collective rather than individualist and inspirational. Therein lies his power, but also the potential seeds of his failure.

If Thabo Mbeki is a bat, most comfortable in the cavern-like recesses of power, then Tokyo Sexwale is a moth, attracted, often fatally, to the flame. Sexwale's criticisms of the Cosatu 'lockout' strike, for example, correct though they might have been, were certainly not politic, and could not have endeared him to a key constituency that could help him in his passage to higher office. Mbeki, it might be remembered, made no public intervention about the strike or the lock-out clause in the constitution: unlike Sexwale, he takes no risks; nails his colours to few masts.

Sexwale is brazen about his aspirations. There is a political cartoon on the wall of his living-room: it shows Thabo and Cyril slugging it out in a boxing ring and there, in the backround, creeping through the ropes, is a little figure with 'Tokyo' stencilled onto his shorts. He speaks, when asked about the presidency, of 'always having been a leader. I will remain in the forefront. But if you're in the forefront you catch the first bullets. I do not believe in having cannon-fodder in front of me. Maybe I must be the cannon-fodder myself.'

He faces a tough dilemma. If he elects to stay in Gauteng in 1999, he will remain the plenipotentiary over an institution with little real power. If he goes national, he might be given an influential cabinet as a passage to post-Mbeki leadership, or he might be given a ticket to nowhere in the form of a deputy-ministership of environmental affairs or a hard backbench.

His success in Gauteng, as a potential testing ground for national office, is hard to measure, if for no other reason than that his power is more in the nature of a figurehead than a true executive. As a figurehead, an inspirational leader, he has done brilliantly. Despite his rather unfair reputation as a 'populist', he has taken a leaf out of the Madiba book and pushed reconciliation above all else. He does not play – or live, for that matter – crude race politics. His administration has provided Gauteng with one of the cleaner and more efficient regional governments. But he remains almost dilettantish in his interests, and does not, say critics within his government, focus realistically on what can actually be acheived in the province.

If he moves onto the national stage, he will have political problems. Despite his massive popularity among rank and file, he is not an operator. A loner by nature, he does not work at sewing up constituencies or regions, and he measures himself by popular sentiment rather than by the opinions of his colleagues in leadership. This, say his supporters, could be his downfall: as Mbeki well understands, it is the party and not the rank and file that votes for its leadership.

Like many great popular politicians, Tokyo Sexwale is supremely confident and palpably insecure in equal measure. He performs so well precisely because he needs to be loved; like Tina, he never believes he's quite good enough. He is Mr Sociable but also – at least in recent years – a real homebody; a teetotaller who, when not at work, can be found at home with Judy and the kids.

He jokes, in our interview, that 'in American politics, you must have some secret to expose! If you don't have a mistress you must find one and pay her to say that she had it off with you and you messed up by going back to your family. That will project you as a family man and you'll be president in no time!'

Back at the Houghton ranch broekie-laced maids bring the guests their tea while Judy serves her husband directly. When he leaves, they embrace dead centre under the portico; more Scarlett and Rhett than Bill and Hill. Glamour is good politics in Gauteng.

MATHEWS PHOSA
Premier of Mpumalanga

The street-fighting premier

I interviewed Mathews Phosa in July 1995. We chose him because his province, Mpumalanga, has frequently come in for plaudits for the progress it has made. Shortly after I published the interview, though, the Eugene Nyati scandal hit the province: Phosa, who must take responsibility for it, got into trouble by making wildly contradictory statements about the affair, although he did finally censure Nyati.

Mathews Phosa

When Mathews Phosa was at high-school in Acornhoek in the early 1970s, he and a group of students were given a chilling ultimatum after disrupting a Parents' Day event: they could choose between expulsion or being stripped naked and lashed with a hippo-hide sjambok.

'Our parents were struggling to keep us at school,' he recalls. 'And so we decided to take the punishment. But we made a pact: no tears. The minimum any of us got was eight lashes. But not one of us cried. I've still got the mark. Look, I'll show you!'

Matthews Phosa believes in transparency. But for our protests, he may well have pulled down his trousers, there and then, in the middle of his premier's office in an ugly old Bantu Administration building on the wrong side of a dorp in the middle of a lush valley that is now the hub of the fastest-growing province in the country.

The choice he and his classmates made says much about their generation and the paradoxes of South African history. They are now lawyers, doctors and one go-get-'em premier. If the incident had happened ten years later, they would have organised a school boycott, joined a self-defence unit, and those who did not become precocious members of Parliament would probably be members of the The Lost Generation by now.

But the choice also says something about Phosa himself – something about his toughness and his ambition. Today, I am with him on a tour of greater White River. There is something about his posture that is classic political boss – Richard Daley, township-style. The way he snaps his fingers at his staff when he wants something; the posture he assumes when consulting with comrades: one hand holding a perpetual cigarette, the other thrust in his pocket, eyes downcast, voice lowered.

Then he is all charm: flirting with an entire hall full of nurses at a hospital, exchanging Afrikaans proverbs with the white councillors, beaming proudly at the democracy of it all when a wild-eyed cultural worker, in some far-flung township, bounds up to him brandishing a hefty document: 'This is the Arts and Culture Task Group Report and I want to make an input! How do we make an input?'

A law graduate from Turfloop, Phosa started Nelspruit's first black law firm and became one of the most prosperous black businessmen in the region: his enterprises included those township staples, a construction company and a mortuary. He left the country 'when I received information that they were going to assassinate me because of my profile as a UDF activist and my work for the ANC. They were going to plant a bomb in my BMW. I had a 735. You see! I often joke to the comrades, How can you call this a gravy train? I had much better cars before!'

Phosa, like almost everyone else in government these days, is also a poet. His verse is archetypally rhetorical, although it has a rhythm about it that is sometimes quite eerily soulful. Perhaps this is because it is in Afrikaans. My favourite, entitled 'Ja-Baas', is about the relationship between power, corruption, and a certain genre of luxury vehicle. It is a parody of a fat-necked bantustan leader who sits straight in his black 'Mercedes-Chrysler' as he goes to and from a beerhall-parliament. Via the Land-Cruiser years of exile in Mozambique (as commander of uMkhonto weSizwe's Eastern Transvaal operations), Phosa has traded in his BMW 735 for the black 'Mercedes-Chrysler' of premiership. In fact, the very car he now cruises about in probably belonged to one of those yes-men he derides (some of whom now sit in his cabinet).

Mathews Phosa

But Mathews Phosa is no Ja-Baas. He is independent in his outlook and sharp in his criticism. The local government provisions of the interim constitution are 'a mess! They undermine democracy and the price is going to be high to pay.' Central government, in the first year of democracy, was 'often weak and indecisive and not co-ordinated at all to the provincial layer'. And the Reconstruction and Development Programme is 'busy churning out tomes and tomes of paper and business plans and implementing less and less. Jay is about to be buried under the paper!'

In fact, of all the ANC premiers, he has been the most outspokenly critical of the way the interim constitution divvies up power. He slams the limitations of provincial competency and calls for a complete overhaul of the Senate as custodian of regional interests. He has already broken the rules – with the frowning approval of central government – by entering the world of foreign affairs: he has signed critical security and trade agreements with two Mozambican provinces, and has also made agreements with a German province, Egypt, Taiwan, and Britain.

Phosa was one of the first four ANC exiles to slip back into the country in 1990 to begin negotiations, and was responsible, as the ANC's in-house lawyer, for dealing with the tortuous indemnity and prisoner-release arrangements. A senior national ANC leader who worked with him then notes that Phosa is 'a bit of a braggart. But I have grudging admiration for him now. His province has been the least problematic in terms of setting itself up. It was the first one to promulgate the necessary laws and to set up productive relations with civil society. He quickly brought a wide range of groups on board, secured capable advisors, and has no problems taking advice.'

Now Phosa runs a province that is at least as hot as the flamboyant trees beginning to bloom along Nelspruit's boulevards. Sure, he inherited the region with the fastest growth-rate in the country (4,5 per cent), but he is determined to push it further, and robust 'economic growth' – rather than flaccid 'reconstruction and development' – is his mantra.

Phrases like 'investor-friendly', 'market economy' and 'the stimulation of entrepreneurs' drop from his lips. There is only one way into the RDP – expanding the economy – and economic planning must be at the centre of all policy. Most impressive, he has just summarily fired the bloated boards of the KaNgwane and KwaNdebele Development Corporations, accusing them of 'earning money for doing nothing at all'.

There's something inspiring about the way Phosa works: the adrenalin is high, even if it does result in over a hundred cigarettes a day, and the operation is hyper-sophisticated, down to the hour-long hotline he conducts every Wednesday night, when people can phone in and get a direct line to him (last week the farmers wanted to know who was tampering with the rainclouds). I haven't come across such efficiency anywhere else in this new South African civil service.

But there's a shadow that lurks, north of Nelspruit, in the densely populated Bushbuckridge; an ex-homeland area that has long been the site of strife – ethnic, supernatural (this is the Witchcraft Belt), and political. Deep-rooted internecine ANC conflict has become superimposed upon an absurd border conflict. Although the region is traditionally part of the ANC's Eastern Transvaal structure, it was allocated to the Northern Province. Last year the two provinces agreed to shift it to the east; in return, the Eastern Transvaal would cede the Groblersdal district to the north. But negotiations between the two provinces and central government have been enmeshed in constitutional difficulties and arcane political agendas.

At a meeting chaired by Thabo Mbeki, the bottleneck was cleared: transfer is to be effected. But, in the interim, trouble erupted in Bushbuckridge, culminating in an incendiary speech, given by Phosa, on Chris Hani Memorial Day this April. Here, Phosa's audience were rural locals. Away from the glare of the national media, he lost his slickness and got heavy, publicly upbraiding dissenters (people who wished to stay in the North) and allegedly calling them *mpanyulas* – a Tsonga word which translates as 'arsehole of an animal'. One of those named, Shiela Sithole, is suing him for R300 000 in defamation damages.

It is difficult for an outsider to make sense of all this. Some senior Bushbuckridge ANC officials accuse Phosa and his right-hand-man, Minister of Finance Jacques Modipane (who is the local heavyweight), of Mafia-like rule through intimidation. Whether or not this is true, one thing is certain: read a transcript of Phosa's speech at the event, and there is a street-fighterliness to his tone which would surprise those urban whites more accustomed to his charm.

There have been other sparks. Although Phosa denies it, former employees of the *Lowveld News* say he managed to get them fired by claiming they were 'part of the old South Africa' and threatening to sue them. 'I've watched Mathews Phosa change,' says someone who knows the notoriously dirty Nelspruit ANC politics inside out. 'He came into this job a real heavy, not tolerating dissent, wanting things his way. But he has begun to mellow. He knows he can't keep playing that way if he wants to be a national contender.'

After lunch, Mathews Phosa takes me on a tour of the R700 000 house he has built on the controversial High Over Estate set up by KaNgwane, just outside Nelspruit. The intention is to quash an article that had just appeared in the Sunday papers accusing the Eastern Transvaal's ANC leaders of using '[the] poor's cash on own homes' by taking advantage of a fraudulent bantustan subsidy scheme. Phosa disputes it and has publicly branded the journalist as racist and libelous.

The house is protected by a vast wall with a gatehouse, and there is an absurdly grandiose false façade into which is set one of the most enormous wooden doors I have ever seen. What troubled me about it was not just how public the ostentation is – it is right on the N4, between Nelspruit and the township of KaNyamazane, on the taxi route home – but how fortified it is. Despite the fact that his property has an exquisite view over the orange orchards of the Crocodile River valley, the house pays no attention to its environment and turns inward upon itself. It is architecturally paranoid, completely at odds with the open, charming and affable man with whom I spent the day. I remembered that, in his office, all his curtains were drawn at midday.

Is it possible to be a regional political leader and not be a 'heavy'? And does it matter if Mathews Phosa is? I came back to Johannesburg, after time with Phosa, singing the praises of Nelspruit. If I were to buy a piece of land outside Johannesburg, it would be in that part of the world: not just because of the landscape and the promise of Sunday lunchtime jaunts to Maputo for prawns and *catembe* and a swim in the sea once the highway is built, but also because I think it would be a good investment. Mathews Phosa may be heavy, but he's doing something right.

EUGENE NYATI
Former Consultant to the
Mpumalanga government

Mr Dial-a-Quote and the gravy boat

'Gravy Train' scandal hit the broadsheets in September 1995, when it was alleged that Eugene Nyati – a consultant to the Mpumalanga government – had pocketed R1,2-million's worth of state money. Nyati, whom I went to see in Nelspruit short-ly thereafter, was not an easy interview. In fact, he so infuriated my good-natured colleague, Henner Frankenfeld, that I found myself physically having to separate them. Following the publication of my interview, Tribute *published allegations that he was not even South African, that his real name was Albert Nina, that all his qual-ifications were false, and that he had been expelled from the University of Zimbabwe for political reasons. Nyati seems to have left South Africa; his threats to sue the* Sunday Times *and* Tribute *have, unsurprisingly, not materialized.*

Eugene Nyati

Here's what Eugene Nyati had to say on 'Newsline' following the April 1994 elections: 'No amount of foreign aid can be a substitute for the internal sacrifices that we ourselves have got to make in order to get South Africa to work. We have to learn to live within our means … Every manager or politician in this country drives a car more expensive than that driven by Bill Clinton, president of the richest country in the world.'

A bare 18 months later finds Nyati in Nelspruit, in a hired, white Mercedes-Benz. He is neither a manager nor a politician: he is a consultant, hired by Mpumalanga, and found with R1,2-million of the province's money in his bank account – handed over to him, in blithe, blank-cheque fashion by a province naive, inept and so desperate for the rapid change Nyati promised (and delivered) it was willing to forgo all forms of financial control.

In the ensuing investigation the following was revealed: Nyati was collecting interest on state moneys; his lawyer had 'mistakenly' added an extra zero to her fee, raising it to six figures; his accountant had hired a pharmacist to play detective after hours at roughly R10 000 a weekend; the chair of the commission, 25-year-old Ntoake Mohape, was paid over R300 000 for just two months' work, while simultaneously drawing a full salary from her employers; and Nyati himself was richer – after three months' work – by the amount a national Cabinet minister or a corporate executive usually earns in a year.

Gravy, finally, has a face. One with volatile features that shift from charm to contempt in the flicker of a moment; one with fiercely intelligent eyes burning above one of those fine-fluted sets of nostrils that exhale arrogance with every utterance. The day after the *Sunday Times* led with 'Gravy high-flyer crashes to earth', I went to Nelspruit to see Eugene Nyati. He was, understandably, prickly and irritable and did not want to do the interview. He gave me two hours of his time anyway.

Adamant that there was no irregularity whatsoever (save, perhaps, the catering account going to his assistant's mother), he insisted – as he had been doing all the previous week – that the *Sunday Times* vendetta against him had pre-empted 'a natural process of reconciliation that would have taken place anyway. All the money not used would have been returned at that point. It's called covering yourself. It's a standard business practice in the private sector.'

Nyati, you see, is a self-confessed 'private-sector man'. The government came to him and said, Do the job! and he did it. 'I walk in here and I find that some civil service employees are happy to spend R20 000 convening three meetings of a tender board to make a decision on how to spend R16 000. Well, I don't work that way. If you're given two months to do a major job, you have to be able to walk into an expert's office and say, Deliver in five days! If that means you put a premium on your rate, then so be it!'

Here's what the *Sunday Times* didn't tell you: Nyati did deliver. This country's first restructured provincial development corporation is about to come into being. On paper it's impressive: run according to private-sector and free-market principles, no guaranteed jobs for lazy civil servants, senior executives on contract, an arm's-length relationship with government; even a provincial development bank that will fund enterprises according to business plans and wean them into the private sector.

No one in Nelspruit – not even his detractors – denies that the job was well done.

That, says Chris McPherson, the National Party representative on the commission, 'was why we were so hurt when the money thing came out. Eugene had credibility: he was excellent at marketing all these ideas about private enterprise to the cabinet. He was charming and friendly and worked very hard.'

But, says McPherson, no way was the job worth R1,2-million. Nyati counters with two cogent points: that he achieved, in two months, what 'a consultative process, costing millions and millions of rand, failed to achieve over fifteen months', and that 'the result of the work will save this province millions of rand in the months and years to come'.

Yes, but should the taxpayer ever be expected to fork out R540 an hour to a consultant? The nostrils flare. The eyes burn. The pages of a rather ragged diary turn furiously, releasing bits of paper that turn out to be evidence. Here, for example, paperclipped to a page, is a fax confirming that Eugene Nyati has been invited to give an hour-long presentation to a major insurance company. Fee: R4 700. 'So you see. I'm actually giving myself on the cheap!'

But isn't there a difference between a once-off fee to the private sector and a continuous fee, over three months, to the public sector? The pages turn again, more furiously. Nyati is a master of releasing information by protesting that he is not. Example: 'If I wanted to, I could tell you that I saw the president of IBM last week. But that's not how I operate.' Or (thrusting a gilt-edged and well-thumbed invitation to dine on HMS Britannia under my nose): 'I'm not the sort of person who goes on a trip and comes back and says, "Oh, by the way, I had lunch with Queen Elizabeth!" I'm not looking for recognition. I've got recognition, whether people like it or not!'

Or my personal favourite (pulling an equally well-thumbed envelope of photos of himself posing with various American politicians out of the diary and laying them on the desk): 'Some guy came and said to me, "That's you with Senator David Boren! That's you with Congressman Howard Wolpe! What are you doing with Al Gore?" Now what sort of bullshit is that? I don't need to sit here and justify why I have contacts all over the world. What the hell for? I provide a service. It's very good. The market pays good money for it. That's all.'

Moving into the personal domain and using the same strategy, he says, when I ask him about his past: 'What relevance is that? I could tell you about how I was born in a village near Newcastle, and how I moved with my parents, who were teachers, to then-Rhodesia, when I was 9 or 10. I could tell you about how my parents died and I was orphaned … But I don't like bringing that into things. I want to be remembered as an issues person.'

He is furious that the *Sunday Times* disputes his Master's degree from the University of Pittsburgh, but he refuses, point-blank, to correct what he calls the 'slander' by telling me anything about his past. Twice he evades the question of where he was an undergraduate. He speaks with a strong accent (Central or East African) but, when I ask where he has lived, he will say only: 'All over the world!'

Why on earth would a man so clearly pleased with himself be so reticent about his background? Eugene Nyati has invented himself, brilliantly and skilfully. With his intelligent, easily understandable and independent commentary, he has built himself up as this country's prime political commentator. At the SABC, he was known as 'Mr Dial-a-Quote': Want comment on the budget? Call Eugene! Slovo dead? Get Eugene!

Eugene Nyati

Winnie fired? Ask Eugene! We journalists loved him because he spoke common sense: he said the obvious thing; the thing we wanted to say but could now attribute to an 'expert'.

When quoted, he was always 'Dr Nyati' or 'Professor Nyati'. He does not have a doctorate, although, he says, he is an 'honorary professor at a university by virtue of the fact that I give occasional lectures there'. Which university? 'Oh, just a university in California.' He tried to tell the people inputting the titles at the SABC that he wasn't really a doctor, but it happens once, and then it's such a big deal to get it changed. 'I'm not into titles. If someone calls me Dr Nyati, why do you blame me? There's an assumption that because I engage in high-flown analysis the way I do, I must be some kind of academic.'

Nyati's analysis is, if not always high flown, always articulate and interesting. He is known as a prophet of the market (who would not be at R4 700 an hour?), and is most critical of the ANC's inability to separate itself from labour now that it is the government. Interestingly, though, his semi-academic writing (published in current affairs journals) is aggressively anti-free-market. In the mid-1980s, writing from Namibia, he was an apostle of the 'mixed economy' and of Zimbabwean President Robert Mugabe, whom he praised for 'far-sighted and pragmatic' leadership.

He arrived in Johannesburg some time in the late 1980s, and was appointed as a contributor to *Tribute* magazine. He set up his Centre for African Studies, first in His Majesty's Building on Commissioner Street, then in a Parktown flat. He was certainly not flush in those days: he drove an old red Jetta and lived with his girlfriend – a night-nurse at a private nursing home – first in a Hillbrow block of flats and then in two rooms at the old Hyde Park Hotel: dingy quarters, right address. A catalogue of the upwardly mobile black professional women he dated would, says a former associate, easily fill an issue of *Enterprise* magazine.

'The world of ideas' was, in those days, not his only entrepreneurial concern. He had a share in a hair salon and a night club; he was involved in plans to sell African art and craft abroad. His greater asset, however – as the Mpumalanga fiasco attests – was his mind and not his bookkeeping skills.

And so his career as a 'consultant' took off. Because of his understanding of economics and his independence – something he quite consciously developed, according to the associate – he became extremely popular on the briefing circuit: ambassadors, visiting foreign missions, foreign companies. It all reached an apex when CNN paid him to be its resident talking-head during the 1994 elections; the BBC did the same during the opening of the first democratic parliament.

Now the night-nurse is his wife; they have a cluster in Fourways – not ostentatious at all – and an 18-month-old baby. The *Sunday Times* claims he has signed a R700 000 housing contract in one of those dreadful new walled cities to the north of Johannesburg: he disputes it.

What will happen to him now? There is, he claims, a 'big picture' that only he and premier Mathews Phosa understand. He will not say what it is, save that 'one of the undercurrents is this goddam racism. It's as if some people believe that certain [money] figures are just not supposed to be associated with a black man.'

Part of the story is the fact that grumpy old white men want to trash him because he is too threatening a change agent. If he can persuade the world that this is all there is to it – a strategy, to his credit, that he is no longer pursuing – then he will bounce back.

It seems a long shot, though. At the end of our discussion, Eugene Nyati and I stopped doing a dance around his past and firing shots at each other about his present dilemma, and lapsed into a discourse more familiar to both of us: I the inquiring and attentive journalist, he the sagacious commentator.

As usual, I found his comments clear and opinionated. But something was different, and it wasn't only that he now says 'us' rather than 'them' when talking of government: there was an exhaustion to this usually ebullient man; a listlessness to his commentary.

His accountant, Maurice Allis (whose R200 000 bill to the commission was subsequently reduced by R150 000), trundled asthmatically into the office. 'Are you winning?' he asked us.

Well, Maurice, no.

MANNE DIPICO
Premier of the Northern Cape

Mama's boy of the Kalahari

I chose to profile the premier of South Africa's sparsest and poorest province as an example of our new government's amazing precocity – in his mid-thirties, he is the country's youngest premier. The interview took place in June 1996, a few months before that year's local government elections, at a time when the politics of local 'transitional' councils were fraught with tensions: those tensions, I found, were Dipico's major preoccupation.

Manne Dipico

The premier of the Northern Cape lives with his mother in a modest township house. Perhaps it is fortunate, says Manne Amsley Dipico (a name that could emanate only from the quirky fringes of the Kalahari), that Kimberley is the only provincial capital without an official residence, for there is nowhere else he would rather be than on Magashule Street, in the home he grew up in – a former shebeen run by his domestic-servant mother to augment her meagre income, its tiny interiors now crammed with the heavily curlicued and thickly upholstered oak furniture of township respectability.

Dipico claims that he stays in the township for political reasons – 'after taking over, people expected a lot from us, and running away from the townships would only cause problems' – but admits that the home he grew up in is something of a sanctuary too: 'When I come in here and close the door, I leave politics behind, because my mother just isn't interested.'

Well, usually not. When Eastern Cape Premier Raymond Mhlaba was seen, on TV, unlocking newly-built houses, Mama gave Mannetjies a piece of her mind: 'Look at that premier!' she clucked. 'He's even opening the door for the people to come in. And what are you doing for our people? When are you going to build some houses?'

He laughs. 'I might be the premier, but to her I am still a child. She is the only one who can really haul me up.' 35-year-old Manne Dipico is one of the most down-home politicians I have ever met – he is genial and playful, hearty and affable, much given to rambling anecdotes and elaborate stage-winks, but pleased enough with himself that it's probably a good thing there's a Mama Dipico around to keep him in line.

He has much to be pleased about. Despite the fact that his province is a developer's nightmare (it is the only one that has inherited no administrative infrastructure, and its small population of 700 000 means that, even though it covers one third of South Africa's land mass, it has a tiny budget to work with), it is being lauded as one of the unexpected miracles of the transition. Mohammed Valli Moosa, the Deputy Minister of Provincial Affairs, spends his life trying to resolve conflict; in the Northern Cape, he says, there is no work for him. This despite the fact that the parliament of the province is hung, with the ANC holding exactly half of the 30 seats.

Moosa says that the Northern Cape is the only province to have stuck to the deadlines for the establishment of transitional local government structures, and its voter registration figures are the second highest in the country. 'No-one would have expected such a tremendous display of political skill from the Northern Cape – in terms of welding people together and building a government that enjoys broad credibility.'

Now, in Kimberley, there is government by consensus – all the more remarkable when one realises that this is Orania-land; the leader of the Freedom Front in these parts is none other than Carel Boshoff. Once the good professor heard that his new premier had been brought up in the church, he slapped him on the back and declared: 'Well, then, we can make a deal. We can trust each other.' That trust has yet to be broken.

Here's the kind of thing Dipico does: after assigning the youth portfolio in his cabinet to the Freedom Front's other member, Jozef Henning, he asked him to organise the province's June 16 ('Youth Day') celebrations. The result: a *volkstater* accompanying hundreds of black youths on buses that he has personally paid for, and publicly and tearfully embracing Dipico for the pain his people have gone through. 'For the first time,' Henning says now, 'I understood the aspirations of black people.'

Henning is 'sympathetic' about the fact that Dipico is a communist, and says, wondrously: 'This premier has a political wisdom and maturity way beyond his years. He is open-minded and without blinkers, and that is part of his success.'

Things like this only happen in the Northern Cape, which sometimes seems to be a province of the imagination rather than one of the nine new regions of our land. Listen, for example, to the rapprochement Dipico engineered in Aughrabies, between striking farmworkers and hysterical grape-farmers about to lose their harvest. After a farmer shot and killed an 11-year-old boy, Dipico rushed over. Eight hours of tough negotiation were followed by a particularly liquid braaivleis. The result: the farm-workers taught their bosses how to toyi-toyi, and the farmers agreed to put a portion of their grape-profits into a Reconstruction and Development Programme fund for schooling, and to stop child-labour.

Chalk it down to the winds of the Kalahari, the landscape of prickly-pear planta-tions and anthills, of reds and ochres and silvery acacia greens through which a white Mercedes slices at 240 kilometres per hour bearing a jovial, tubby former-unionist who honed his negotiating skills, as a former National Union of Minework-ers organiser, at the elbow of Cyril Ramaphosa. It was Dipico, in the mid-1980s, who got trade unionism going in the Northern Cape, reining in the frontier-cowboys who ran the mines in Kimberley, in Okiep and Nababiep, in Springbok and Sishen.

And so the last thing he is scared of is 'the boerboys' as he still delights in calling them. The provincial legislature's sole Democratic Party member, Ethne Papenfus (yet another name that leads one to believe that the Northern Cape is an invention of Garcia Marquez or JM Coetzee rather than the negotiators at the World Trade Cen-tre) attests that 'he is hearty and full of fun, but don't be deceived, he is a skilled and tough negotiator who knows exactly what he wants and how to get it.' She should know: he got her to be Speaker, thereby preventing a coalition that would have kept the ANC out of power.

He is the Ramaphosa of the provinces, suave urbanity replaced by amiable folksi-ness, but with the same net result. I saw this side of Manne Dipico when I chased his white Mercedes through the prickly-pear plantations and anthills to Petrusville, the next dorp over from Orania, and one of the average of five towns he visits every week, to hold public meetings, talk with the transitional local council, and spread the gospel of reconciliation.

Another Northern Cape vision stolen from fiction: A convoy of cars makes a night-time tour of Petrusville's pitch-black township, led by a group of young comrades in a fancy BMW ('BMW!' the kids cheer, 'Bob Marley *en die* Wailers!'), and tailed by Dipico's overzealous security, weaving unneccessarily behind the premier and open-ing the doors of their car to push back screaming children, many of whom are clear-ly inebriated. The convoy stops at a shack, and everyone gets out, to examine a fam-ily who live with their goats. They get back into their cars, and weave their way to the community hall, where Manne Dipico climbs on to the stage to address the peo-ple.

Don't tell Valli Moosa, but there's trouble going on down here – the ANC is riven with faction-fighting, the white members of the council are not playing ball, and the township folk are refusing to pay rent. 'Why', asks one of those formidable old African women who fear nothing, 'should we pay rates when we are forced to drink the same water as donkeys?' She is dressed in the squatter fantasia of rags, blankets, pink-rimmed sunglasses, and other found objects, and, like Mama Dipico, she is not scared of the Premier – he is a little boy now, and she tells it like it is.

He responds to her as he did to the white members of the transitional council earlier, with a rasping and harsh Afrikaans that raps them all over the knuckles. 'There's a lot of foreign interest in South Africa, but I can't take them to Petrusville if you are still fighting each other.'

At times he was so stern and preachy that he was rather unpleasant, a young Mandela on a bad day. But one had to admire him for not taking the populist option. How easy it would have been to side, full of righteous indignation, with the members of his own constituency – whose votes he needs – and lambast the old white council.

After berating them for their lack of reconciliatory impulse, he leads these dirt-poor people through a blow-by-blow account of Mandela walking ('if you've been fortunate enough to see Mandela, you would see that he puts his feet in front of each other very properly, like a real president'), eating ('properly, the fork going deliberately into the mouth, like a real president'), sleeping ('he sleeps *lekker* straight *nê*, just like a real president') and even dreaming ('I sneaked in to see him at 2.30 in the morning and I saw him dreaming, like such an *oulike* president, dreaming of all the good things he can do for his people').

It is a clever ploy, showing his constituents that, even if he will not support them in their rent boycott, he is close enough to the great old man to watch him dream. But perhaps it also says something about the closeness with which Dipico observes his man, the way in which he, the apprentice, is trying to learn that particularly Mandela-esque combination of gravitas and *oulikheid* that makes a president.

It reminds me of something Dipico told me earlier in the day, when he was recounting how he locked horns with the Kuruman Conservative Party. When they threatened to fight the new order just as the ANC had the old, he stared them down, and won. 'I reminded them that when Mandela took up the armed struggle, he was prepared to go to the ultimate, to life imprisonment or even death. I said that prison had made Mandela into what he is, a reconciliatory figure, and I only hoped that if they were lucky enough to go to prison, the same would happen to them.'

Manne Dipico was trained by Cyril Ramaphosa, but blessed by Nelson Mandela. The former is his mentor, the latter his saint. He too went to prison (sentenced to five years for furthering the aims of the ANC – he was the leader of an uMkhonto cell in Kimberley). He went in a bitter and angry young man and came out a leader. What happened in betweeen is that he was touched, directly, by Nelson Mandela.

Manne Dipico is a member of the South African Communist Party Central Committee devoted to developing private sector industry in his province so that raw materials stop leaving the region and jobs are created. He is free-willed and independent; highly critical of central government and the ANC for not backing up the provinces. He is ambitious. He doesn't have half the poise of the president, but I imagine that, in terms of drive, he is much like the Mandela of the early 1960s. He is one of those young men who believes he can change the world, and probably will. Watch this (wide open) space.

RAYMOND MHLABA
Premier of the Eastern Cape

Oom Ray in the Wild East

'Oom Ray' Mhlaba and I had a wonderful, free-ranging chat in his Bisho presidential residence. I left, humbled, by the breadth of his involvement in the South African struggle: his quiet maturity was a welcome balm to the arrogane of youth I so often encounter in my profiles. In the months before we met – in January 1996 – there had been much publicity about what a mess the Eastern Cape was and how badly Mhlaba was managing things. It was in that context that I went to see him.

Raymond Mhlaba

Y ou catch the similarity first in the tone: the ponderous and spare mode of delivery, a schoolmasterish stress on each syllable. Then you catch it in the ability – perhaps borne of a half-lifetime in captivity – to control a large, even gangly, frame with the smallest of gestures; in the wry self-deprecatory humour that nonetheless never intimates self-doubt; in that archaic mission-school language where men are 'fellows' or, if a little younger, 'chaps'.

Nelson Mandela and Raymond Mhlaba are almost exact contemporaries: they were born, two years apart, on opposite ends – socially and geographically – of what is now the Eastern Cape. They both landed up at Healdtown Mission School, the Thembu princeling by right and the policeman's son by pluck.

Mandela went to university, became a lawyer in Johannesburg, assumed his position of leader. Mhlaba drifted into Port Elizabeth, found the Communist Party on a dry-cleaner's shopfloor, and was working as a clerk in a lawyer's office when Mandela recruited him into u Mkhonto weSizwe in 1961. They stood trial together in 1964, spent 25 years in jail together. Now the one governs the country and the other the Eastern Cape.

Although they share many mannerisms, Mhlaba is as down-home as Mandela is patrician. Mandela is 'Tata', the father adored, revered and sometimes also feared. Mhlaba is 'Oom Ray', the uncle, loved too, but a little distant, a little less directly engaged in the destiny of his subjects.

In Mandela's autobiography – and, indeed, in most accounts of the Rivonia trial and life on Robben Island – Mhlaba is something of a conundrum: he is always around, yet somewhat invisible; he is always very senior (he was one of the four-man 'High Organ' on the Island), and yet one knows very little about his personality, his style, his responsibilities. He is part of the trail of names, Mhlaba–Motsoaledi–Mlangeni, that follow in the typographical wake of Mandela and Sisulu. Of the Rivonia generation, however, he is the only one, apart from Mandela, to hold a position of significant responsibility in the new government.

Mandela does give us one little clue when he describes how he consulted his inmates about negotiating with the government. 'Ray was always a man of few words, and for a while he digested what I had said. He then said to me, "Madiba, what have you been waiting for? You should have started this years ago."'

He is indeed a man of few words, no-nonsense and common-sensical, staunch in his belief in the common man, unwavering in his commitment to socialism (he replaced Joe Slovo as the National Chairman of the party), and given to workaday but quite compelling homilies, often with a martial tinge (he was sent for extensive military training in China in 1962). He and his comrades in government, he tells me, are 'untrained to govern … like a man in a war situation who has never used a gun before, but is handed one and told to fight'.

We sit in the banal, face-brick, suburban box that Lennox Sebe deluded himself into believing was a Presidential Palace. All in all, Bisho is a pale imitation of Mmabatho (say what you like about Lucas Mangope, he knew how to buy style). The Ciskei capital used to be infuriating, outrageous, deadly. Now its stone leopards are pathetic and without the omnipresent crunch of soldiers' boots giving the illusion of order and sovereignty, the sound of peasant women announcing their freshly roasted corn dominates.

Raymond Mhlaba

Now, the incongruously classicist lines of the buildings are smudging into a true post-modernity that proclaims that order is unattainable and reflects the bewilderment of is current political occupants – democrats! modernists! communists! In a world of stone leopards, they are trying to clear a new society out of a hinterland that is vast, populous, underdeveloped. It holds within it South Africa's own Wild West, our very own tragic caricature of a Banana Republic, the Transkei, the poorest part of the country, the logical end product of apartheid; lawless, corrupt and undernourished; R9-billion in debt, serviced by 90 000 civil servants who do … well, very little indeed.

Oom Ray, the commoner from New Brighton, chuckles about Transkeians: 'Oh yes,' he says, 'they have their own history … They'll tell you, We have always governed ourselves, we know how to govern. Even when I was at Healdtown, people from Transkei spoke about how they were from the Black England: We are elite, we are special. Yes, if you want to approach a Transkeian you handle him with care.'

But there are dangerous politics lurking behind the gentle mockery. For the system he inherited boasts not only bone-idle civil servants but also puffed-up chiefs. They privately scorn Mhlaba as a deracinated commoner and, while he would never publicly admit it, those close to him say he sees them as precisely the kind of feudal scourge socialism was supposed to do away with. But they, like the senior ranks of the civil service, are key ANC power-brokers. They are thus not easily discarded, they all have vested interests in the status quo, and all have (or believe they should have) a hotline to Cousin Madiba.

The evidence of graft grows by the day: paycheck embezzlement in the health department was so entrenched that the government has had to tender an outside contractor to manage the payroll; phantom teachers at phantom schools were paid very real salaries; the Transkei government defrauded itself in a bizarre scam where it charged itself illegally high interest through its own bank.

Little wonder the civil service is, by Mhlaba's own admission, 'very hostile to us'. The cause of the 'mistrust,' he believes, 'is that this is a bloated administration that will have to be trimmed. So they know they will have to be retrenched'. Indeed, on the day I interviewed Mhlaba, the province's Director General, Thozamile Botha, announced that around 18 000 civil servants could lose their jobs in a plan aimed at bringing the province's impossible civil service into line. His goal is to reduce the numbers from 155 000 to 124 000.

By completely restructuring the province, thereby rendering everybody redundant and forcing everybody to reapply for their jobs, Botha believes he has provided the rest of the country with a model for how to circumvent the sunset clause. 'We are the first province', he says, 'which is facing the reality of bloated administrations head on and which is trying to deal with it, rather than using delaying tactics.'

In my interview with national Public Administration Minister Zola Skweyiya in December, he pointedly contrasted the Eastern Cape with Mpumalanga. The former, he said, 'was very negative towards old public servants already there, from South Africa and the bantustans. They tried to chop everyone, and the result was hostility. Mpumalanga never had that problem: from before the elections, [Mathews] Phosa interacted with all the different stakeholders to set things up. So, from the beginning, they had a vision shared by everyone. There has thus been less tension there.'

The result: things have moved quicker in Mpumalanga. One example is that both provinces made significant agreements with Germany shortly after the 1994 elections. According to the Germans, most of the agreements have been implemented in Mpumalanga, but nothing has happened in the Eastern Cape. Mhlaba acknowledges this: 'There is some delay I cannot put my finger on.'

Answers like that are testimony to the premier's straightforwardness and honesty. They also lead many to believe that he does not have a grasp on his province's issues. 'He is', says one senior official, 'very good on the big picture but very fuzzy on the detail.' Several of his advisers acknowledge that there is a general impression that he and the province are not doing a good job, but insist this has to do with the impossibility of the situation.

It is unfair to blame Mhlaba for the excesses of a system that rotted while he was sitting in prison. He is industrious, engaged, and wise. But one key player notes: 'Oom Ray inspires loyalty and love in those who know him. I, for one, can honestly say I love him. But he is not a charismatic figure. He doesn't have the verve to be able to say, 'Come on, we're all in this together!''

One of the more irrational laws of politics is that if you make people believe you are doing things, you encourage a confidence which actually makes things start to happen. Almost every other ANC premier, for example, has taken a leaf out of Mandela's book and deflected attention from service delivery by flourishing the magician's rainbow cloth of reconciliation. At least, they say, we've got everyone working together! Both Mhlaba and the Eastern Cape don't seem to be interested in this rhetoric – perhaps because the region is so overwhelmingly dominated by one ethnic majority; perhaps because Mhlaba, a man truly reconciled after 25 years in prison and a communist to his bones, can't bring himself to play games with racial identity.

'I think more than anything', says another senior politician from the region, 'that Oom Ray is trapped by the fact that he is not Steve Tshwete.' This is a reference to the fact that the hugely popular Tshwete was expected to be given the province. Some say Mhlaba's appointment was the direct intervention of Mandela, a combination of the Old Man's loyalty to an old comrade and his sentimental attachment to his own province. Others point to the fact that the province is an amalgamation of three very powerful ANC regions – the old Eastern Cape, Border and the Transkei – each of which believes, fervently, that it is the cradle of the liberation movement. The competition between the many leaders from these three regions was so severe that Mhlaba had to be called in as the elderly statesman compromise.

In every other province the ANC won, it installed a young, charismatic, ambitious man as premier. All of them are a good three decades younger than Mhlaba. The provinces were given to the young 'chaps': no-one really expected them, anyway, to have much power in a centralised state.

But, because the 'chaps' are ambitious and the constitution ambiguous, the provinces have become reservoirs of political testosterone. The archetypal premier is as pop as Tokyo, as cocky as Manne, as main-man as Mathews and as tuned-in as Terror. A Tshwete or a Holomisa would fit right in to the profile. There's something quite incongruous, and not a little moving, about Oom Ray Mhlaba, with his dove-white hair and his blue-flecked cataracting eyes among them.

BANTU HOLOMISA
Deputy Minister of Environmental Affairs and Tourism
More Biggles than Bokassa

Former military dictator turned populist crowd-pleaser, Bantu Holomisa is one of the more enigmatic of our new leaders. I profiled him in February 1996, partly, to assess his role in the disaster zone of the Transkei and partly to understand the source of his power. The fact that Pallo Jordan was made Minister of Environmental Affairs and Tourism, following the NP's departure from government in May 1996, reinforces the impression that Holomisa remains marginal to the ANC's centre of power, despite his popularity.

Bantu Holomisa

'**M**y friend,' says Bantu Holomisa with his trademark imp-twinkle when asked about his role as deputy minister and his political ambitions, 'you must remember that I have already tasted power. *Absolute* power. I've been there. I've had it all. Now I'm just responding to a call to help out.'

His particular way of ribbing, rather too dry to be a wisecrack, falls somewhere between self-deprecation and self-adulation. Responding to the fact that he constantly seems to be in trouble these days for speaking his mind, he urges this fledgling democracy to take a leaf out of his own book. 'This new democratic government can learn one or two things about accountability from our military regime. Compared to this democracy, we [in the Transkei] were much more transparent.'

We find General Holomisa, military dictator turned environmentalist, sitting in the garden of his ministerial home, reading the Sunday papers. Fully aware that we are coming to photograph him, he is wearing shorts; his 9-year-old's basketball has been placed strategically nearby. It's all very Boys' Own; more Biggles than Bokassa.

A few years ago, political columnist Hugh Roberton compared Holomisa to Constand Viljoen, ascribing to both the 'irrational naivete which afflicts so many military men who enter politics'. Both, like all good military commanders, have the common touch; both have a sentimental attachment to the common man, in whose name they moved from war to politics: Viljoen to save the Afrikaner from obliteration, Holomisa to save the Transkeian from corruption.

Coming from the classless security forces, Africa's military leaders have often been – or claimed to be – the common-man antidotes to excessive neo-colonial emperors. I remember seeing him at Umtata airport in 1991. In jeans and a leather bomber-jacket, he picked up his luggage, jumped into a small car and drove off. No fanfare, no lackeys, no fuss. I thought of the legendary Thomas Sankara who took over Burkina Faso in a military coup, and then tried to institute a Marxist revolution from behind the wheel of a self-driven Renault 5.

There are some marked differences, though: there was no repression of dissent in Holomisa's Transkei, and there was no ideology. The latter, perhaps, is the best way of understanding his present role, as loyal and disciplined maverick, in national politics. He is a very recent comrade indeed. He learnt about revolution and the African National Congress not on the Soweto streets or in Angolan camps, but from the other side: at Army College at Voortrekkerhoogte.

Matriculating in 1976, he went to Kaiser Matanzima's army – recruited into an officers' programme for the sons of chiefs – rather than leaving the country to join uMkhonto weSizwe. He was virulently opposed to sanctions, and said, in 1988, that it would 'not be wise' to unban the liberation movements as 'we have an agreement with our neighbour, South Africa, that we will not use each other's territory as a springboard to attack the other'.

But Holomisa was quick on the uptake: he sought confrontation with Pretoria and allowed the ANC and the Pan-Africanist Congress to operate freely in his 'liberated zone'. The watershed came in 1989, when he presided over the burial of exiled Thembu chief Sabata Dalindyebo and announced that he would seek a referendum to rejoin South Africa. The funeral, festooned in ANC colours, stole FW de Klerk's thunder and provided the first tangible sign of pending liberation.

Holomisa became a hero; the figure behind the scenes was none other than Winnie

Bantu Holomisa

Mandela. In conversations and meetings over two years, she had nurtured him, brought him on board. Little wonder he is so fiercely loyal to her; that he regards her as South Africa's primary 'kingmaker': he is one of her kinglets.

In partnership with her and the other men she drew close to her – Chris Hani, Peter Mokaba, Tony Yengeni – he attained immense grassroots popularity, coming first at the end of 1994 in an election for the ANC's national executive committee. But he has never been a struggle-insider. He doesn't obey the protocols.

And so he gets into trouble: by jumping to Winnie Mandela's defence after her dismissal, by publicly challenging Nelson Mandela on a statement he made about corruption in the Transkei; and, more recently, by railing against the 'elitists' in the ANC for trying to get rid of him.

This latest allegation was dispatched to the media, last November, in a turgid pages-long release replete with menagerie metaphor ('one cannot send a jackal to represent sheep in a conference of jackals where the subject matter is the slaughter of sheep'), in which Holomisa accused his enemies within the ANC of using the National Intelligence Agency (NIA) in an attempt to discredit him. It 'chimed well', he added, with the campaign against 'so-called populists' in the party – and proceeded to upbraid the ANC for not taking action against those who would call him such.

There may well be an attempt to marginalise his clique within the ANC. But to put the two together, as Holomisa did, is nothing short of paranoid. His paranoia, notes one senior government source, 'is the result of him being a bit cut off. He is not in the thick of things, and so he perpetually feels he is being left out.'

Some in the ANC say he has marginalised himself by publicly identifying himself with Winnie while her other 'friends' dived for cover; others say that he has forgone a pivotal role in government by not being more active, either as deputy minister or as a National Executive Committee member.

But even those who disapprove of him find it very difficult to dislike him. One member of the Eastern Cape government, angry at Holomisa for the appalling state of affairs in the Transkei, remembers being seated next to him at an event: 'His opening gambit was an incorrigible smile: "I've left you with a real mess, haven't I?", he said. What could I say?'

Is Holomisa responsible for the mess? On several levels, he clearly is not: South Africa deliberately kept the Transkei in penury, and Holomisa had no option but to swell the ranks of the civil service. He was pretty much the homeland's only employer. He certainly opened up the society, and tried valiantly, in his first couple of years, to stem the corruption that had set in under the Matanzimas. His first fallout with South Africa was over the extradition of Sol Kerzner after the casino-king was charged for paying R2-million to George Matanzima for gaming rights.

No one has ever accused Holomisa – as they have the Sebes, the Mangopes and the Matanzimas – of being corrupt. But if his reason for seizing power in 1987 was to stamp out corruption, then the assessment must be, eight years later, that he failed miserably. His regime did not come close to stopping the rot.

Zam Titus, the Eastern Cape's legal adviser who served Holomisa in the same capacity, gives two reasons for this: because there was 'the lack of auditing on an annual basis', and because the military council's focus shifted, after only being in office for a year or so, from fighting corruption to 'national politics and the unbanning of the liberation movements'.

Holomisa is very critical of the way the provincial government has handled the transformation, most of all the announcement that civil servants are going to be retrenched in droves: 'The central government said, "You'll have your job guaranteed," to civil servants. But so far, my friend, the only people who have their jobs guaranteed are whites in South Africa. You can take me on record and I'm not apologetic. We are going backwards and forwards trying to make sure they are happy in their workplace. We don't care about our blacks!'

People say he's a populist as he plays to the crowds. Perhaps another way of putting it is that he speaks basic truths. But while his analysis might be correct, it is shadowed, once more, by dark conspiracies lurking at the gate. Disregarding the fact that it is none other than ANC stalwart Thozamile Botha who is wielding the axe in the province, Holomisa blames white National Party bureaucrats for deliberately plotting to alienate the ANC from its supporters in its strongest province.

He maintains that if the Transkei is a Wild West, this is only post-April 1994. 'If you had come before to the Transkei, you would have seen all was going well; although we were strangulated, we were managing. One town would have one police van to service half-a-million, but we slept peacefully.' What changed was that the government alienated the civil service, and so there was a breakdown in delivery.

His image of an Edenic 'Kei under his command is hopelessly romantic. It is certainly true that, with a strong authority in Umtata, there was a semblance of control. But one Eastern Cape official said he was 'horrified to discover how little was happening outside Umtata. What little money came into the homeland seemed to stay in the capital.' The people may well have loved Holomisa – but this is because he was a canny politician, and not because he was a good administrator.

Apart from an over-use of certain adjectives ('nefarious', 'nauseating'), Holomisa speaks a simple, ungrammatical, but sensible English. His grasp of environmental issues is impressive. But, say players in the sector, his record is patchy: sometimes he gets very involved, and drives things politically – like when he took up the cudgels against toxic waste dumping last year – but equally often, he's just not around.

There was talk, following his tirade last November, that he was finally to be dumped from the cabinet. There is no sign of it, though: his political lifespan is closely linked to his relationship with the Mandelas, which verges on the Oedipal. In many ways he is a son Mandela never had. Like a stern but loving father, the old man chastises him – sometimes publicly – but keeps him close to his bosom and often uses him to say things that he cannot. Like a loving but ambitious prodigal son, Holomisa both respects Mandela and chafes against his authority.

In this context, Holomisa's refusal to attend rallies 'explaining' to the people why Winnie was fired has familial as well as political reverberations: he is determined to remain close to both his political parents.

The royal 'we' is one verbal tic he has picked up from his mentor. He also refers to himself in the third person, as in: 'Holomisa is not one to turn the other cheek when he is struck. Oh, no. Holomisa hits back.' This may well be born of arrogance, but it is also a sign of the man's distance from his own actions; as if, almost Chaplinesque, the little man is trying on roles – the military dictator, the popular politician, the cabinet minister – and seeing how they fit.

ZOLA SKWEYIYA
Minister of Public Services and Administration

An unlikely Tarzan for our red-tape jungles

Zola Skweyiya is one of those very powerful politicians the public knows very little about: he is politically responsible for overhauling the public service. He is not renowned for his garrulousness and affability – but he turned out to be one of the most refreshingly straightforward politicians I have ever met. When we spoke – December 1995 – a power conflict had erupted between himself and the Public Services Commission. It has been somewhat resolved: the Commission has been rendered an advisory body and Skweyiya now wields the executive power he did not have when I interviewed him. It remains to be seen how he exercises it.

Zola Skweyiya

To drive into Transvaal House, where the behemoth Public Services Commission looms over its kingdom of Pretoria, you need to ascend a ramp and go through a security check next to a trash-filled dumpster. The pungent concoction of *kop-toe* security guard and rotting produce is a fragrance peculiarly appropriate for the work that goes on in the building, for this is the factory where they make the spokes to throw into wheels; where 435 people spend their lives preventing good government in the name of good government. Responsible for all decisions that involve staffing the national civil service, these are none other than the people who have set out to make reconstruction and development quite as inefficient as apartheid ever was.

At the very top of the building, on the 22nd floor, are the offices of Zola Skweyiya, Minister of Public Services and Administration. He has what is perhaps the most difficult and most important job of anyone in Cabinet: to transform the civil service. At a recent press conference, he admitted that he didn't even know exactly how many people his government – this country's largest employer – had working for it: the bantustans managed to fold gravy into the most inaccessible of crevices. No wonder he carries with him, as a colleague describes it, 'the air of a Dostoevsky novel, morose and austere, but with more than a little wry understanding of the situation he is in, a situation with a lot of responsibility and no power'.

His impotence stems from having no sway over the Public Services Commission (PSC), a statutory body over which he expected to wield political control, but which has been using him, rather, in his own words, 'as a messenger boy between itself and Cabinet whenever they want something'. Until recently he did not even have his own staff. In fact, he had to apply to the PSC to get a staff so that he could begin to do the job that he felt they weren't doing; little wonder they gave him the runaround too. This ain't Dostoevsky. This is Kafka!

The minister himself has the demeanour of another age: on a balmy summer's day he is to be found in a three-piece black woollen pinstripe suit. It's funny to think that he is the exact contemporary of Chris Hani, with whom he left the country in 1962. Hani – perhaps because of his early death – is freedom's Peter Pan, perpetually youthful; Skweyiya, on the other hand, possesses the dour mission-school gravitas of those who went through Lovedale and Fort Hare a generation before him – the Tambos, the Mandelas, the Govan Mbekis.

He was born in Simonstown in 1942, in the midst of several forced removals his family underwent during the de-Africanisation of the Western Cape. He understands grit: 'If I had stayed in South Africa,' he says, 'I would have landed up in jail or a drunkard, like everyone else I grew up with.'

He has a reputation for honesty and principle that, one colleague notes, 'almost borders on the precious'. He is known for his inflexibility and his doggedness: 'If he makes up his mind to do something, he does it doggedly. And if you stand in his way, he can make life very uncomfortable indeed' – a reference to his legendary temper. He is emotional: this comes out in the way he speaks, in spasms almost, as he describes his work and – more reluctantly – his life. Both have been difficult.

Another close colleague says that 'he is not very articulate. So you measure him not by his words but by his actions.' In an interview he is affable and forthright. There is no slick politician here, no jive talker, no spin doctor. When the eyes twinkle

– as they do periodically – one senses that this is the result of some internal motivation, rather than the external need to be pleasant to a journalist. He does not seem to have the ability to dissemble.

Recently married to Thuthu Mazibuko, the Deputy Director-General of Foreign Affairs, he lives in a flat atop Yeoville Ridge; he is happy there, but has been told by security to move. This has made him grumpy. 'I thought of defying them and staying where I am,' he says, 'but I was advised against it.' It is a measure of how long African National Congress exiles have been back that he talks of 'community' in Yeoville – now abandoned by the new political elite – with the same nostalgia as exiles once spoke of Lusaka.

Despite his low profile – he hates publicity – he is one of the most important decision-makers in the ANC: he sits on its National Working Committee and is a close confidante of Thabo Mbeki. One of his best friends and ideological sparring partners is Pallo Jordan. He has always been a 'social democrat', he says, even when it was unpopular. Some of his colleagues have accused him of 'anti-communism'; the roots of this may have been a particularly difficult decade studying in East Germany, where he was profoundly troubled by the pervasive control of the state. 'I don't', he says now, 'like people telling me what to do.'

He is known as an 'Africanist' – perhaps, he says, because of his 'insistence that black empowerment should be part of democratisation. I don't see progress or development without ensuring the economic upliftment of the oppressed people. Blacks must be part of the restructuring of the economics of this country and not only its politics. The ANC shouldn't shy away from blacks becoming capitalists. The only question is – how do we achieve it?'

Perhaps it is his belief in the value of a black middle class that has made one part of his job – the rationalisation of the bantustan public services – so troubling. He acknowledges how difficult the issue is for the ANC: 'These people, unlike the civil servants in Pretoria, are within the ANC's own constituency. But when retrenchments begin to happen, these will affect them more than anyone, because people in the TBVC states simply don't have the skills. They cannot compete.'

By no means is that the voice of a crude Africanist. Later in our conversation he mentions that 'when we came here and we realised we were now employers [as opposed to freedom fighters], we had to see that we were employing human beings who, irrespective of their colour, have to be treated equally.' Indeed, his critics within the ANC feel he has gone too far in accommodating white civil servants (he has excellent relations with the largely white Public Servants' Association, and troubled ones with the Cosatu-affiliated unions representing public servants).

Much criticism of Skweyiya comes from Cosatu and from his own comrades in Parliament – specifically the powerful Public Services Portfolio Committee, with which he has frequently clashed over the speed of the transition of the civil service. Many parliamentarians feel his worries about counter-revolution from within the ranks of the civil service led him, at first, to attempt too much to accommodate public servants. He is, they say, entirely responsible for the predicament he is in: his inherent conservatism and his legal background (he has a doctorate in law from Leipzig) made him too cautious. He thought he could work through the PSC, and he did not act quickly enough or decisively enough to put into place the overhaul of the civil service so necessary for delivery of the ANC's promises.

There is, in his recent moves, a tacit acknowledgement of this. Beware! Zola has stirred. He has gone about setting up his own department and – most important – he has belatedly announced the establishment of a Presidential Review Commission, to be chaired by Mandela, charged with rationalising and restructuring the civil service.

In the early days of his tenure, he would hear no criticism of the PSC, to which he had appointed three new black people to serve alongside the two white men who ran it. Apart from that and a name change (it used to be the Commission for Administration), the institution has remained exactly the same and Skweyiya is now the first to admit it. 'One cannot run away', he says, 'from the fact that these were the people who determined the administration of the former apartheid regime, and we have set them up in our interim constitution without looking at their effect on the whole of the public service.'

The PSC is 'too rigid and inflexible. There is not a single minister, from any of the parties, who has not complained about how obstructive he or she finds them.' They are far too powerful; far more powerful, in fact, than similar commissions in other countries. 'You can't do anything in the public sector without consulting them, and so there's a lot of tension around them.' He has come around to believing that they should simply have the power to monitor and maintain standards; executive and policy-making power must rest with him and his department.

Skweyiya does speak his mind, even when his opinions are unpopular. He feels, for example, that the provinces must have more powers and that federalism has become unnecessarily demonised. He acknowledges too that, when the new government came in, 'there was more emphasis on representivity within the public service than in changing the way the public service works', and is particularly harsh on his party for its lack of preparation in the arena. The ANC has always been more interested in policy than in management, and so, while it had brilliant plans to bring housing, water, jobs, schooling and health to the people, it did not stop to think about what needed to happen institutionally to do this.

Once more, his critics feel that he must take at least some of the rap for this: he was given the responsibility for running the ANC's Civil Service Unit. Remember, however, that he was simultaneously running the critical constitutional committee – the ANC has a tendency to overload its reliable workhorses.

In the next year, we'll see whether Skweyiya can play the role of Action Man. Phumzile Mlambo-Ngcuka, chair of parliament's committee on public service, speaks of how, in countries like Malaysia and New Zealand, 'reforming the public service became a national obsession. We need T-shirts, slogans, a campaign, a profile, because nothing else happens until the civil service changes.'

Oy, vey. Please God, not another RDP or Masakhane campaign, all smoke and mirrors signifying state ideology rather than action. Perhaps Skweyiya's trademark sobriety will prevent this: not even the spin-doctors who invented Clinton and Thatcher could transform him into a bushwhacking Camel Man, slashing through the red-tape vines of the bureaucratic jungle to bring a little light to the public service.

Skweyiya's new salesperson is the glamorous ex-journalist, Thandeka Gqubule. If she can portray him, rather, as the trustworthy accountant, bringing reason and efficiency to the public service, she will have acquitted herself well.

BRIGITTE MABANDLA
Deputy Minister of Arts, Culture, Science and Technology

Wild woman, big soul

My first profile in this series – done in April 1995 when Brigitte Mabandla was appointed to replace Winnie Mandela as deputy minister of arts, culture, science and technology – it remains one of my favourites.

Brigitte Mabandla

You walk into the deputy minister's office in the Oranje-Nassau Building on Schoeman Street and you feel, immediately, the Winnie touch – mediated, of course, by the brigade of government interior-decorators without whom aesthetic life in Pretoria would grind to a halt.

Instead of the standard brown netting stitched with floral appliqué there are flouncy over-pleated peach curtains; instead of heavy imbuia armchairs there is tasteful upholstery over which vaguely Afro abstractions float in mauves and greens.

It's all just so. And sitting behind a desk is a large, exuberant, sloppy, chain-smoking, back-slapping, loudmouthed, kindly woman who only half-jokes about her first days in office: 'Mrs Mandela's staff just packed up and left, leaving me all alone, quite overwhelmed, in an office big and empty but for some brown files. I didn't know what to do with those brown files. I just stared at them ...'

Brigitte Mabandla, the new Deputy Minister of Arts and Culture, Science and Technology, is a mensch. She is so straightforward she kind of takes your breath away. She is one of those rare people who touches strangers. She defies the conventional boundaries of women in power. She will not get dressed up (even though she was spotted in a hat when Queen Elizabeth came to town). She will not sit down and be a good girl. She will drink; she will smoke.

But her emotions are very close to the surface – she will cry, publicly, when upset. 'If you try to get ahead by imitating maleness,' she says, 'you'll land up imitating the stereotype of the macho man. That's not for me. I'm very comfortable with my womanhood, thank you.'

She blames none other than Oliver Tambo for her gender liberation. When the African National Congress leader asked her to join the ANC Legal Department as its only woman, 'he encouraged me to be critical and outspoken. He didn't approve of lackeys.'

She sometimes exasperates her colleagues. Her parliamentary shouts of '*Bua!*' are often the loudest, and she has been accused of being undiplomatic in the caucus. She can be chaotic and disorganised; she tends to overcommit herself.

But she is, says one fairly critical colleague, 'completely down the line; principled to the core'. She clearly commands her peers' respect – she was, after all, chosen by her caucus to be their candidate for Cyril Ramaphosa's deputy in the Constitutional Assembly, a position which in the end went to the National Party's Leon Wessels.

As the only woman on the ANC's pre-negotiations Constitutional Committee, she played a central role in the drafting of the Bill of Rights – and, according to a leader of the women's movement, 'has perhaps been the most effective female voice in the ANC for gender equality'.

During the negotiations, she came to the fore in the customary law debate; she has also pioneered children's rights in South Africa. She currently sits on the government Constitutional Committee and the Constitutional Assembly's Management Committee, two positions she will not give up now that she joins the Cabinet.

She is a human rights lawyer and says, quite frankly, that this remains her passion – she was, in fact, preparing to give up politics for a position in the Human Rights Commission.

'But then Madiba said he had a task for me, and that we need first and foremost to govern this country. That was that.' It makes one realise, once more, the supreme power of Nelson Mandela: will good people find it as difficult to say 'no' to Thabo Mbeki or Cyril Ramaphosa?

Mabandla is aware that the politics of culture are treacherous indeed – 'I do read the *Mail & Guardian*' – but she is genuinely impressed with the 'winning team' in her ministry. By all accounts, the admiration is mutual.

With the recent appointment of Director-General Roger Jardine, what was formerly a dormant ministry – unforgivably so, since it is one of the few new ones, and thus able to invent itself without having to stumble over the hallways full of recalcitrant civil servants – is now kicking into gear.

Although nothing has been decided yet, the indications are that Mabandla will take responsibility for arts and culture, while minister Ben Ngubane will stick with science and technology.

Already, the voracious new deputy minister is devouring the reams of documentation in which cultural policy is currently swamped. 'I'm trying to like my new post. I take it very seriously indeed. And after just a few days I see its possibilities. This is a field in which I truly believe we can measure success.'

She might feel she would have been put to better use as a human rights commissioner, but she doesn't say it. Rather, she points to the example of her old colleague Kader Asmal: 'Here is a man who, in his heart of hearts, is committed to human rights law. So what does he do? He handles water and forestry from a human rights angle! And look how successful he is.'

She tries, unconvincingly, to persuade me of her interest in the arts – she saw a brilliant play at The Market but can't remember its name; she bought an artwork but is not sure who painted it – and then capitulates: 'Listen! I am not a connoisseur. I'm a consumer. I go to jazz clubs. I buy South African art.' She laughs. 'That's not really enough, is it?'

Actually, it is. But only because she brings something far more important than connoisseurship to her new portfolio: 'I don't want to sound vain,' she says, 'but I do think that I'm actually ...' she pauses. A visionary? Yet another poet? An undiscovered prodigy with mountains of canvases in the closet, or a demo tape that she is now going to submit me to? No. '... a humanist.' Hallelujah!

This, after all, is a woman who started off as a South African Students Organisation heavy at Turfloop in the late 1960s, but had her true political awakening a few years later, running an encounter group of black and white students for the South African Institute of Race Relations in Durban.

'For the first time,' she says, 'I got to see the damage that apartheid did not only to blacks but also to whites. There was one boy in the group who had had an experience in the army and who was completely traumatised.

'I came to see that South Africa belonged to all its citizens, and that there were young whites who also wanted a better future.'

The person who found her the job was historian Luli Callinicos. Both women were pregnant – they bonded over health food and ideology. Mabandla and her husband Lindelwe – then a teacher and now a honcho at Kagiso Trust – would spend long evenings in passionate debate with Callinicos and her husband, the sociologist Eddie Webster.

'Luli had the most important transforming role in my life,' says Mabandla. 'She empowered me; she moved me towards the ANC.'

'Later, when I was detained, I was beaten and accused of consorting with a communist. All I could think was that if Luli was a communist then communists must be lovely people …'

Mabandla's association with the Websters – and with the white liberals of Race Relations – meant that she fell foul of her old Saso comrades. 'I took a lot of flak. But I was resolute. I loved my job; I loved working with those young people. I was not going to give it up.'

One of those young people was a 16-year-old girl called Pippa Green. Green, now head of SABC radio's parliamentary team, recalls: 'I was a white schoolkid from the white suburbs, but I never felt white in front of Brigitte. She had this incredible ability to deal with you, whoever you were.

'She opened the world for me. She took me into communities I'd only read about. She really listened to people, and held together this incredible multiracial group for over two years. I've yet to meet again such an egalitarianism of spirit.'

Mabandla had her first child and then, a month later, was detained following a pro-Frelimo rally in 1974. She was brutally beaten and tortured. After five months she was released, and made plans with her husband to leave the country.

Then came the trauma that has haunted her ever since – the only thing in her life about which she can honestly say she has regrets: the circumstances of her departure meant she had to leave her baby, less than a year old, alone in her house – it would be picked up the following day by her sister.

'I have never cried like that. Lindelwe had to pry me off the baby. The worst was that we had to move out of the house, and then pass by the house disguised as two men. So there I was, dressed as a man, weeping, as I knew my baby was inside all alone and I was not able to do anything about it.'

Two years later her baby was delivered to her, in Botswana, via the underground. But by then she was 'bananas with anxiety'. Ever since, she and her husband have resolved, successfully, to keep their family intact no matter what – despite the fact that they live once more in separate cities.

Sitting behind her new desk, the deputy minister is uncharacteristically contained. You can read the furrows on her forehead: 'How does a deputy minister comport herself?' they ask. She is smoking fewer cigarettes, and her arms are not flying all over the place.

Has Brigitte Mabandla succumbed to an attack of gravitas? Madiba has given her a task and she will acquit it.

HUGH MASEKELA
Assistant Chief Executive, Performing Arts
Council of the Transvaal
Strijdom Square's Merry Prankster

I went to see Hugh Masekela in August 1995, days after his controversial appoint-
ment as assistant chief executive of Pact. Since then, the landscape has changed dra-
matically: the monolith still stands, but the 'old guard' with whom Masekela had a
strategic alliance have all left, to be replaced by people like John Kani as chairman
and Alan Joseph as chief executive. Masekela has become something of a concert-
organiser and artist-in-residence. His long-awaited album, released a month or so
after the interview, received mixed reviews and, in public utterances since then, he
has been even crabbier about South African cultural life than he was when we spoke.

160

Hugh Masekela

'Seventh floor!' shouts a voice in campy, elevator-lady pitch as the crowded State Theatre lift bumps to a halt. Its occupants lower their eyes embarrassedly as a grim Pretoria cultural apparatchik pushes his way forward and the voice continues, 'ladies underwear and apparel!'

As the lift closes, the newly appointed Assistant Chief Executive Officer of the Performing Arts Council of the Transvaal says, 'Laugh, guys! Anyone who doesn't laugh will report immediately to me in my office on the eleventh floor!'

Earlier, as we bounded down to Strijdom Square for a photo-shoot, I watched with delighted amazement as Hugh Masekela transformed our own Nuremberg Parade Ground into a laughing circus through the mere force of his personality. No one ever lingers on the marbled expanses over which JG Strijdom's monolitihic head looms; no one would ever dare. But around Masekela a crowd gathers and, within moments, there is a one-man show. 'Masekela? I'm not Masekela! I'm Lucky Dube. I shaved this morning!' All around, laughter swells, shattering Strijdom's serene vacuity.

Would he like to see the statue removed? 'No fuckin' way, man! When I come here with my grandchildren and they say, "Who's that guy?" I'll tell them that it's Strijdom and what a bastard he was. If he wasn't there to remind us we'd just forget. If we knock everything down, we're gonna forget and our children won't know shit!'

Back in the building he leads me through the underbelly of official South African culture. 'Where are we going?' I ask. 'To Goebbels's secret palace!' he responds, and touches his access card to the monitor on a security door with a click of a heel and a Nazi salute.

A merry prankster has been let loose in the pompous corridors of the State Theatre. The wardrobe-queens are aflutter, the Brunhilde at security is trying her own attempt at a theatrical wisecrack, and even the tea lady is finding it hard to suppress a smile. Masekela's laughter is neither simple nor reassuring; it is edgy and even derisive at times, empathetic but not gentle; Rabelaisian in that it is lewd and subversive in equal measure. It could bring a building down, yea even the monolith of apartheid culture that is the State Theatre, by the sheer force of its reverberation.

But Masekela insists that he is no buffoon. 'Don't get me wrong. I know what I'm doing. I just like people to rela-a-a-x. To have fun, man. It's easier to deal with people that way.' In Masekela's transatlantically inflected world, people earn 'bread', and 'vibe' is the measure of quality. At times I feel I'm in the Village, circa 1965.

Masekela riffs and raves in a way more appropriate to 'Round Midnight at Kippies than the State Theatre interiors that pass for High Culture. At times, too, it is tinged with showbiz hype: 'I'm gonna take Strijdom Square and fill it with dancers from the north. I'm gonna have choirs coming out of every fucking balcony. We're gonna bring theatre. We're gonna bring cripples. We're gonna bring kids. We're gonna take theatre and satellite it out into the townships.

Pin him down to specifics and you'll get: a collaboration with Pieter-Dirk Uys in which 'black and Afrikaner families can come together and laugh at each other'; a Rebecca Malope concert; a Rainbow Festival of Tolerance next year, in which, Masekela proposes, a ten-block radius around the theatre will be transformed into an international festival that will culminate with an event at the Voortrekker Monument amphitheatre.

'But is that politically correct?' asked Bra Hugh's Main Man, CEO Louis

Hugh Masekela

Bezuidenhout. 'Hey,' Hugh responds, 'the amphitheatre is the best motherfuckin' venue in the land, and we gonna use it, man!'

Hughie and Louis are tight – 'I'm loose with him, man, we laugh together' – and therein lies the surreal drama of the appointment of Hugh Masekela, the man with the golden trumpet, to the post of change-manager at Pact (Performing Arts Council of the Transvaal). He came in, he says, after being approached by 'friends of Louis, who said he was very worried about the future of this place [because] there are elements who'd like to see everything from the past destroyed ...'

The thing about Louis, however, is that he and his Pact board have long had the reputation for being aloof, arrogant and recalcitrant. In fact, Bezuidenhout has resigned after a scrap with the Ministry of Arts and Culture over budgets, and is staying on, temporarily, at the request of both Minister Ben Ngubane and Masekela.

Basically, Pact is fighting tooth and claw the recommendations of the Arts and Culture Task Group (Actag), which suggest that all the performing arts councils cease to be producers and become, instead, funding agencies that disburse state money for the arts in all provinces. This would mean that the State Theatre would become the property of Gauteng, and Pact's companies (Ballet, Drama and Opera) would be unbundled, becoming independent entities that would have to compete with everyone else for resources and space at the complex.

And, in Pact's arsenal, Masekela has become number one cannon. No wonder there is much consternation in the always-turbulent world of cultural politics. There are strong rumours that the ministry itself disapproves, even though it is saying nothing at the moment.

'Forgive me for being cynical,' says one major player, 'but why did Pact have to go and appoint Masekela now, just weeks before a new board, charged with restructuring the council, is to be put into place? Masekela might well change the face of Pact. He might well bring wonderful concerts into the State Theatre. But under him, the monolith will have stronger cause to remain intact. What we have been doing, for years, is trying to decentralise it, to make its resources accessible to all in a transparent and fair manner.'

Characteristically, Masekela is nonplussed by all this. He – like Bezuidenhout – thinks the Actag proposals are 'unrealistic', and says: 'I'm 56 years old. I was offered a plum job. Why do I need permission to take it? Didn't I vote to be able to take the job I want?'

Politics aside, it remains to be seen whether Masekela has the wherewithal to run an institution like Pact. He has shown himself, in the past, to be an excellent organiser, but he does not reveal himself to be interested in, or moved by, the kind of serious or innovative art an institution like Pact would be expected to produce – in fact, he dismisses the very differentiation between 'serious art' and 'popular entertainment' as a Western construction.

Masekela's passion is, in his own words, 'to introduce South Africa to South Africa. There is no music industry in this country any more. No venues, no recording industry, nothing. We have to create an infrastructure for recreation and entertainment, a thing that was crushed during apartheid because the natives of this country weren't meant to have a good time. They were meant to go to work, and come back, and rest for the next fucking day's work.'

Hugh Masekela

The story of his return from exile is instructive: 'I came back on a Wednesday, waiting for the weekend. I expected all the noise of the weekend to fill the air. The Pedi drums. The wedding bands practising. The music that is part of life in the townships I grew up in. And all I heard was silence.' This is the perpetual riff of Masekela's conversation: 'We are the one country in the world that neither hears itself nor sees itself. If you land in Johannesburg you could be in Milwaukee or Vienna.' And the crescendo: 'There is no country that is as dead recreationally and entertainment-wise as South Africa. For the infrastructure we have, we must be the dullest fucking country in the world!'

Contrast this with the South Africa Masekela left in 1960, the Kofifi world that made him, and one understands immediately his romantic nostalgia, his desire to turn the State Theatre into 'a pilot place to create certain things that are lost, things that we all need in the future. The place of renaissance.'

My colleague, Meshack Mabogoane, notes that musically, Masekela is 'not an innovator, he is a conservative. His genius is that he took South African traditional forms and put his own voice to them, thereby immortalising them. But unlike someone like Miles Davis, who found a way to bring fusion back into jazz, Masekela has reacted to contemporary muscial styles like bubblegum by harking back to the past.'

When he returned to South Africa, 'he realised that the social world that had brought about his generation of music had been destroyed.' This, says Mabogoane, has made him into a romantic; 'a musical expression of the alienation exiles feel in South Africa'. Perhaps, indeed, Masekela has carved for himself the niche of South Africa's primary cultural emcee because he is, since his return from exile, undergoing a paradoxically dry time in terms of his own creative development.

Masekela's move to arts management is, the trumpeter insists, neither permanent nor full-time. He will still play live; he will still record. 'Hugh's Place' is currently being erected on Rockey Street, and a new album, written and produced by Cedric Samson, is expected out next month. Is all of this good for the State Theatre? And will the State Theatre be good for Masekela's trumpet? Unless he is able to achieve a drastic new relationship between the theatre and the people of Pretoria in the next few months, my tendency would be to agree with the sceptics: I can't really see how it will change the allocation of cultural resources in this country if, instead of having five operas a year, we have three operas, one Caiphus-and-Letta concert, and a street fair – all still produced by one performing arts council that continues to devour the lion's share of arts funding.

But then again, is it such a bad thing if Masekela wishes to introduce us to one another; if his objectives revolve around entertaining South Africans? For as long as I live I will remember his 'Sekunjalo' concert of 1991; his immense generosity as he played backup for a host of guests far less illustrious than himself; the illusion of a casual, easy-going event that was always meticulously controlled, from the wings, by a tubby, mischievous little man in rumpled clothing, who seemed to gain so much pleasure by the mere fact that he was bringing so weirdly diverse a group of performers together.

Masekela wishes to reconstruct a world, perhaps mythical, where people interact through culture. He wants to build a Sophiatown around Strijdom Square. Perms are probably flopping all over Waterkloof at the mere thought of it.

Independent film producer and creator of
'Cry, the Beloved Country'

The Sam Goldwyn of South Africa

I profiled Anant Singh in October 1995, as his latest and biggest film, 'Cry, the Beloved Country', was being released. In the profile I fantasise about how Singh's face would look, in close-up on TV, when James Earl Jones wins the Oscar for his role as Stephen Khumalo. It was not to be. In fact, the film did just okay in South Africa and bombed in the United States. No matter. The industrious Singh is onto his next project: he has acquired the rights to Nelson Mandela's autobiography, Long Walk to Freedom, *and has begun working on it.*

Anant Singh

You want to know what chutzpah is? I'll tell you what chutzpah is. Chutzpah is being a little nudnik from South Africa at Cannes and getting Whoopi Goldberg to be in your next low-budget movie by promising her a cut of the profits – and then making enough off 'Sarafina!' to be able to pay her more than she would have ever earned as a fee.

Chutzpah is going off to interview President Nelson Mandela for promotional material for his book launch (for which you are footing the bill) and, at the end of the shoot, quietly keeping the camera rolling while you sit next to him showing him the stills you happen to have with you from your upcoming picture, 'Cry, the Beloved Country' – and then using the footage of Mandela looking at the stills to help promote the film. Chutzpah is then, on top of that, getting Mandela, the busiest man in the world, to be guest of honour at your New York première by making it a benefit for his Children's Fund.

The New York event is on Monday [October 23]. On Wednesday, he'll be back, with stars Richard Harris and James Earl Jones, for the local première, hosted by Tokyo and Judy Sexwale. The thing about Anant Singh is that he doesn't look or behave like a mogul: there's none of that brandy-guzzling cigar-chomping 'Buy! Sell!' swagger about him. His style is Spielberg rather than Mayer: a jeans and sneakers guy, studied informality masking a shrewdness and a toughness that have made him, in our little corner of the firmament, a shimmering star; a phenomenon whose rags-to-riches story equals at least that of a Chaplin, a Mayer, a Goldwyn.

Granted, he didn't arrive penniless off the boat from Riga, and his father was a bourgeois doctor, but the trajectory of his own life is a property so hot that Anant Singh should snap it up immediately: the Indian kid in a racist South Africa who started off rewinding movies in a hire shop on West Street, made an early fortune buying up rights to 'action' and soft-core porn movies, took a chance by backing anti-apartheid movies that were banned, and landed up being one of the most respected and successful independent producers in the world. One scene, however, has yet to be written: the slow pan of his face in the audience – sharp, focused, dispassionate – breaking briefly into the discomposure of victory as James Earl Jones goes up to collect his Oscar for the role of Stephen Kumalo in 'Cry'.

In Singh's mogulspeak, 'pictures' are known only by their abbreviations: there is 'Cry', there is 'Gump', there is 'Kane'. Once a 'property' has been 'greenlighted', you hope it doesn't 'stiff'. When talking about his work, Singh has an accent, American in genesis, with roots more in some celluloid studio-lot than in any geographic location. According to Ken Kaplan, an independent film-maker who is currently working with Singh: 'Anant can speak the speak and do the deal. He does bring a little bit of Hollywood here, a little bit of maturity to this very naive film industry.'

Do the deal Singh does – preferably by speaker-phone, his preferred instrument of communication. In our face-to-face discussion, Singh, while courteous to a fault, was evasive and uncomfortable. When we picked up later, on the phone, it was like we were old friends. He works, says his lawyer David Dison, a double day, 'one in South Africa and then, starting in the late afternoon, one in LA. He is an incredibly hard taskmaster. The reason for his success is that he's such a detail person.'

He has tried the studio system – he produced a Patrick Swayze bomb called 'Fatherhood' for Disney in 1992 – and he doesn't like it. He wants to remain an independent. He wants to keep on financing films himself – taking the risks and making the profits. He sees no reason to leave his native Durban. He hates Hollywood.

But one can see, in Anant Singh's Durban-based Videovision, the beginnings of a classic studio, even if there isn't yet a studio-lot up on the Berea: the tight-fisted boss who rules with firmness and demands absolute loyalty; the family-business feel of it all (his brother is in charge of marketing, a cousin does financial management, 'connections' come in with plates full of samoosas to be tasted in the hope of securing catering contracts for premières); the small circle of creative staff he works with, at the head of which was Darrell James Roodt, a young anti-apartheid film maker Singh picked up in 1984 with 'Place of Weeping'.

Roodt made Singh; Singh made Roodt: 'Cry' follows 'Sarafina!' as the apex of their collaboration. They made eight films together. They have now parted ways, after Roodt went elsewhere for his next film, 'Spear' (not an abbreviation; that's its name). There is pain, there is bitterness, there is recrimination. Classic studio-system stuff.

'Sarafina!' made over $10-million (it cost $4-million), largely due to Singh's marketing nous: as he has done with 'Cry', he roped Mandela into the act, getting the legend to endorse a product about the legend. He has an uncanny instinct for the right movie at the right time. He jumped at 'Place of Weeping' just when the anti-apartheid movement was gathering steam: it put him on the map. He did 'Sarafina!' in the wake of worldwide euphoria about Mandela's release and at the peak of Mbongeni Ngema's career. Now he has identified the fact that the world is weary of the celluloid commodification of the South African struggle and so he is offering, instead, a human interest story set in South Africa that makes of 'black' and 'white' universal properties seeking overarching reconciliation – Miss Daisy being driven along that 'lovely road that runs from Ixopo into the hills'.

'Cry, the Beloved Country' is an emotional and beautiful film that is not in the least bit challenging. In terms of production value, it is the best film that has ever come out of South Africa. Which is not to say that Singh hasn't made some clangers in his time: his first film, 'Deadly Passion', was, in his own words, a poor man's 'Body Heat'. After 'Sarafina!', he made 'The Mangler', an adaptation of a Stephen King horror story. 'Cry', on the other hand, is a classic crossover art movie. It has the highbrow performances, the incomparable literary pedigree, the soupçon of political conflict, the soaring and artful cinematography, to ensure that it is taken seriously. But it also has the schmaltz and sentimentality to ensure that American audiences will weep, from the moment they first set eyes on the pained and stoical face of James Earl Jones to the last soaring shot that trips off the Drakensberg, the hills alive, quite incongruously, with the sounds of 'Enya'.

Singh, when talking about film, reserves his highest praise for such crossover products: he wants for 'Cry' what happened to 'Forrest Gump' or 'Driving Miss Daisy': a quality film that can move the masses. He may well get it. I imagine that when he looks in the mirror, he sees (or would like to see) Ismail Merchant: an independent producer who makes high art that sells. One difference, though, is that he has no disdain for shlock: 'I guess,' he says with his usual diffidence when I ask him what moves him, 'there's a little more passion in "Cry" than there is in "Mangler", but you have to be passionate about any film, or you might as well not make it at all. Critics might not be as kind to "Mangler" as to "Cry", but hey, audiences responded to "Mangler". It's already shipped 150 000 videos in America. I'm not complaining.'

I can honestly report that I don't know what moves Anant Singh. I hand him a question on a plate: what movies does he love? His answer: 'Oh, everything from "Citizen Kane" to "Star Wars" to Charlie Chaplin, from "The Jungle Book" to "Siddhartha".'

Kaplan makes the point that 'Anant's come to appreciate movies by making them, rather than the usual way, which is to make movies because you appreciate them. It started off with, "Oh! I can make these things! And there's a market out there for them!" And then people said to him, "We like the movies you make." Only now is he beginning to discover what exactly he likes about films, what his sensibilities are.'

Even though Singh is adamant that 'there's only one person in the world I need to prove things to, and that's myself', there is something, in his drive, of the outsider needing to show that he can make it. His enigma is that he does this without swaggering. His Hills are Reservoir rather than Beverly; here is where he lives with his mother. His Beach is Tongaat rather than Malibu; here is where he bought a seaside property a year or so ago, twenty minutes north of Durban. By all accounts it is comfortable and modest: the Videovision gang often gathers there to drink cokes and play pool. In his late thirties, he is unmarried: his employees are his friends; he does not appear to have a social life outside of his work environment.

He is one of Indian Durban's most famous sons. People come up to him at the Royal Hotel squash courts, ask him what he's doing, and talk to him about how an Indian kid has been dropped from the Natal cricket team. He likes being known, being part of a community – that has as much as anything to do with his decision to remain in Durban.

Sure, he lets you know that he is important: in the folder of publicity bumf he gave me there was, discreetly tucked in towards the back, a xerox of a handwritten inscription on the title page of *Long Walk to Freedom*,: 'To Anand Singh ... a comrade who has rendered impressive service to the democratic forces of our country and helped to bring about a historic victory. N Mandela 9.1.95.'

But in the few hours we were together there were only two gratuitous name droppings. Granted, they were big ones (Attenborough, Tarantino), but in the world of hype that Singh inhabits, that's a good innings. He did drop a third, but asked me not to publish it: 'We talk once a week, but I don't want you to mention it, because I don't want it to be perceived that I'm using other names to bolster myself.' I was impressed with the finesse, and began to understand how he works: he established his cred with me, the paparazzo, while remaining circumspect about his friends in the industry. It is upon precisely that combination of marketing savvy and in-house discretion that he has built his name.

Anant Singh has just been rereading Alan Paton's autobiography, and he found an account of the 1951 South African première of the first 'Cry, the Beloved Country', starring a Sydney Poitier who was not allowed to attend. Paton sat next to the Malans. At intermission, Mrs Malan said, 'Surely, Mr Paton, things are not like this.' He replied: 'They are much worse, Madam.'

On Monday night at the Ziegfeld, New York's grandest moviehouse, Comrade Anant will sit, in a star-studded crowd, next to President Mandela. There's an ever-spiralling circularity to it that is quite breathtaking.

BRENDA FASSIE
South Africa's bad-girl singer

Weekend Special bites back!

What is Brenda Fassie doing in a book entitled Portraits of Power? *She is, if any-thing, a tragic icon of fallen power; a goddess who will not make it into the New South Africa. Whatever her current state, she still gets them hopping in the town-ships: if nothing else, she is a portrait of libidinal power. I profiled her in December 1995, when she attempted to make a comeback with her 'Brenda's Back' tour. I have seen her twice since then: once upstaging Sibongile Khumalo at the Civic Theatre and once bowing to the traffic on Rockey Street in Yeoville. She is as dissolute and as fabulous as ever.*

Brenda Fassie

'How can I make you smile?' I asked an enraged Brenda Fassie, dressed in baby-pink denim cutoffs and throwing the contents of her handbag around my car with the jerky impetuousness of a seriously cold turkey as we drove away from her latest humiliation – a no-show from Bob Mabena for a radio interview.

'How can you make me smile? Go home. Leave me alone.'

There's no more pretty to Brenda's pink. There's not even that raunchy 'I-like-it-here-in-the-dirt' sexuality of her Quirinale drug-den days. She vonts to be alone, more Marlene than Madonna nowadays: bitter, prematurely aged ... until you make a connection with her. Then she's your best friend. Whatever she says, the cynicism is a thin crust: break it open and you'll hear her scream, as she did several times during our day together: 'I wanna be loved. I just wanna be loved!'

Since her July crash – when her girlfriend Poppy Sihlahla was found dead next to her in their room in a Hillbrow bordello and she was checked into rehab – she swears she has been clean. She is living in hotels for the moment; she drinks, she smokes, but no more coke. Three weeks ago she hooked up with Paul Tillsley, the mercurial former head of M-Net's ill-fated news programme 'Camera 7' and current owner of The Shebeen. There are sparks already, though, and by the time you read this Tillsley might be the latest in a long and illustrious line of Brenda's ex-managers.

Rehearsing on stage at the old Melodi Theatre in Orange Grove, which Tillsley leases, she poses for the camera, playing the superbitch. Today her targets are the five young men who make up her shimmying, vogueing, campy chorus-line. You could crack a coconut in the swivel of their hips.

'You bloody gays!' she screams at them, gratuitously, for the benefit of myself and the photographer. 'You don't know how to work! You think this is just a rehearsal! Quincy Jones could walk through this door any minute. I am a superstar!!!! You don't like it? Leave! Walk out that door right now. You're fired! I hear Yvonne Chaka-Chaka needs some back-ups. Go to her. She's your standard!'

She is 31, but she can be, at times, a parody of all the parodies of all the washed-out has-beens who have ever marched down Sunset Boulevard. She has always been difficult, but in the past she has also always ultimately complied. In township subculture she was revolutionary, not only because she stripped down to Lycra underwear, but because she was, figuratively, an easy lay for her listeners. This is the woman, remember, who burst into public consciousness as your Weekend Special, as the mistress who might complain that you never visit on weekdays, but who is nonetheless faithfully waiting for you come Friday.

She commanded intense libidinal power too: remember those incidents when people would trash the stadium – and even kill each other – when Brenda didn't turn up for a concert? At her 'Brenda's Back' concerts – her first live gigs in nearly a year – South Africa's greatest pop star performed with characteristic energy, the beauty and power of her voice peeking occasionally through the histrionics. You could see, as always, the contours of her genitalia beneath two layers of Lycra as she swaggered across the Melodi's shabby stage. Her sexuality is more aggressive than ever. Sure, there are flashes of the ingénue, of the coquette. But now, when Brenda performs the sex-kitten, she does it with thinly veiled derision, or with vampish venom, as if to say: 'Look, but don't you dare touch!'

Brenda Fassie

She did not want pity – in fact she did a sneering imitation of people hypocritically commiserating with her – and she did not want concern. She wanted respect. The Weekend Special was finally fighting back: she had become an embodiment of Gloria Gaynor's anthemic 'I will survive'. But Brenda is never simple: she taunted and swaggered all the same. She played, as she has never done publicly before, with her sexuality: 'I wipe the toilet-paper on both sides!' she yelled once, with clear delight, in reference to her bisexuality.

She told me that she owed it to Poppy to be upfront about her sexuality now. At another point in her concert, she cast an imperious hand back along her chorus line: '*Stabane*! [the township word for queens],' she declared, again with delight. 'There are more people here than in the Skyline [Hillbrow's famous black gay bar] tonight! Why', she challenged her audience (most of whom probably drive a Skyline rather than drink in one) 'do we not give gay people their rights? It's high time we did!'

There was no applause for this peroration. In fact, there was no applause at all. At one point she received a note written by one of her fans clamouring at the foot of the stage, and sang it aloud, weeping: 'Brenda, we love you! We are behind you all the way!' For an instant, there was a spontaneous burst of compassion in the 700-strong crowd: all the hands went up. For the rest, though, the audience – largely young and black – seemed to be profoundly ambivalent about Brenda. They did not dance to her music; they did not clap; they gaped with awe, rather, at the spectacle their icon had become: the lesbian addict beyond the pale; the glamour-dream they bought stripped bare to reveal a banshee howling out all the angst those CCV soapies edit out of their metropolitan fantasies. Brenda's fans, like Brenda, are creatures of the city: look what the city did to her. Who's next?

Interestingly, Brenda's plummet down beyond the pale has not unduly affected her record sales: her latest single, 'Umuntu Uyashintsha' ('People Change') has already sold more than 30 000 copies. With characteristic bolshiness, she dedicated it to township rapper Senyaka, who recently came out with a song called 'Brenda ke Mampara' ('Brenda is a fool' for taking drugs); she disses him as a country bumpkin and, in one mix, she sings 'Umuntu Uyashintsha' while a ragga voice-over declares, 'You cannot change Brenda Fassie Girl. She's a fine musician, but she cannot change! You can't predict her! She's fuckin' wicked!'

The voice-over is clearly a caricature of Senyaka, but – brilliantly and characteristically – Brenda turns it round to work for her so that she can have her cake and eat every one else's too : she can sing the repentant soprano harmonies of how she's going to be good now while an insistent vocal bassline tells us she is b-a-d!

Backstage at the Melodi, she and I sit in the shabby make-up room. Brenda positions herself so that, while talking to me, she can look at her reflection in the dirty mirror framed with holes where the lightbulbs should be. There couldn't be a better place to discuss the rise and fall of Brenda Fassie. She tells me: 'Senyaka did drugs with me, so what the fuck is he on about?'

She has an understanding of social hypocrisy so sharp it could slit a wrist. She catches me being disingenuous before the words have finished leaving my mouth, brands me a 'fake', and refuses to talk to me for a while. Everyone is fake and hypocritical: her clan-cousin Nelson Mandela, for promising so much and delivering so little; Desmond Tutu, for telling kids to stay away from school while sending his own kids to America; journalists, for pretending to like her when they just want a scoop; managers, for pretending to like her when they just want a buck.

When Tokyo Sexwale announced, at the press conference he held for her at his home in Houghton after Poppy's death in July, that she was a 'diamond withering away … in the spirit of Masakhane, we must build up what has been destroyed', Fassie caught the populism lurking in those mixed metaphors, doubted the Gauteng premier's sincerity, and replied, ungratefully, 'I'm doing it for myself.'

As for black people who say there is no homosexuality in their culture: 'They're lying! They're fake! They don't wanna come out with the truth! People do things in their bloody rooms and then come out and wipe their mouths and say, 'I did nothing!' Why do it if you won't talk about it? Why do people not talk about sex?'

Brenda does talk about sex. She once said of Yvonne Chaka-Chaka: 'She thinks she's white. She says, "I stay next door to the Oppenheimers." Who the fuck wants to know that? "I'm married to a doctor." Who the fuck wants to know that? Call Brenda Fassie, I'll tell you who I fucked last night!' Now she tells me, with derision, about the husbands and wives she sleeps with simultaneously, 'and they don't even fucking know they're cheating on each other!' She tells me, with even more derision, about how 'lesbianism is becoming a fashion in Soweto. All these girls pretend to be gay just so they can be seen with me.' She then goes on to recount, in graphic detail, how she makes them go down on her, but how she'll never go down on them.

No wonder she calls herself the Madonna of Soweto. Inside every dominatrix is a pussycat who wants to be loved. But, even though Brenda insists, 'I'm in control,' she isn't. She is spot-on when she identifies the hypocrisy of her fellow muzos who also do drugs but who pontificate sanctimoniously about her demise. The tragedy is, though, that they can control their habits and she can't. They can control their emotions too. Would Madonna ever allow herself to say to a journalist, as Brenda does: 'No, I just can't be with a girl since Poppy died. Every time I touch a girl I see Poppy, and I just can't take it. I am more lonely than ever'?

So is the voracious sexual appetite simply a foil? She insists that she does what she does 'because I'm a shocker. I like to create controversy. It's my trademark.' I'd venture to guess that there has become, over the years, a fatal interdependency between Brenda Fassie and the paparazzi. She is ultimately a creature of the *Sunday Times Extra*, which has faithfully emblazoned her woes in banner headlines, from 'Fassiemania swamps wedding!' through 'Brenda smashed by jealous husband!' all the way down to 'Brenda took our baby, says grandpa' and 'Brenda's pal dies of drugs'. She is a textbook tabloid commodity: her fix, and her downfall, has been notoriety, not cocaine.

MARK FISH
Bafana Bafana superstar

Go, Feeeesh!

I'm neither a sports spectator nor a soccer fan, but I couldn't resist the patriotic frenzy around the Bafana Bafana in the Africa Cup finals that took place in January 1996: I found myself, twice in one week, at the FNB Stadium bellowing 'Feeeesh!' with the rest of them. Feesh pulled a fast one on me, though: the week I published this profile, along with a poem by Fish called 'Changes', I got calls from outraged Jim Morrison fans throughout the country: at least half of the poem, which I earnestly lit-crit in the profile, was quoted directly from the guru. I was faced with the dilemma of ethics versus patriotism: if I exposed Fish as a plagiarist, perhaps he'd fall apart and we'd lose the finals. I kept quiet. We won.

Mark Fish

Monday afternoon at the Old Eds Health & Racquet Club in Houghton. It's only 48 hours after they were crowned national heroes, and the Bafana Bafana seem bemused, rather than irritated, by the fact that only a few autograph-hunting children recognise them. 'Excuse me!' calls a fluorescent kugel, 'what team are you?'

Doctor and Shoes have led an invasion of the aerobics class, pealing with laughter as they throw their gold around. Zane, meanwhile, is throwing indignant teenage girls off exercycles. Augie is primping his pecs down in freeweights. Coach Clive is gamely puffing his way through a circuit. The Feesh, it goes without saying, is in the water, doing laps.

Later, signature bird's-nest hair tamed by a back-to-front baseball cap, the youngest member of the South African squad – and the one most likely to hit the international bigtime – lopes across the floor to laugh at his buddies in the aerobics class.

There's something mesmerising about Mark Fish. The gangly white boy's jerky, too-long limbs sometimes seem to be caught in adolescence (he is 21), beyond his control, until they snap, in a moment, into the machine-like precision that earned him the 'Man of the Match' vote last Saturday when South Africa trounced Cameroon.

There's no white player black South Africans love more; there's no South African defender who gets as much attention from the crowd. 'Feeeesh!' the supporters cried every time his boot tapped the ball on Saturday. 'Feeeesh' they cry every time he plays for Orlando Pirates.

And it's not just because his name, like 'Shhhhooooees', rolls easily off the collective tongue of a stadium-full of people. It's not just because he is a defender who never loses a tackle, no matter how aggressive the striker; who is given to blazing lone storms across the length of the field into the other team's goal-box; who reads a game like no-one else on the field. No; it's because he is raw, a rebel, easy to find (that hair!), easy to read.

There's something intimidating about the artistry of a Khumalo or a Mosheou, something inaccessible about the lofty Masinga; through Feesh, though, you can live the match, following the fortunes of your team as they ripple through his posture and register on his features.

Coach Clive Barker puts it best: 'What impresses most people about Mark Fish is his body language. He's unpredictable, a character. A Jonty Rhodes, a James Small. He betrays to the crowds what we're trying to get across.'

Barker clearly adores his youngest ward: 'He's not my first choice for the national team! He's my first, second and third choice!' The bluff, no-nonsense coach plays his part so perfectly you wonder if he hasn't stepped off the pages of *Whizzer & Chips*. But Fish stirs even the coach to poesy: 'If I were in the trenches of World War I and I had Mark Fish next to me, even if there were 1 000 soldiers storming us, I'd be convinced we'd still win. He's a fighter.'

It's no secret there are talent scouts from the European clubs here for the African Cup of Nations, and they've got their eyes on Fish. There have been rumours about Manchester United, and it's believed that the Italians are also showing interest. Soccer writers caution, though, that a star in malnourished South Africa might not even register a blip on the Italian or British landscape.

173

Barker believes that Fish 'may have the potential to hit the jackpot, to make the big league if he manages things right. But he may yet go into the category of the George Bests.' Fish, you see, is Party Animal Number One in the South African squad. He loves to drink, and he can get unruly. The squad still chuckles at how he told Mike Atherton he was 'ugly'.

'He loves a good party,' says Barker, 'and his parties go on longer than anyone else's.' As does his hair, even though Barker's caught wind of a rumour that, if the Bafana Bafana get to the finals, a certain Feesh might be sporting an 'exotic, punk, short, blue do'.

There's none of that Mark Fish sitting opposite me at the bar of the Sunnyside Hotel this week. He is the consummate Pretoria Boy's High alumnus: well-spoken, very polite. He talks, for example, of 'Mr Barker' and 'Mr Mandela'. It's clear he doesn't really like the limelight, but he plays ball anyway, attempting to answer questions and admitting, sheepishly, that his mind is elsewhere. Despite his youth, he is one of the most popular members of the squad: it's hard not to like him.

He is not self-conscious about being a white boy in a black sport. His best buddy – and room mate at the Sunnyside – is Pirates captain and fellow Pretoria homeboy (and rabble-rouser) Edward Motale. 'Fish', says Motale, 'is not like other whites. I take him to Mamelodi, to Tembisa, and he'll get up and dance, even though he's the only white. He won't give a damn, he'll just boogie, and then others will join him. With other whites it's different. They need that special attention one cannot afford.'

After Saturday's victory, Fish chose to go with his mates to a bar, 'Tings and Times' in Pretoria, rather than joining the team at the Randburg Waterfront. Johannesburg, he says, is 'flashy and phoney and false, all these guys who dress to impress'. Motale often accompanies him on his Pretoria sorties – a place not known for its mixed venues – where the couple have become known as 'New South Africa'.

Fish lives in one of our land's strange interstices, unrecognised by his home culture, but a folk hero to millions. 'I'll go to a restaurant with a girlfriend and the only one who'll recognise me is the waiter, and he'll insist I go into the back and meet all the kitchen staff.'

Perhaps his ease with this is a function of his youth: he was in nappies during the Soweto uprising. He is, truly, a post-apartheid babe. Although he is 'not rushing to join the ANC', he acknowledges that, because soccer has taken him across the railway line, he does have an insight into the ravages of apartheid his white peers may not have. But there is something a little too defensive – or perhaps just young – in his comment: 'I know about apartheid years, but I wasn't there. It's got nothing to do with me. I never hated blacks.'

Fish, like Eddie Motale, spent most of his childhood playing soccer at Pretoria club, Arcadia Shepherds. But, while Fish remembers the Shepherds with unqualified warmth, Motale's stories are full of the slights of petty apartheid: he was left behind in the showers when the white boys went off to the pub, he was dropped from the Colts team even though he was clearly the best player, and then, at rival Berea Park, he was not even allowed to use the facilities.

Fish – like most white South Africans – wants to erase race; Motale – like most black South Africans – can't. Motale lives with his parents in Mamelodi; Fish lives with his grandparents in Arcadia. Motale's mother is a cleaner at Pretoria University;

Mark Fish

Fish's mother is a sales manageress at Edgars. Motale had a hard time finishing school and, aged 29, lives for and through soccer. Fish is in the middle of a Unisa marketing degree and thinks he may want to move into sports psychology.

There are intimations that Fish had a difficult childhood – his parents are divorced, and those who know him well say, elliptically, that his drive on the football field is related to his 'background' – but he does not talk about this. The greatest conflict of his youth seems to have been that timeworn one of white South African schools: soccer versus rugby.

Pretoria Boys' High is a great rugby-playing school. They wanted him to play rugby, he wanted to play soccer. At primary school, he was head boy. But in white South African high schools, soccer – the terrain of dagga-smoking rebels – is positively unpatriotic, so at Boys' High Fish assumed a more marginal existence. He speaks, now, with indignation, about how the school 'did nothing for me, and now has the cheek to ask me to donate money to a new library. When Robbie Brink made the national rugby team, they said he was Boys' High's first Springbok. Well what about me? I was already playing for the national soccer squad!'

He clearly doesn't like authority. Soccer administration in this country is 'corrupt … the administrators get all the money and the players don't get the respect they earn. I tell you, if I get picked for a European club, if it's Clive Barker as coach I might consider coming back to this country. Otherwise, forget it.'

Right now he's listening to the group LIVE on his walkman, particularly 'this one song, "Lightning Crashes", about the world and how fucked up it is'. It figures that his favourite movie is 'What's Eating Gilbert Grape?': even though he is as gregarious as Johnny Depp is dark, there's something unmistakably teen-rebel about him. It's not nihilistic, wear-black, fuck-you or gangsta-rap rebellion; it's rather the indie-rock rebellion of vague social conscience, long sideburns and mellow attitude – REM and the Red Hot Chilli Peppers are two of his favourite bands.

And yes, he is a poet. A promising one at that. His poem, 'Changes', is filled with the nostalgic romanticism of an alienated Generation-X yearning for more essential times, when there was nothing to mediate our experience and we were mad bodies 'dancing on the hillsides' rather than 'pair[s] of eyes' staring, through the dark, at TV sets.

He wrote the poem to Clive Barker's wife, a ballet dancer, but it is clearly a meditation on his own career. We are no longer all 'dancers', but now 'cleaved' into 'actor and spectators', soccer stars and fans. 'We are obsessed with heroes who live for us/ and whom we punish.'

Mark Fish must know that he has now become one of those heroes.